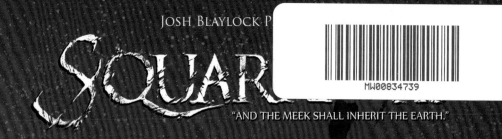

Josh Blaylock P

SQUAR

"AND THE MEEK SHALL INHERIT THE EARTH."

MW00834739

CREATED/WRITTEN/LAYOUTS BY

ASH MACZKO

ART/LETTERS/COLORS BY

ASHLEY WITTER

DEVIL'S DUE COMICS

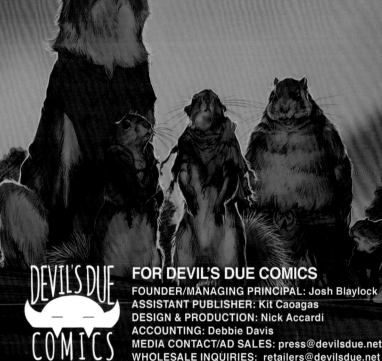

FOR DEVIL'S DUE COMICS

FOUNDER/MANAGING PRINCIPAL: Josh Blaylock
ASSISTANT PUBLISHER: Kit Caoagas
DESIGN & PRODUCTION: Nick Accardi
ACCOUNTING: Debbie Davis
MEDIA CONTACT/AD SALES: press@devilsdue.net
WHOLESALE INQUIRIES: retailers@devilsdue.net

www.DEVILSDUE.net

ROBERT SMALL, ALLY OF THE AMONI · JOHN CAMPOS, ALLY OF THE MAW · ALEX FISHER, ALLY OF THE TIN KIN

SQUARRIORS: Vol. 2 Summer May 2022. Published by Devil's Due Comics. Office of publication 1658 N. Milwaukee Ave #100-5850 Chicago, IL 60647.

DEDICATED TO

ALEX FISHER
ALLY OF THE TIN KIN

JOHN CAMPOS
ALLY OF THE MAW

ROBERT SMALL
ALLY OF THE AMONI

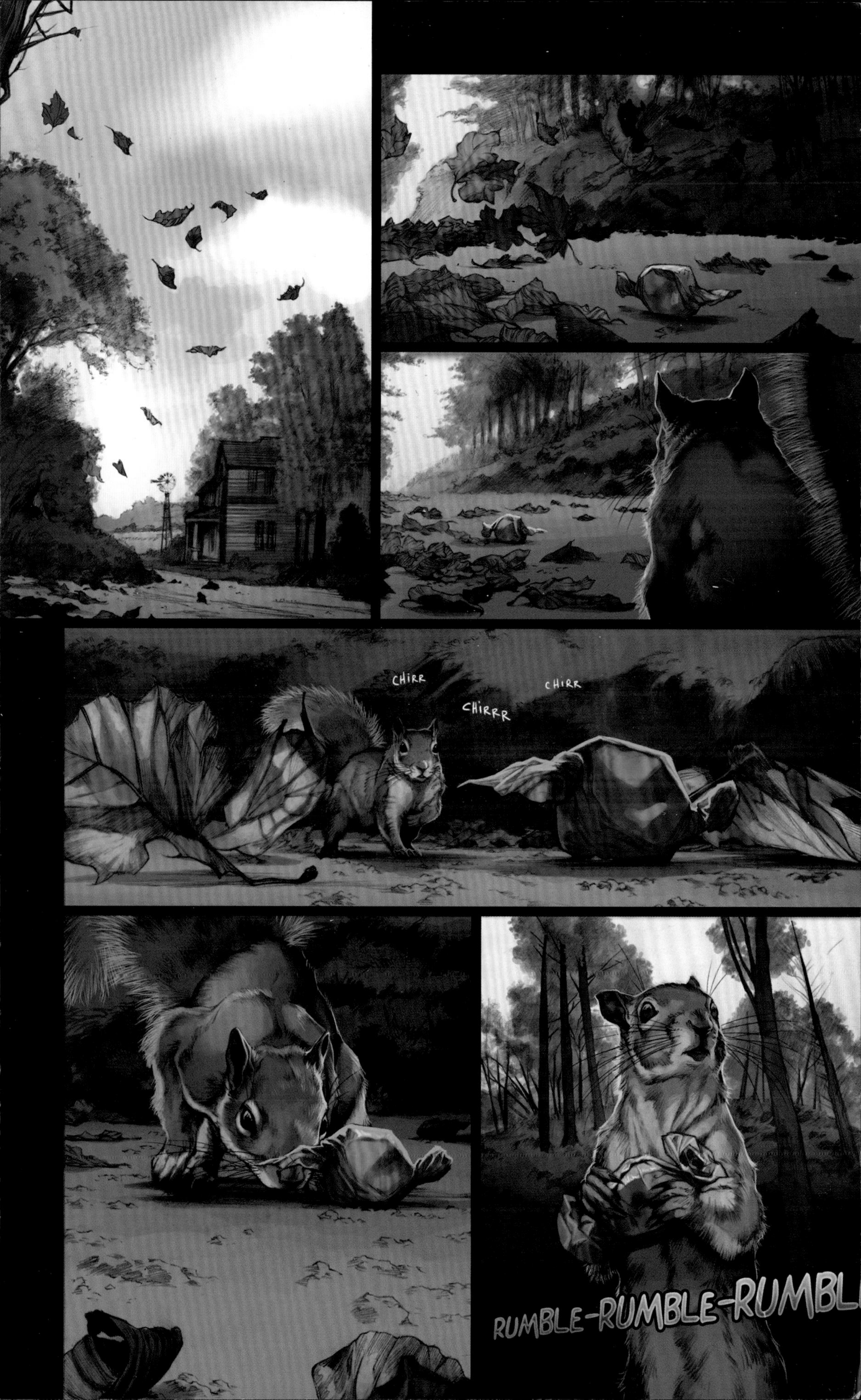
CHIRR
CHIRRR
CHIRR
RUMBLE-RUMBLE-RUMBL

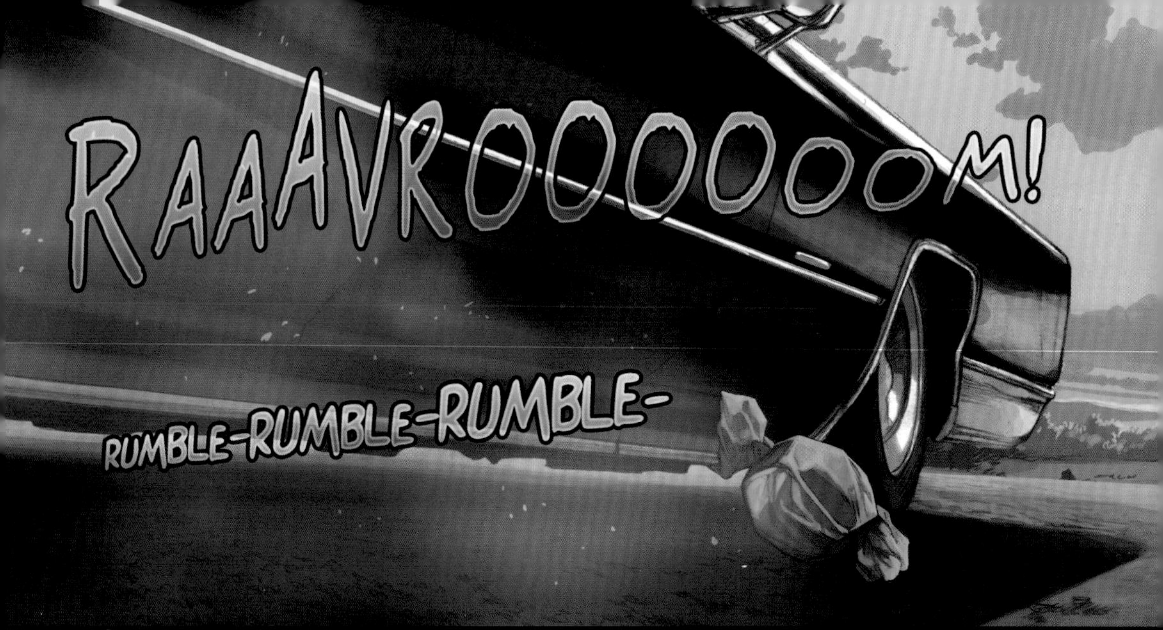
RAAAVROOOOOOOM!
RUMBLE-RUMBLE-RUMBLE-

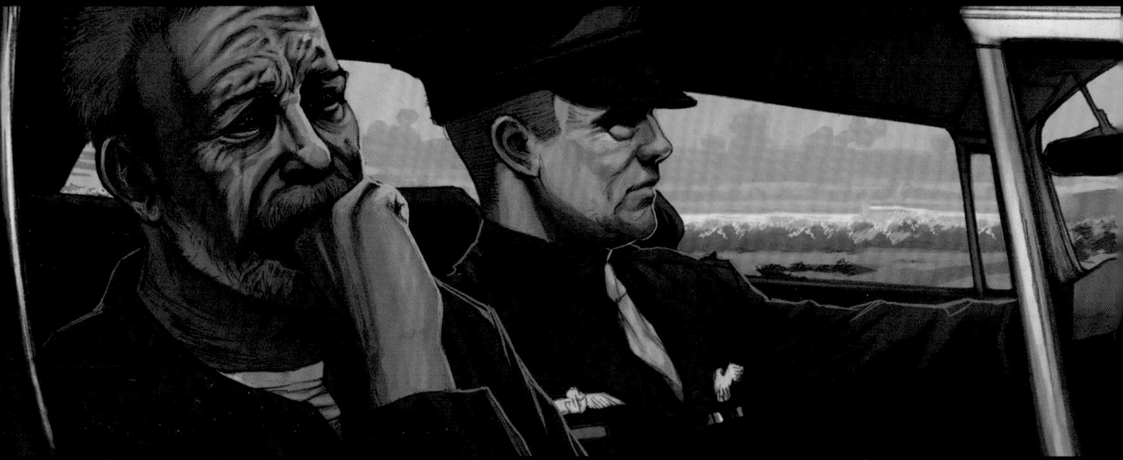

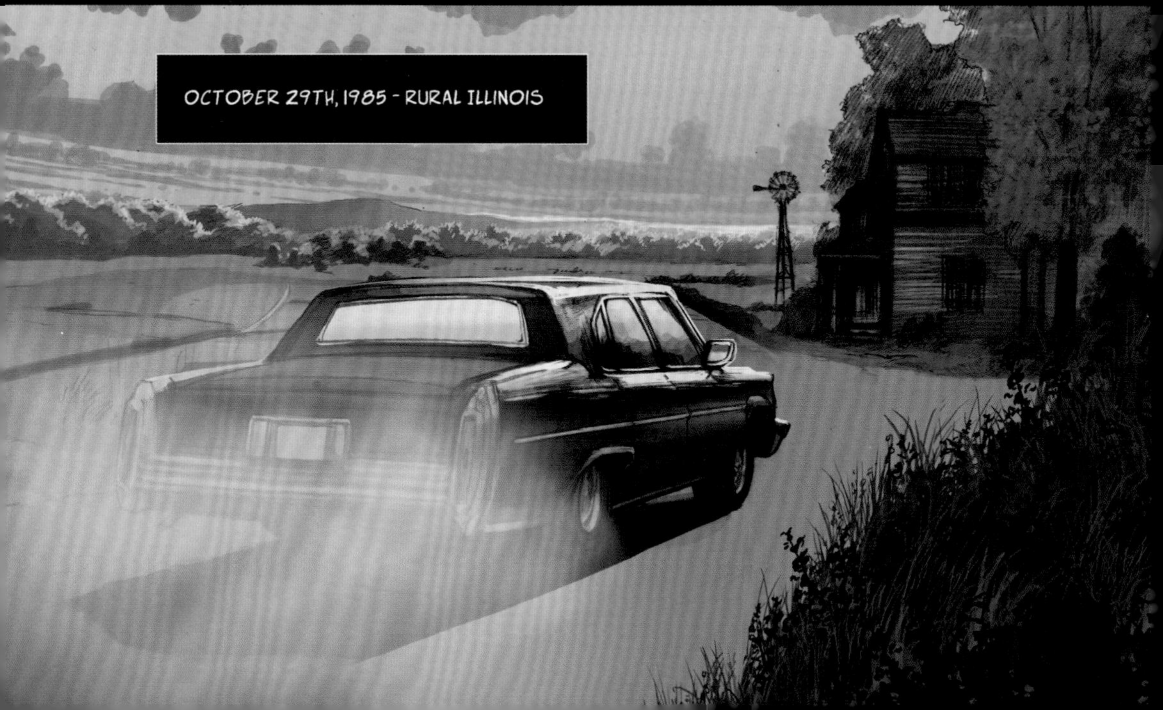
OCTOBER 29TH, 1985 - RURAL ILLINOIS

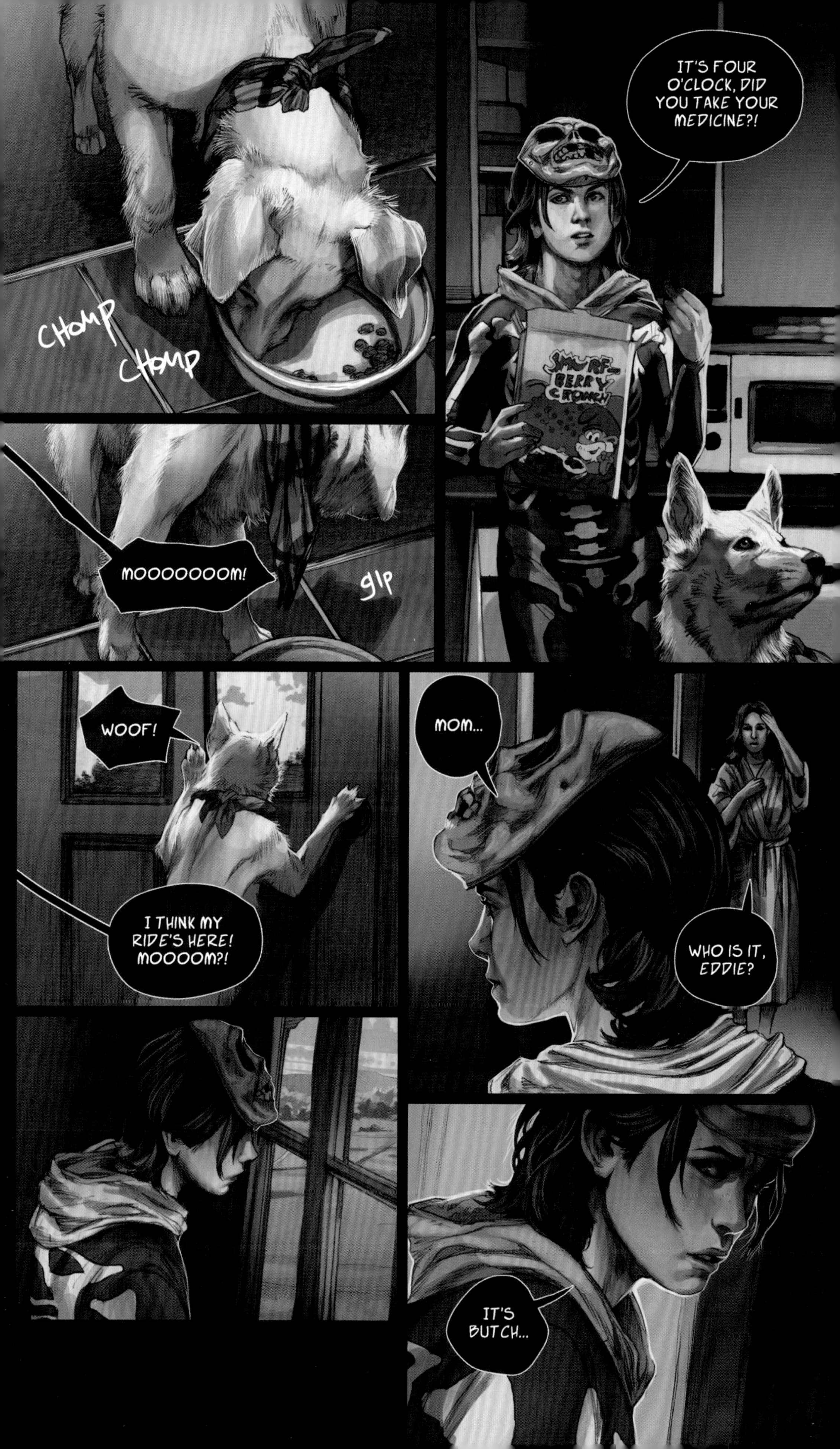
CHOMP
CHOMP
IT'S FOUR O'CLOCK, DID YOU TAKE YOUR MEDICINE?!
SMURF-BERRY CRUNCH
MOOOOOOOM!
glp
WOOF!
I THINK MY RIDE'S HERE! MOOOOM?!
MOM...
WHO IS IT, EDDIE?
IT'S BUTCH...

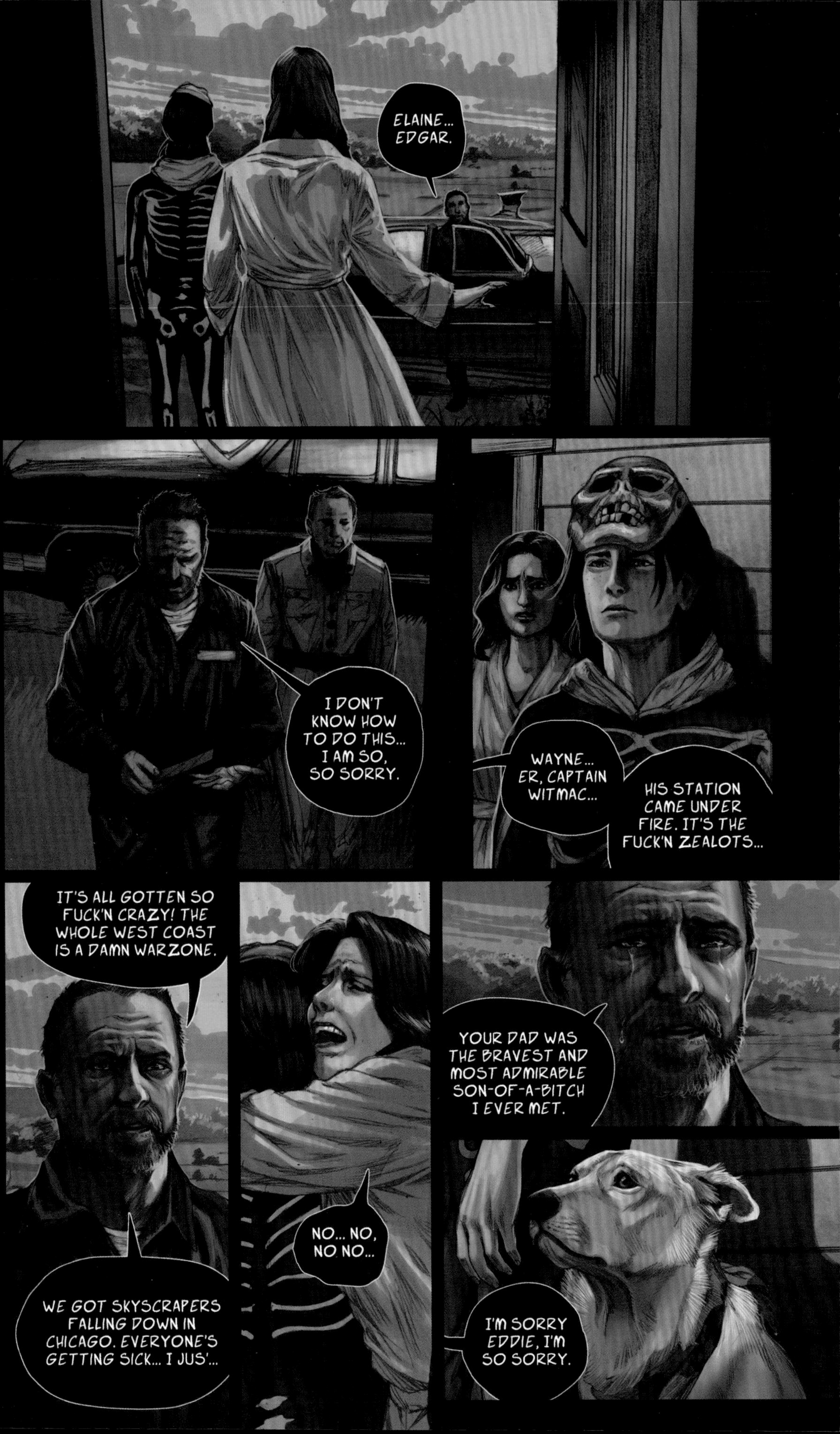
ELAINE... EDGAR.
I DON'T KNOW HOW TO DO THIS... I AM SO, SO SORRY.
WAYNE... ER, CAPTAIN WITMAC...
HIS STATION CAME UNDER FIRE. IT'S THE FUCK'N ZEALOTS...
IT'S ALL GOTTEN SO FUCK'N CRAZY! THE WHOLE WEST COAST IS A DAMN WARZONE.
WE GOT SKYSCRAPERS FALLING DOWN IN CHICAGO. EVERYONE'S GETTING SICK... I JUS'...
NO... NO, NO NO...
YOUR DAD WAS THE BRAVEST AND MOST ADMIRABLE SON-OF-A-BITCH I EVER MET.
I'M SORRY EDDIE, I'M SO SORRY.

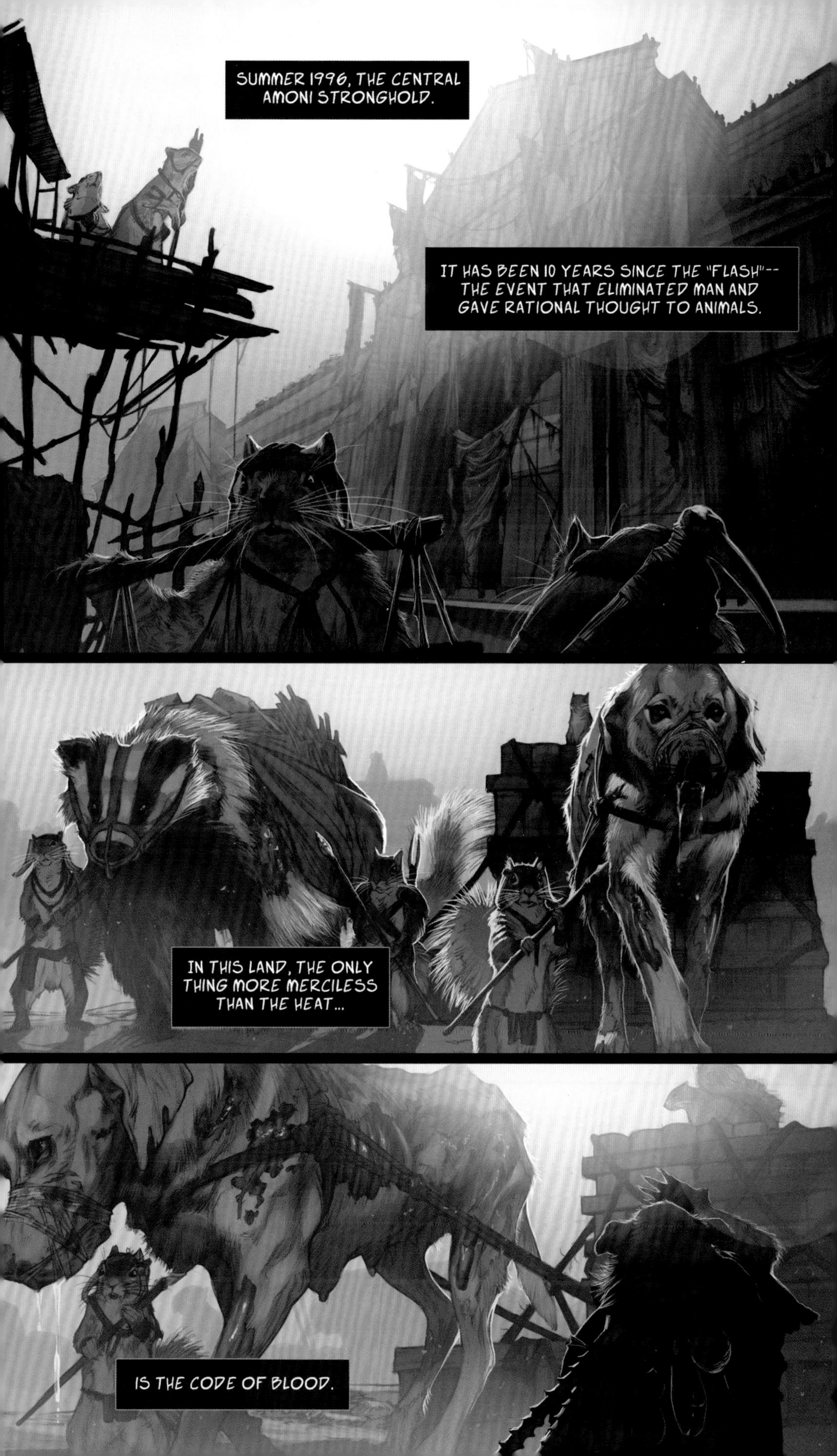
SUMMER 1996, THE CENTRAL AMONI STRONGHOLD.
IT HAS BEEN 10 YEARS SINCE THE "FLASH"-- THE EVENT THAT ELIMINATED MAN AND GAVE RATIONAL THOUGHT TO ANIMALS.
IN THIS LAND, THE ONLY THING MORE MERCILESS THAN THE HEAT...
IS THE CODE OF BLOOD.

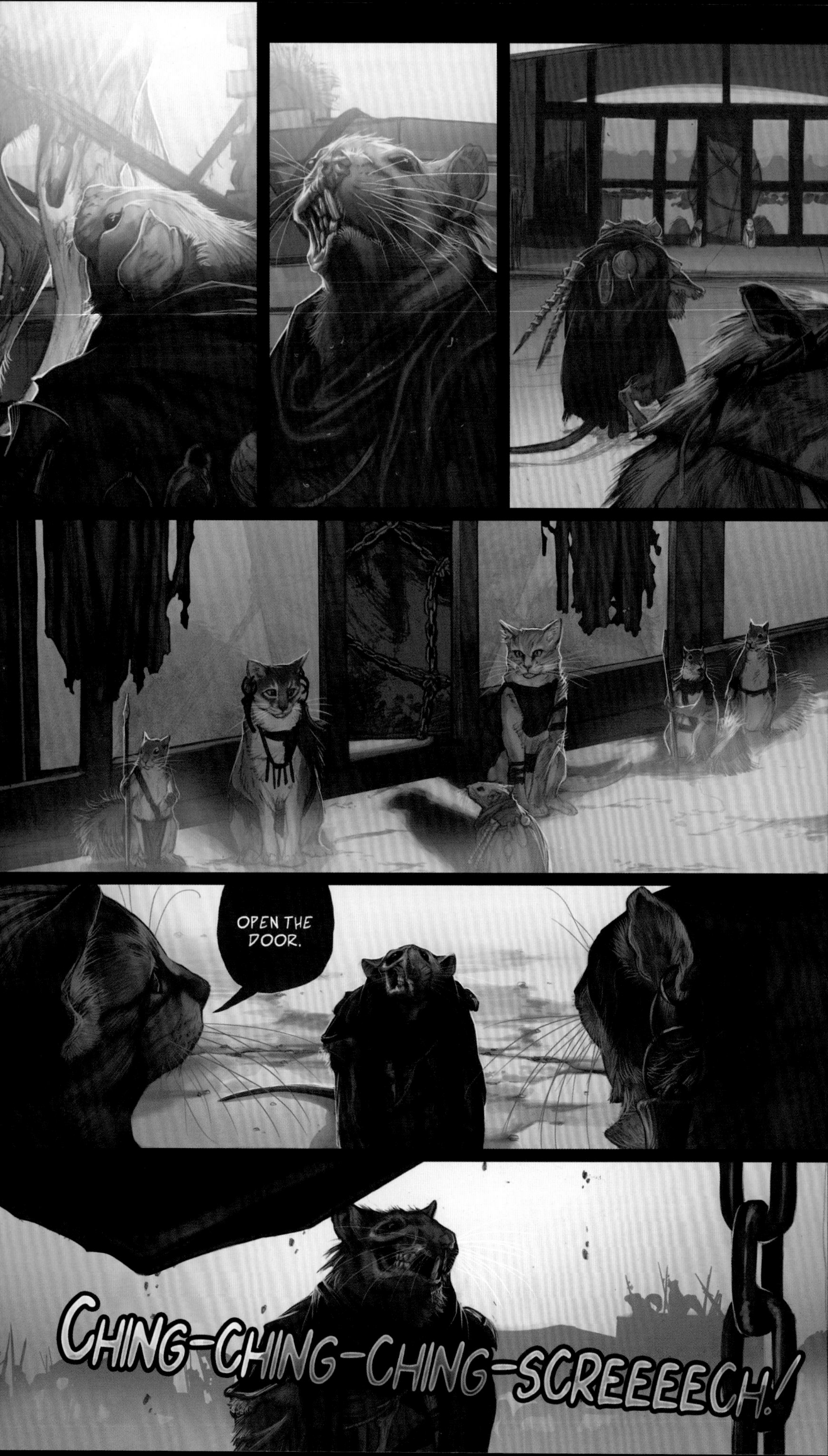
OPEN THE DOOR.
CHING-CHING-CHING-SCREEEEECH!

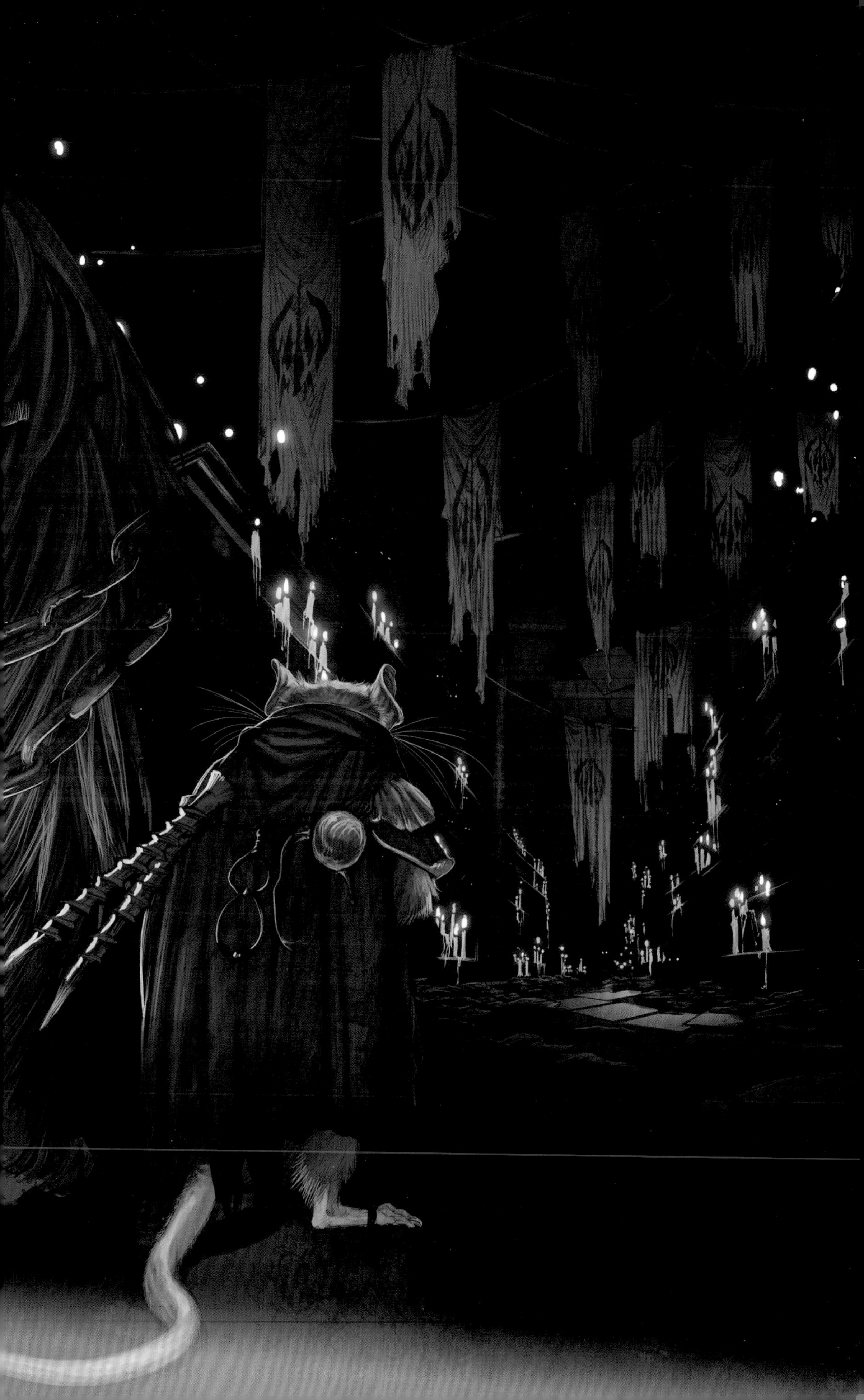

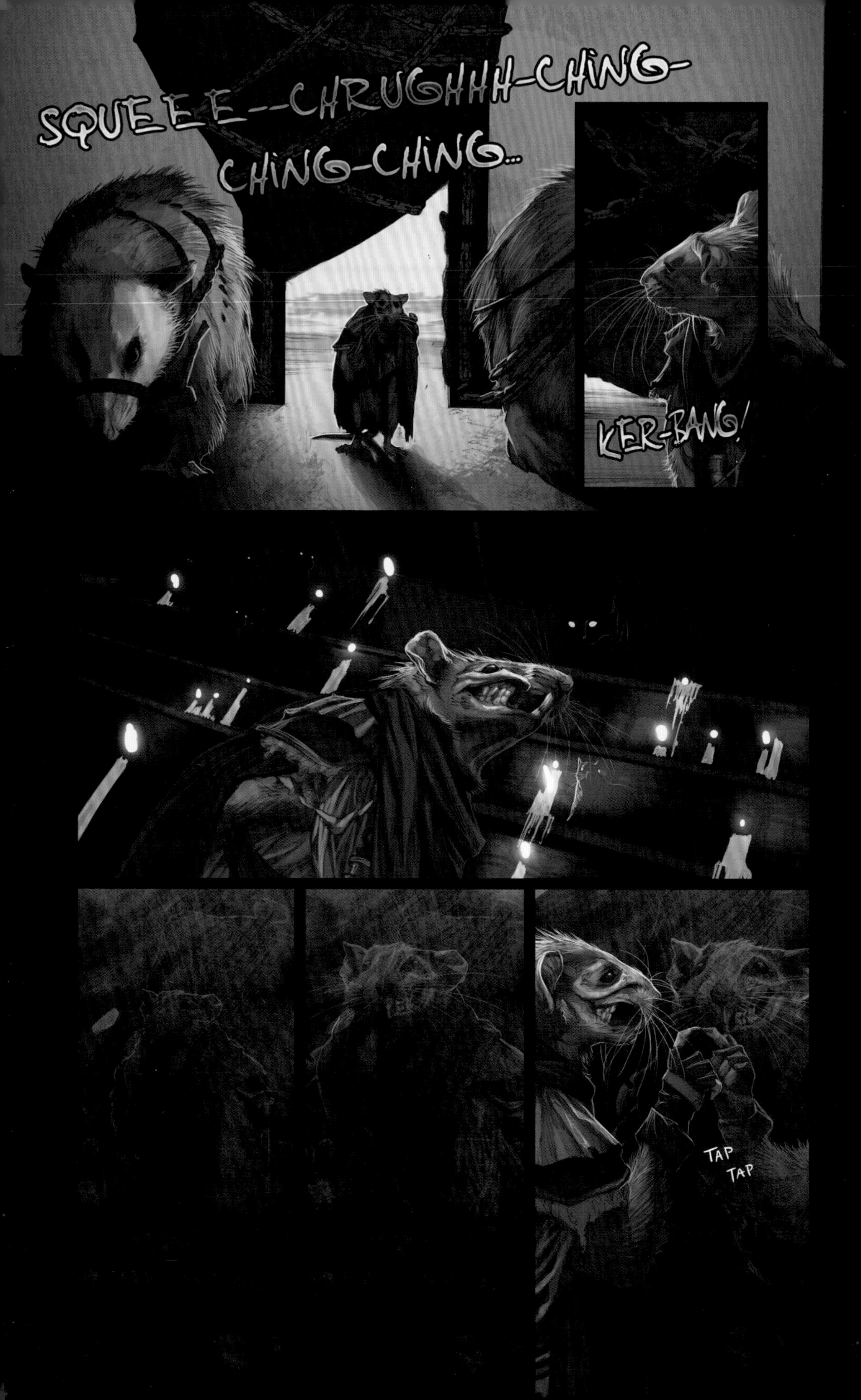
SQUEEEE--CHRUGHHH-CHING-
CHING-CHING...
KER-BANG!
TAP
TAP

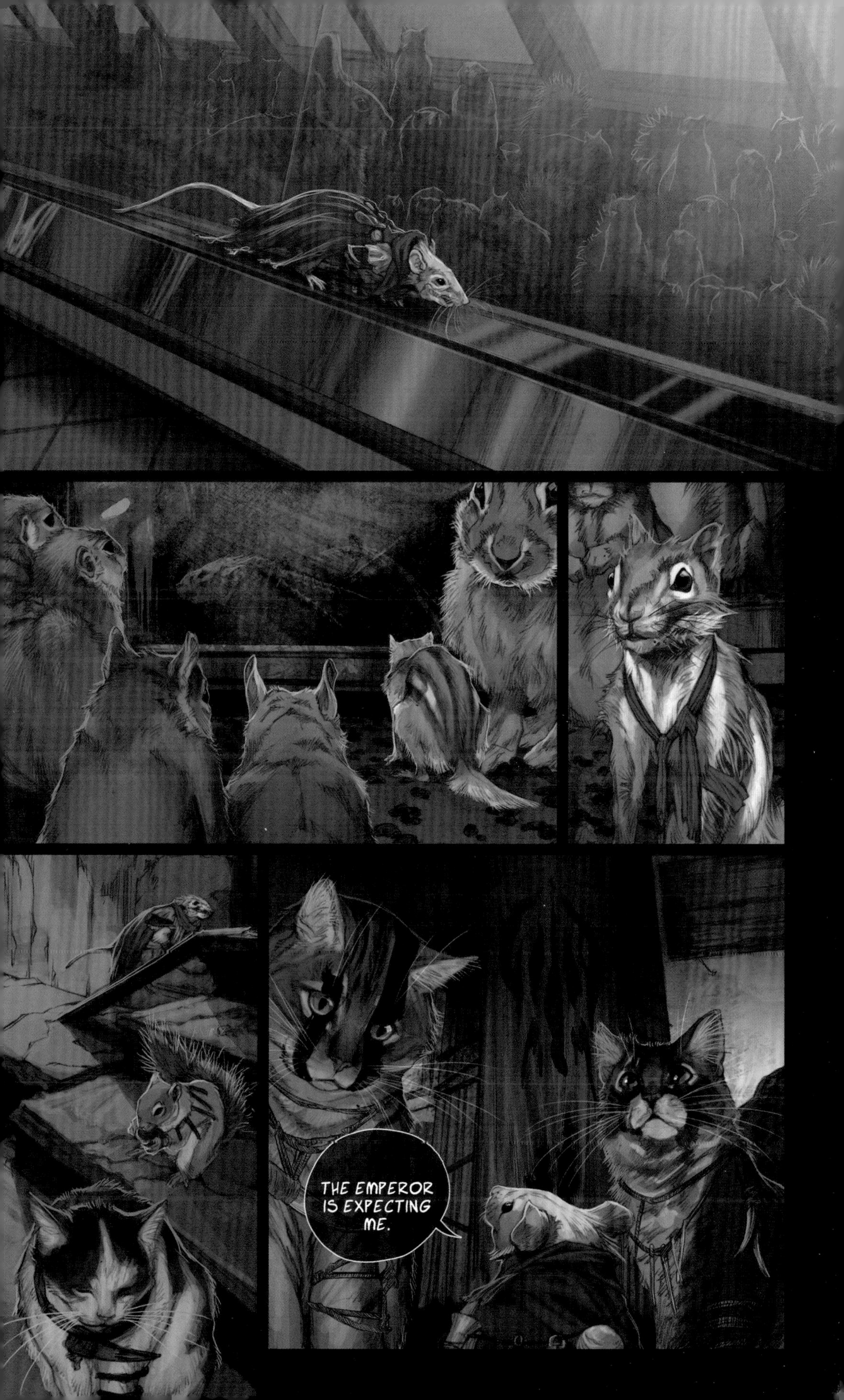
THE EMPEROR IS EXPECTING ME.

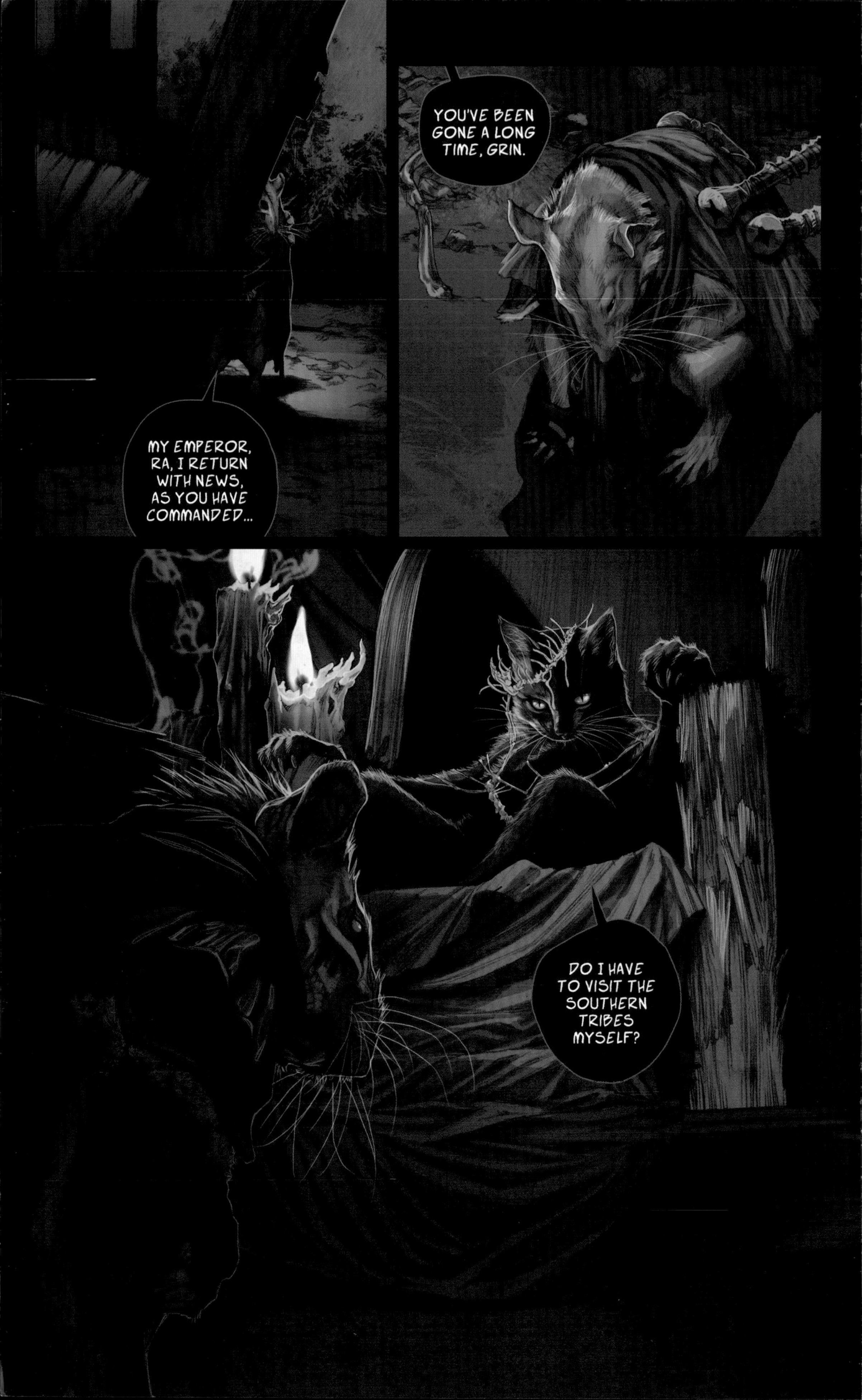
MY EMPEROR, RA, I RETURN WITH NEWS, AS YOU HAVE COMMANDED...
YOU'VE BEEN GONE A LONG TIME, GRIN.
DO I HAVE TO VISIT THE SOUTHERN TRIBES MYSELF?

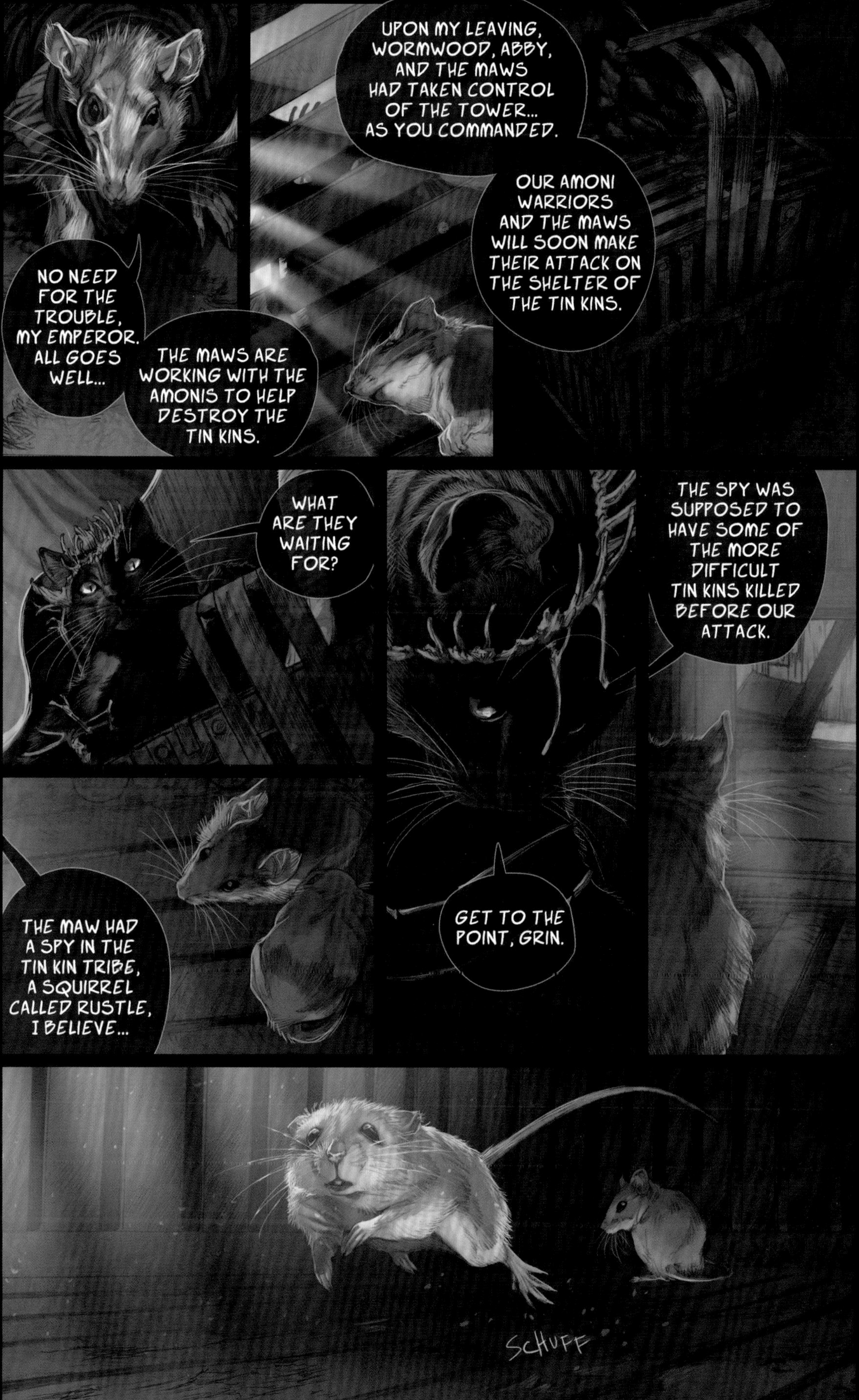
UPON MY LEAVING, WORMWOOD, ABBY, AND THE MAWS HAD TAKEN CONTROL OF THE TOWER... AS YOU COMMANDED.
OUR AMONI WARRIORS AND THE MAWS WILL SOON MAKE THEIR ATTACK ON THE SHELTER OF THE TIN KINS.
NO NEED FOR THE TROUBLE, MY EMPEROR. ALL GOES WELL...
THE MAWS ARE WORKING WITH THE AMONIS TO HELP DESTROY THE TIN KINS.
WHAT ARE THEY WAITING FOR?
THE SPY WAS SUPPOSED TO HAVE SOME OF THE MORE DIFFICULT TIN KINS KILLED BEFORE OUR ATTACK.
THE MAW HAD A SPY IN THE TIN KIN TRIBE, A SQUIRREL CALLED RUSTLE, I BELIEVE...
GET TO THE POINT, GRIN.
SCHUFF

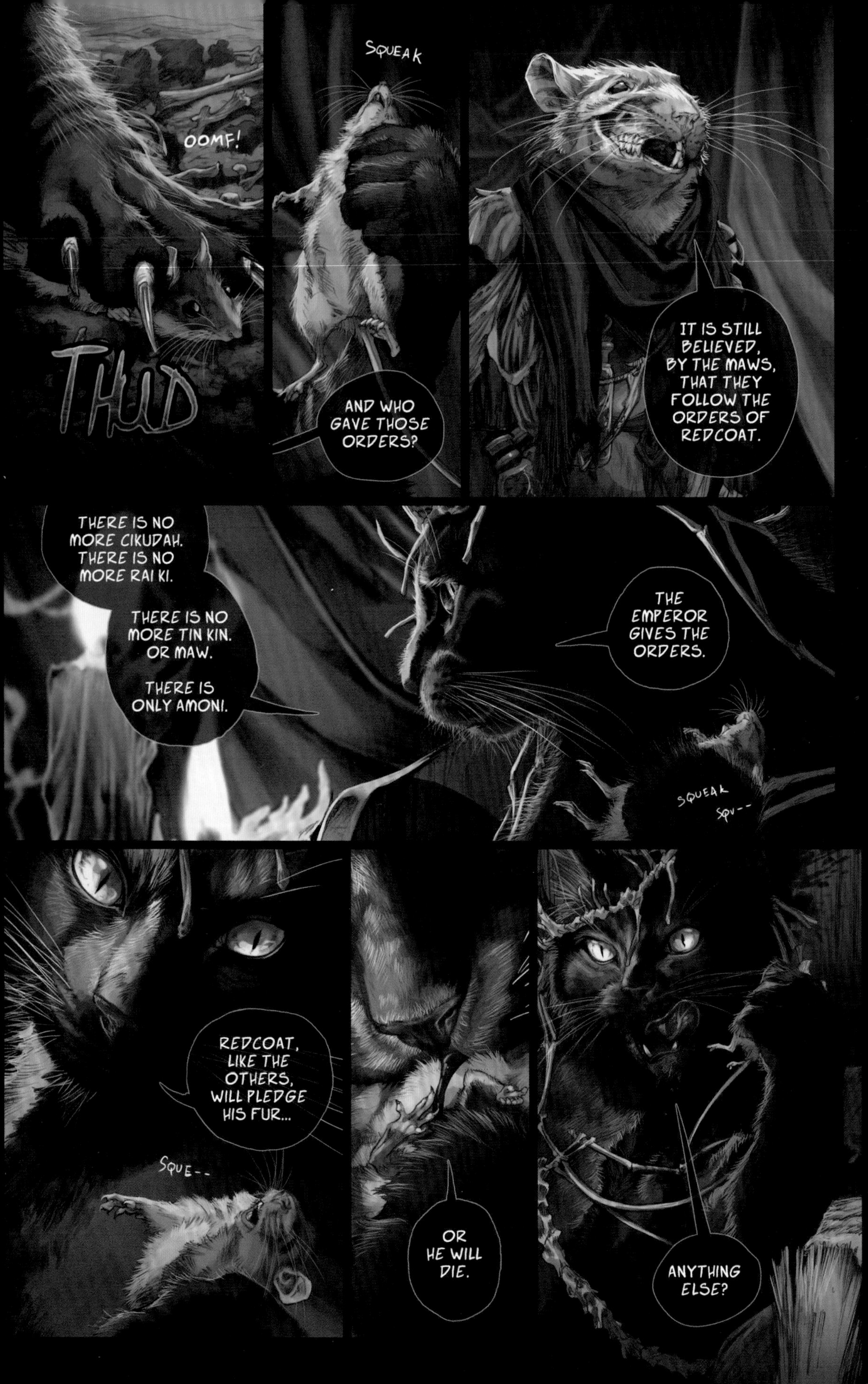
OOMF!
THUD
SQUEAK
AND WHO GAVE THOSE ORDERS?
IT IS STILL BELIEVED, BY THE MAWS, THAT THEY FOLLOW THE ORDERS OF REDCOAT.
THERE IS NO MORE CIKUDAH. THERE IS NO MORE RAI KI.
THERE IS NO MORE TIN KIN. OR MAW.
THERE IS ONLY AMONI.
THE EMPEROR GIVES THE ORDERS.
SQUEAK
SQU--
REDCOAT, LIKE THE OTHERS, WILL PLEDGE HIS FUR...
SQUE--
OR HE WILL DIE.
ANYTHING ELSE?

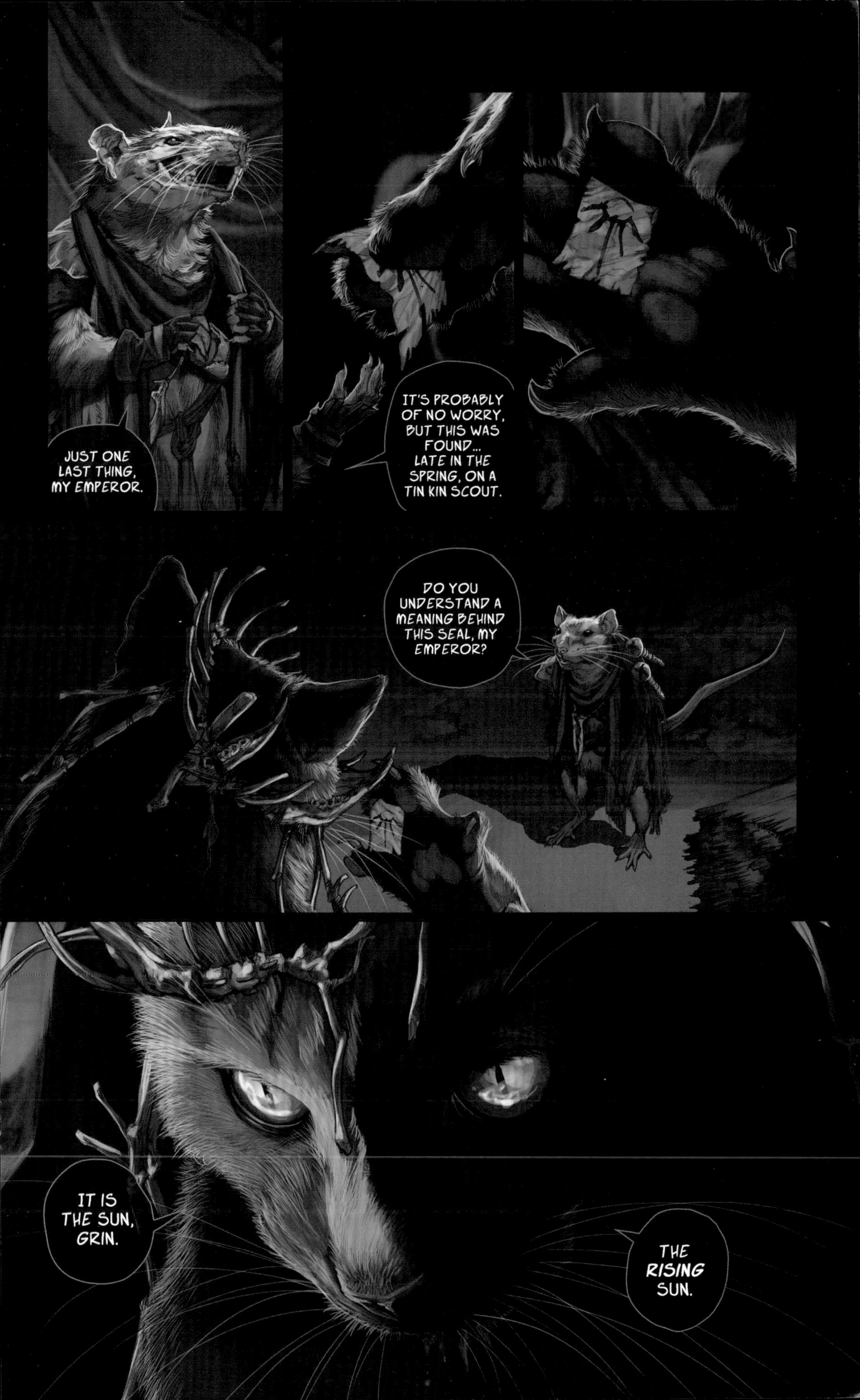
JUST ONE LAST THING, MY EMPEROR.
IT'S PROBABLY OF NO WORRY, BUT THIS WAS FOUND... LATE IN THE SPRING, ON A TIN KIN SCOUT.
DO YOU UNDERSTAND A MEANING BEHIND THIS SEAL, MY EMPEROR?
IT IS THE SUN, GRIN.
THE *RISING* SUN.

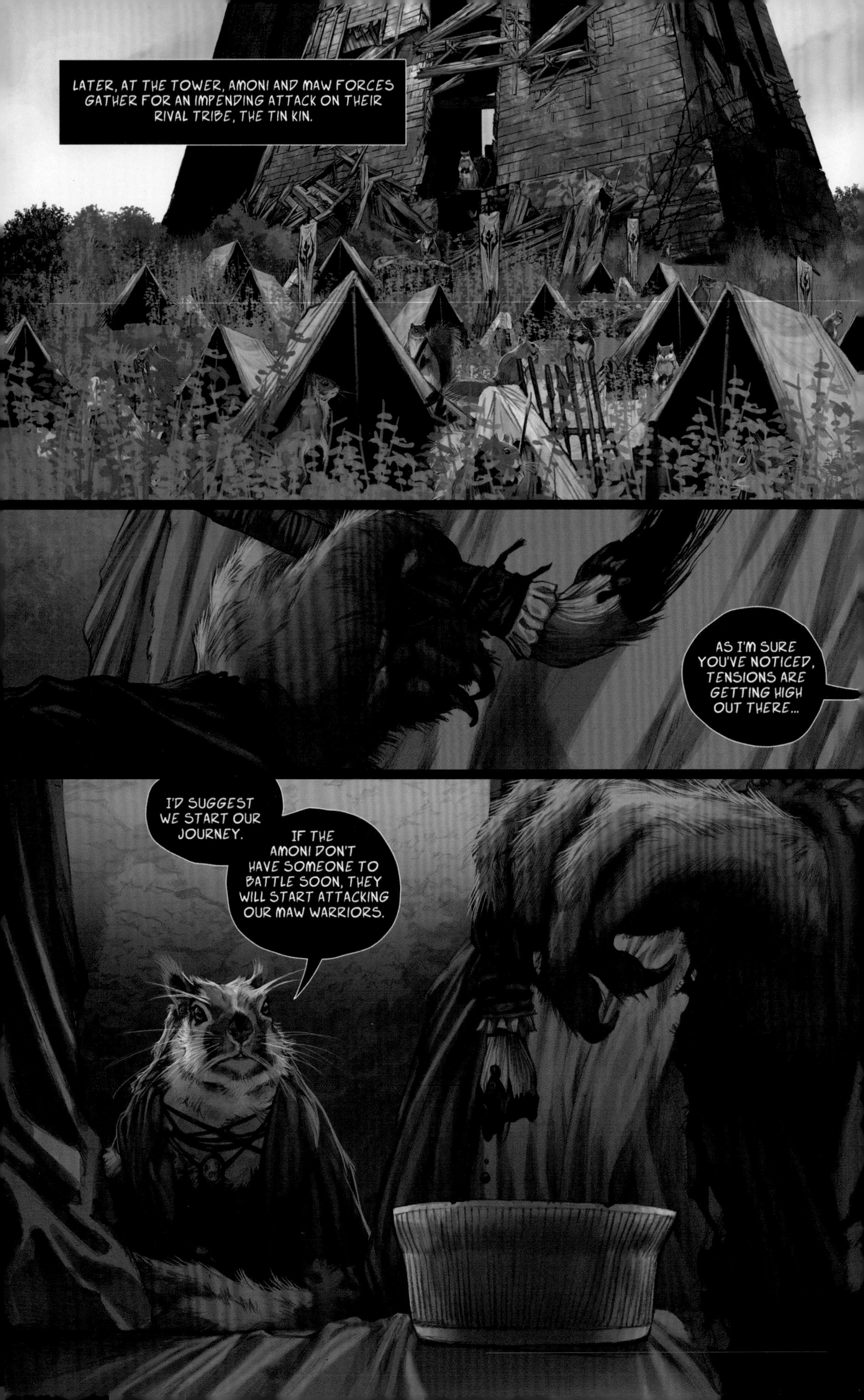

LATER, AT THE TOWER, AMONI AND MAW FORCES GATHER FOR AN IMPENDING ATTACK ON THEIR RIVAL TRIBE, THE TIN KIN.
AS I'M SURE YOU'VE NOTICED, TENSIONS ARE GETTING HIGH OUT THERE...
I'D SUGGEST WE START OUR JOURNEY.
IF THE AMONI DON'T HAVE SOMEONE TO BATTLE SOON, THEY WILL START ATTACKING OUR MAW WARRIORS.

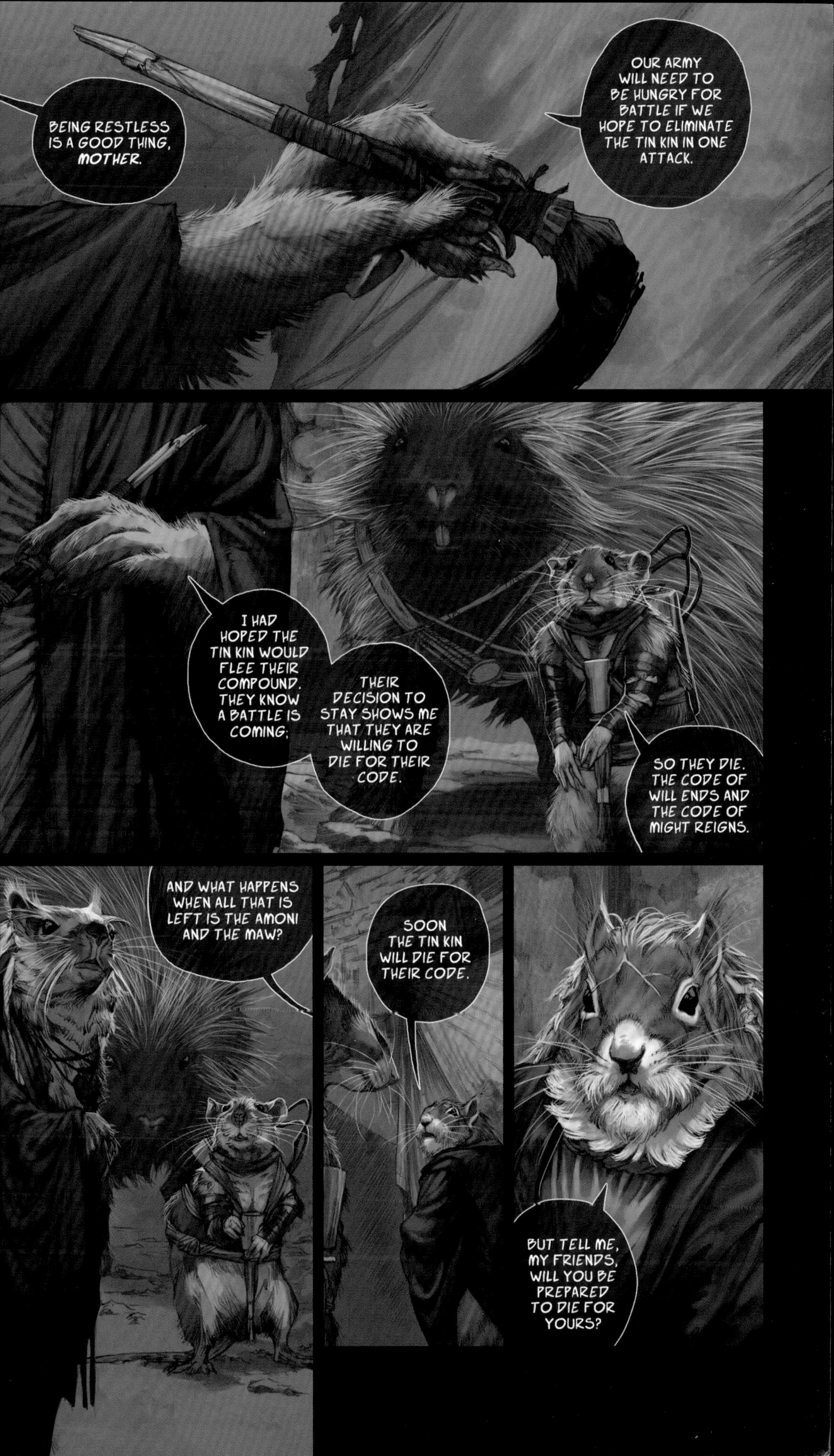
BEING RESTLESS IS A GOOD THING, MOTHER.
OUR ARMY WILL NEED TO BE HUNGRY FOR BATTLE IF WE HOPE TO ELIMINATE THE TIN KIN IN ONE ATTACK.
I HAD HOPED THE TIN KIN WOULD FLEE THEIR COMPOUND. THEY KNOW A BATTLE IS COMING;
THEIR DECISION TO STAY SHOWS ME THAT THEY ARE WILLING TO DIE FOR THEIR CODE.
SO THEY DIE. THE CODE OF WILL ENDS AND THE CODE OF MIGHT REIGNS.
AND WHAT HAPPENS WHEN ALL THAT IS LEFT IS THE AMONI AND THE MAW?
SOON THE TIN KIN WILL DIE FOR THEIR CODE.
BUT TELL ME, MY FRIENDS, WILL YOU BE PREPARED TO DIE FOR YOURS?

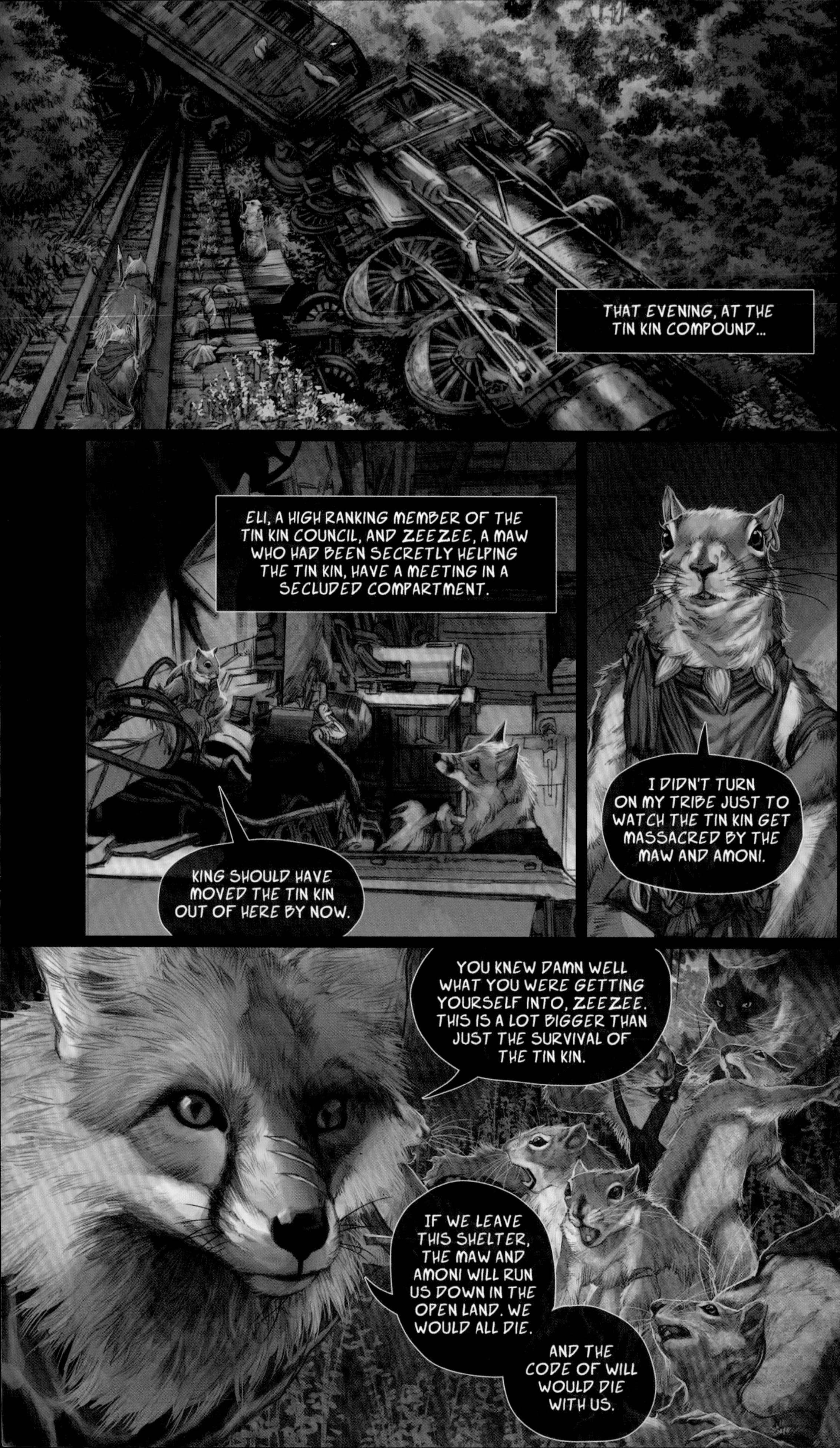
THAT EVENING, AT THE TIN KIN COMPOUND...
ELI, A HIGH RANKING MEMBER OF THE TIN KIN COUNCIL, AND ZEEZEE, A MAW WHO HAD BEEN SECRETLY HELPING THE TIN KIN, HAVE A MEETING IN A SECLUDED COMPARTMENT.
KING SHOULD HAVE MOVED THE TIN KIN OUT OF HERE BY NOW.
I DIDN'T TURN ON MY TRIBE JUST TO WATCH THE TIN KIN GET MASSACRED BY THE MAW AND AMONI.
YOU KNEW DAMN WELL WHAT YOU WERE GETTING YOURSELF INTO, ZEEZEE. THIS IS A LOT BIGGER THAN JUST THE SURVIVAL OF THE TIN KIN.
IF WE LEAVE THIS SHELTER, THE MAW AND AMONI WILL RUN US DOWN IN THE OPEN LAND. WE WOULD ALL DIE.
AND THE CODE OF WILL WOULD DIE WITH US.

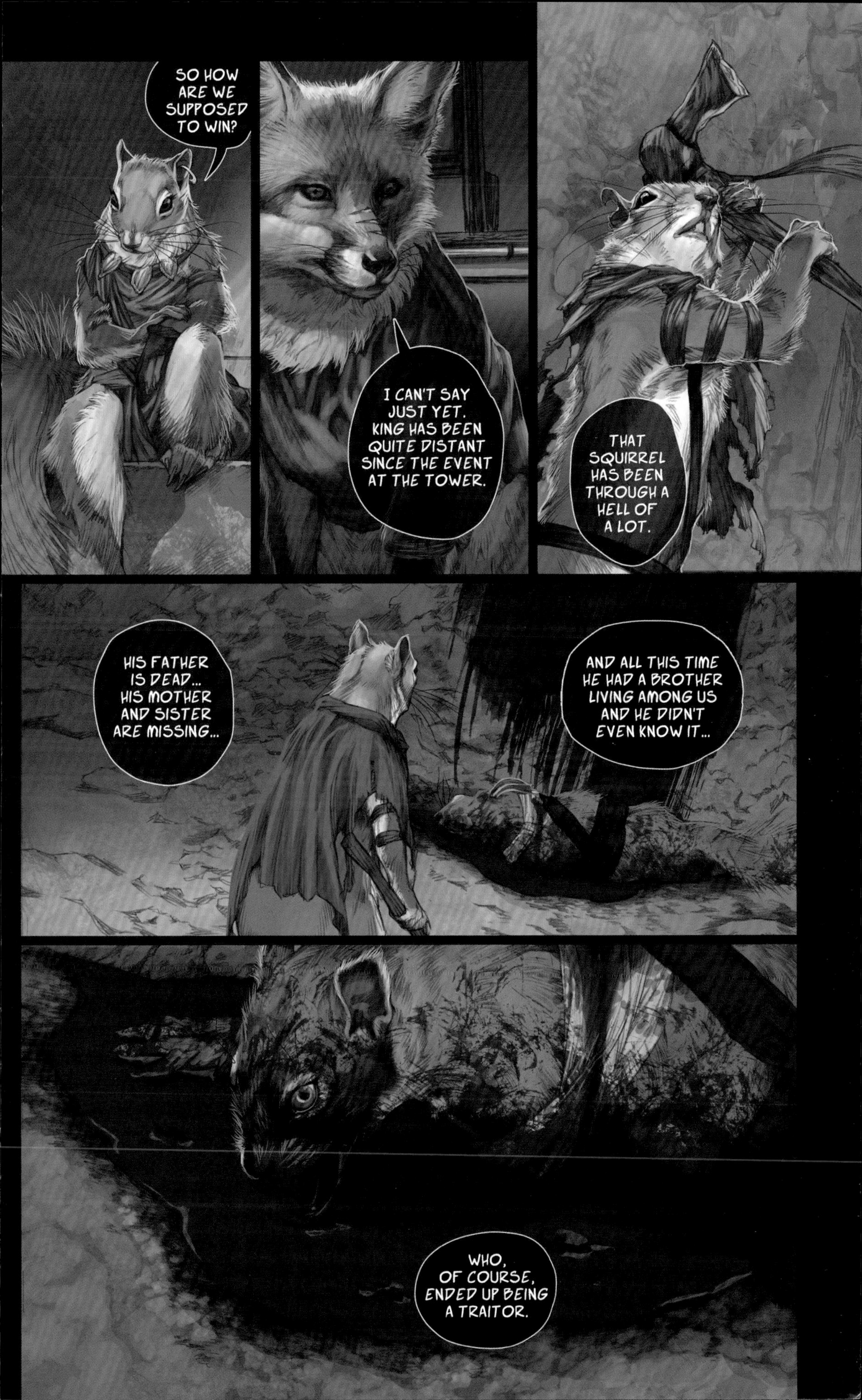
SO HOW ARE WE SUPPOSED TO WIN?
I CAN'T SAY JUST YET. KING HAS BEEN QUITE DISTANT SINCE THE EVENT AT THE TOWER.
THAT SQUIRREL HAS BEEN THROUGH A HELL OF A LOT.
HIS FATHER IS DEAD... HIS MOTHER AND SISTER ARE MISSING...
AND ALL THIS TIME HE HAD A BROTHER LIVING AMONG US AND HE DIDN'T EVEN KNOW IT...
WHO, OF COURSE, ENDED UP BEING A TRAITOR.

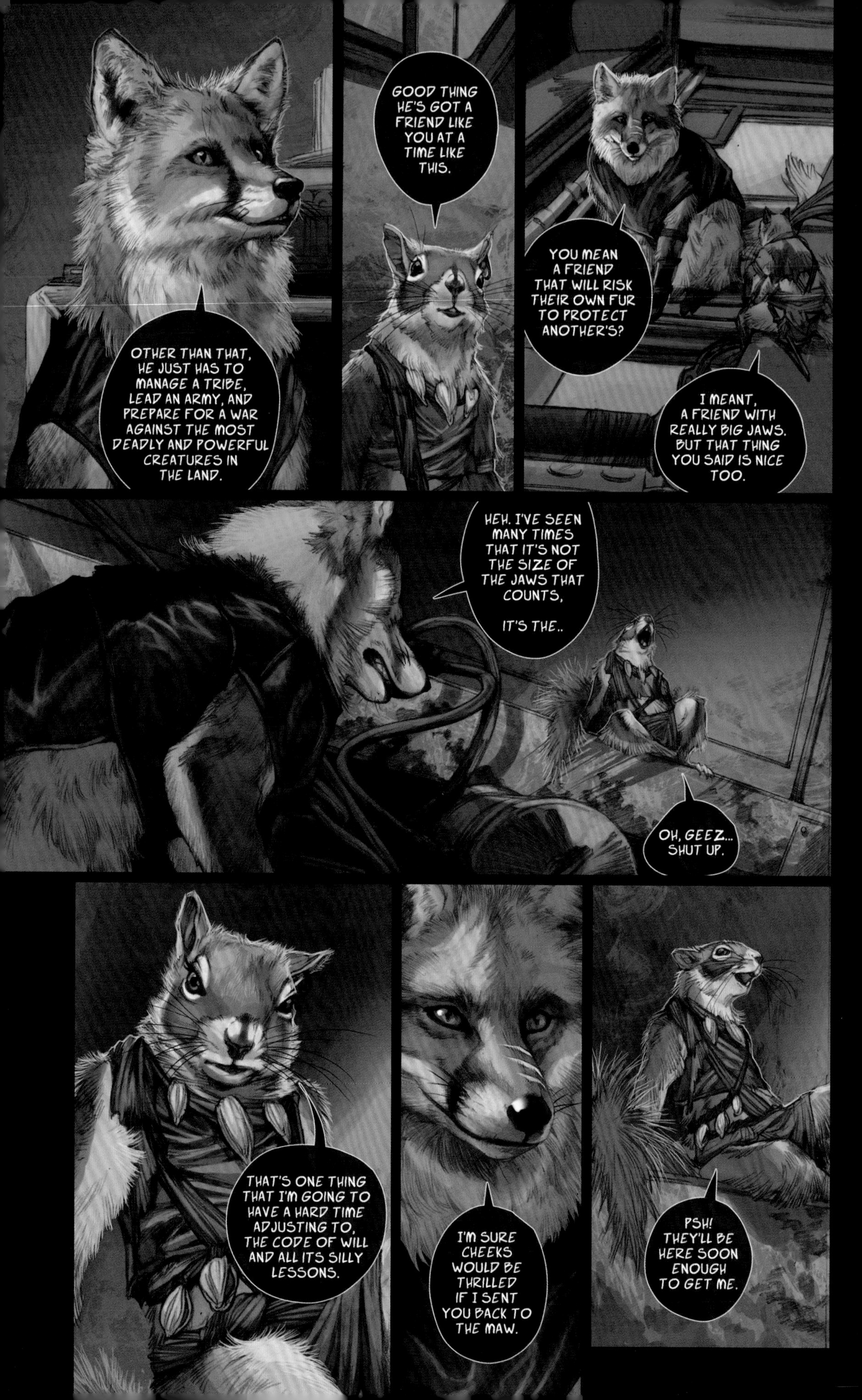

OTHER THAN THAT, HE JUST HAS TO MANAGE A TRIBE, LEAD AN ARMY, AND PREPARE FOR A WAR AGAINST THE MOST DEADLY AND POWERFUL CREATURES IN THE LAND.
GOOD THING HE'S GOT A FRIEND LIKE YOU AT A TIME LIKE THIS.
YOU MEAN A FRIEND THAT WILL RISK THEIR OWN FUR TO PROTECT ANOTHER'S?
I MEANT, A FRIEND WITH REALLY BIG JAWS. BUT THAT THING YOU SAID IS NICE TOO.
HEH. I'VE SEEN MANY TIMES THAT IT'S NOT THE SIZE OF THE JAWS THAT COUNTS,
IT'S THE..
OH, GEEZ... SHUT UP.
THAT'S ONE THING THAT I'M GOING TO HAVE A HARD TIME ADJUSTING TO, THE CODE OF WILL AND ALL ITS SILLY LESSONS.
I'M SURE CHEEKS WOULD BE THRILLED IF I SENT YOU BACK TO THE MAW.
PSH! THEY'LL BE HERE SOON ENOUGH TO GET ME.

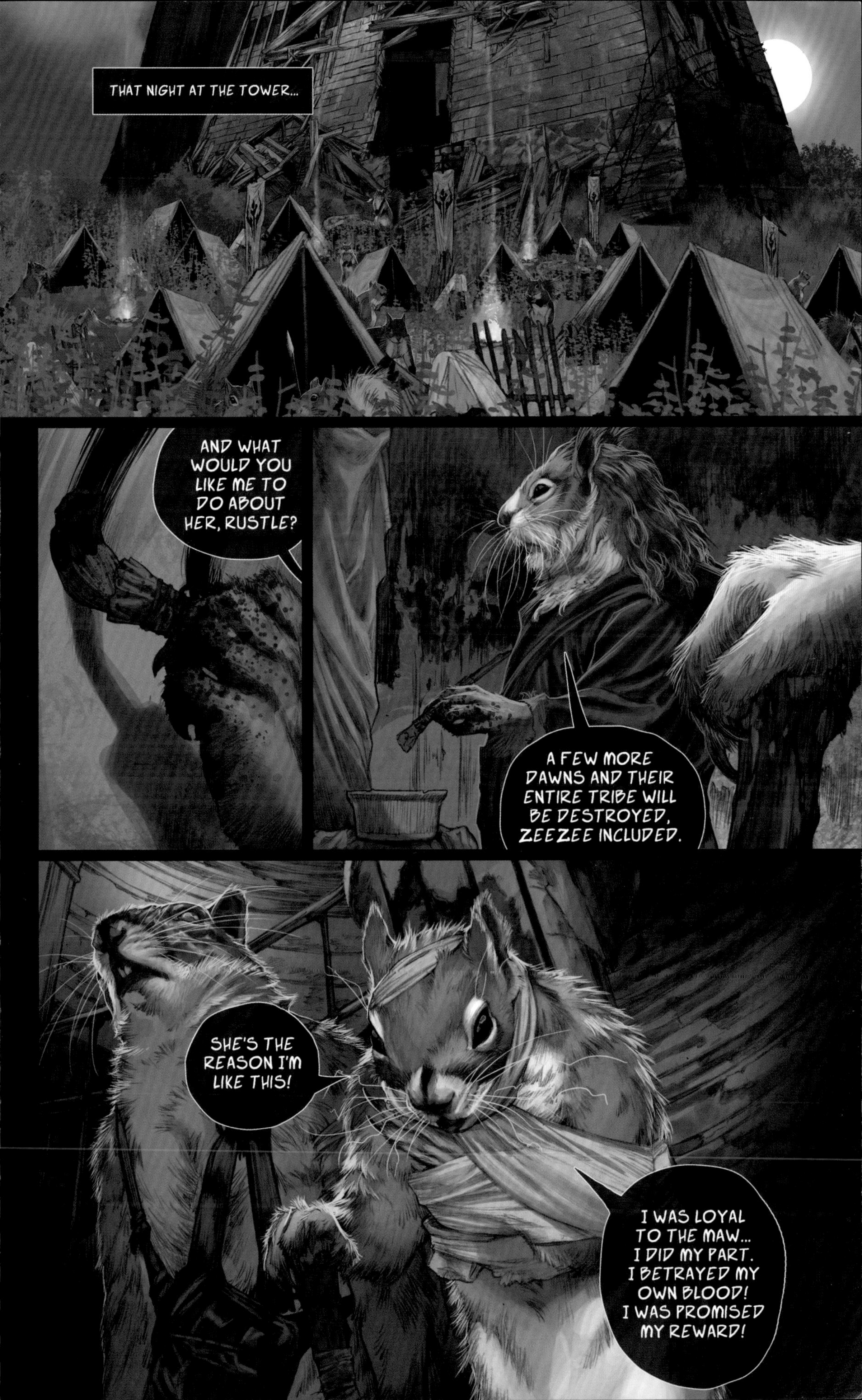
THAT NIGHT AT THE TOWER...
AND WHAT WOULD YOU LIKE ME TO DO ABOUT HER, RUSTLE?
A FEW MORE DAWNS AND THEIR ENTIRE TRIBE WILL BE DESTROYED, ZEEZEE INCLUDED.
SHE'S THE REASON I'M LIKE THIS!
I WAS LOYAL TO THE MAW... I DID MY PART. I BETRAYED MY OWN BLOOD! I WAS PROMISED MY REWARD!

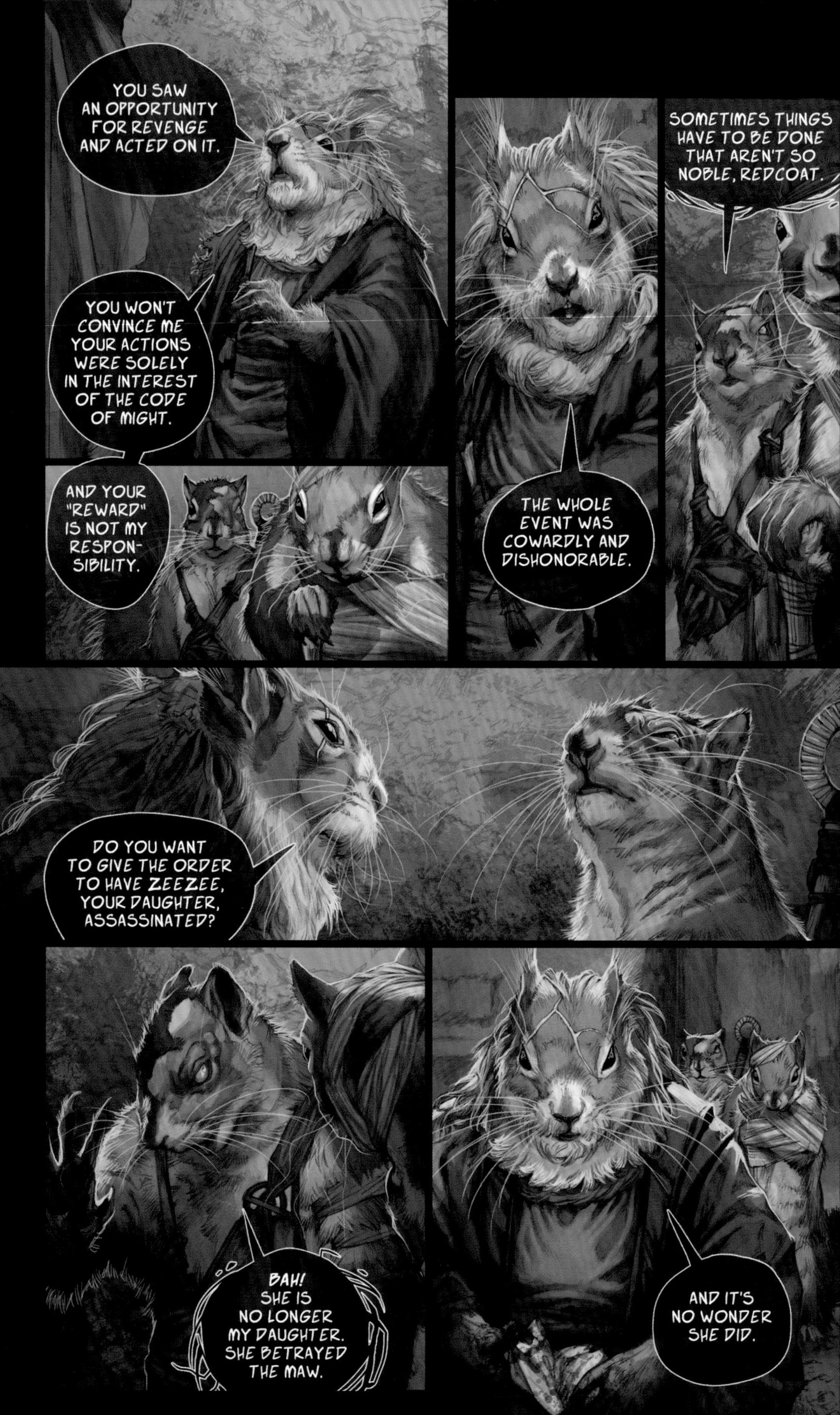
YOU SAW AN OPPORTUNITY FOR REVENGE AND ACTED ON IT.
YOU WON'T CONVINCE ME YOUR ACTIONS WERE SOLELY IN THE INTEREST OF THE CODE OF MIGHT.
AND YOUR "REWARD" IS NOT MY RESPON-SIBILITY.
THE WHOLE EVENT WAS COWARDLY AND DISHONORABLE.
SOMETIMES THINGS HAVE TO BE DONE THAT AREN'T SO NOBLE, REDCOAT.
DO YOU WANT TO GIVE THE ORDER TO HAVE ZEEZEE, YOUR DAUGHTER, ASSASSINATED?
BAH! SHE IS NO LONGER MY DAUGHTER. SHE BETRAYED THE MAW.
AND IT'S NO WONDER SHE DID.

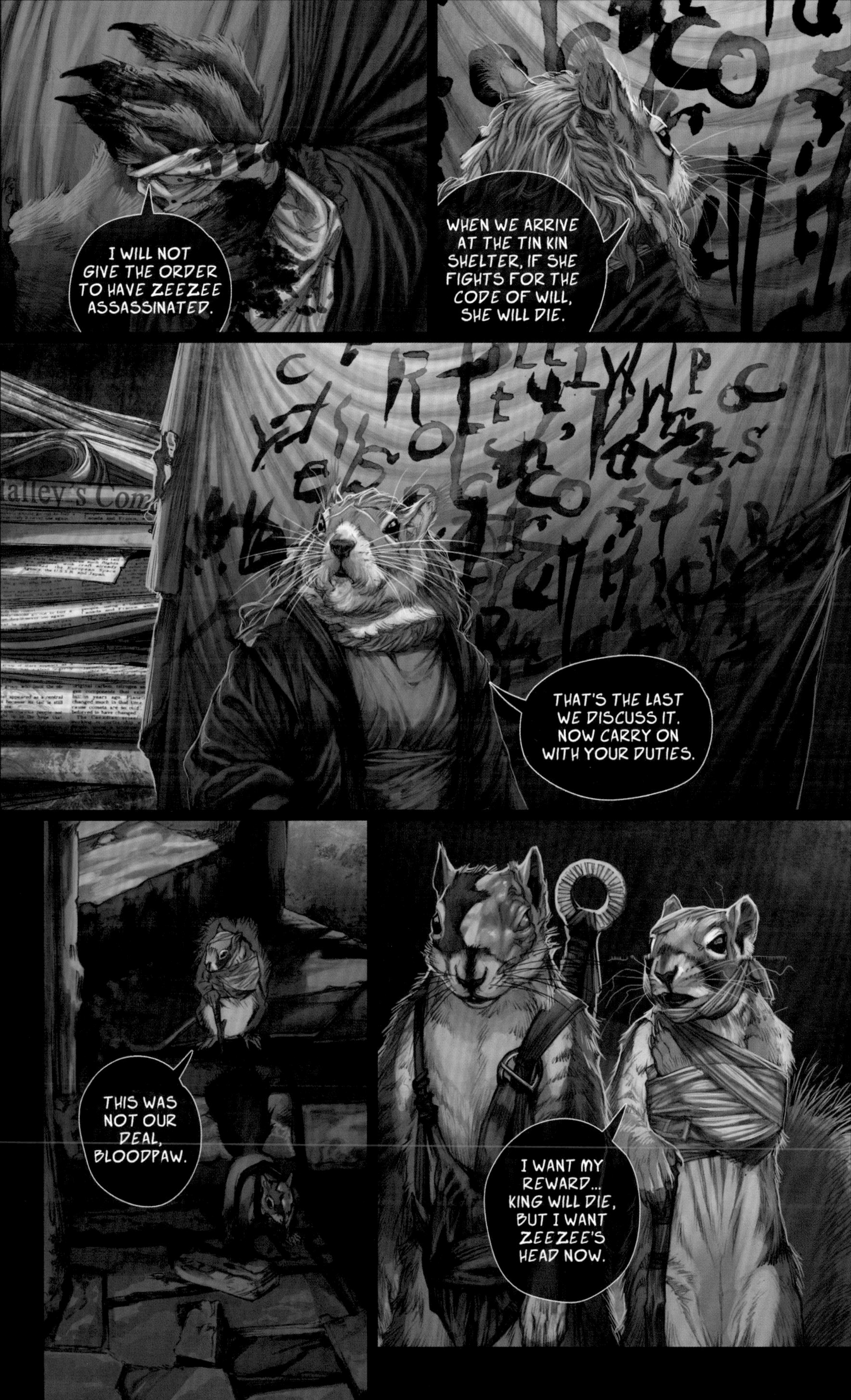
I WILL NOT GIVE THE ORDER TO HAVE ZEEZEE ASSASSINATED.
WHEN WE ARRIVE AT THE TIN KIN SHELTER, IF SHE FIGHTS FOR THE CODE OF WILL, SHE WILL DIE.
THAT'S THE LAST WE DISCUSS IT. NOW CARRY ON WITH YOUR DUTIES.
THIS WAS NOT OUR DEAL, BLOODPAW.
I WANT MY REWARD... KING WILL DIE, BUT I WANT ZEEZEE'S HEAD NOW.

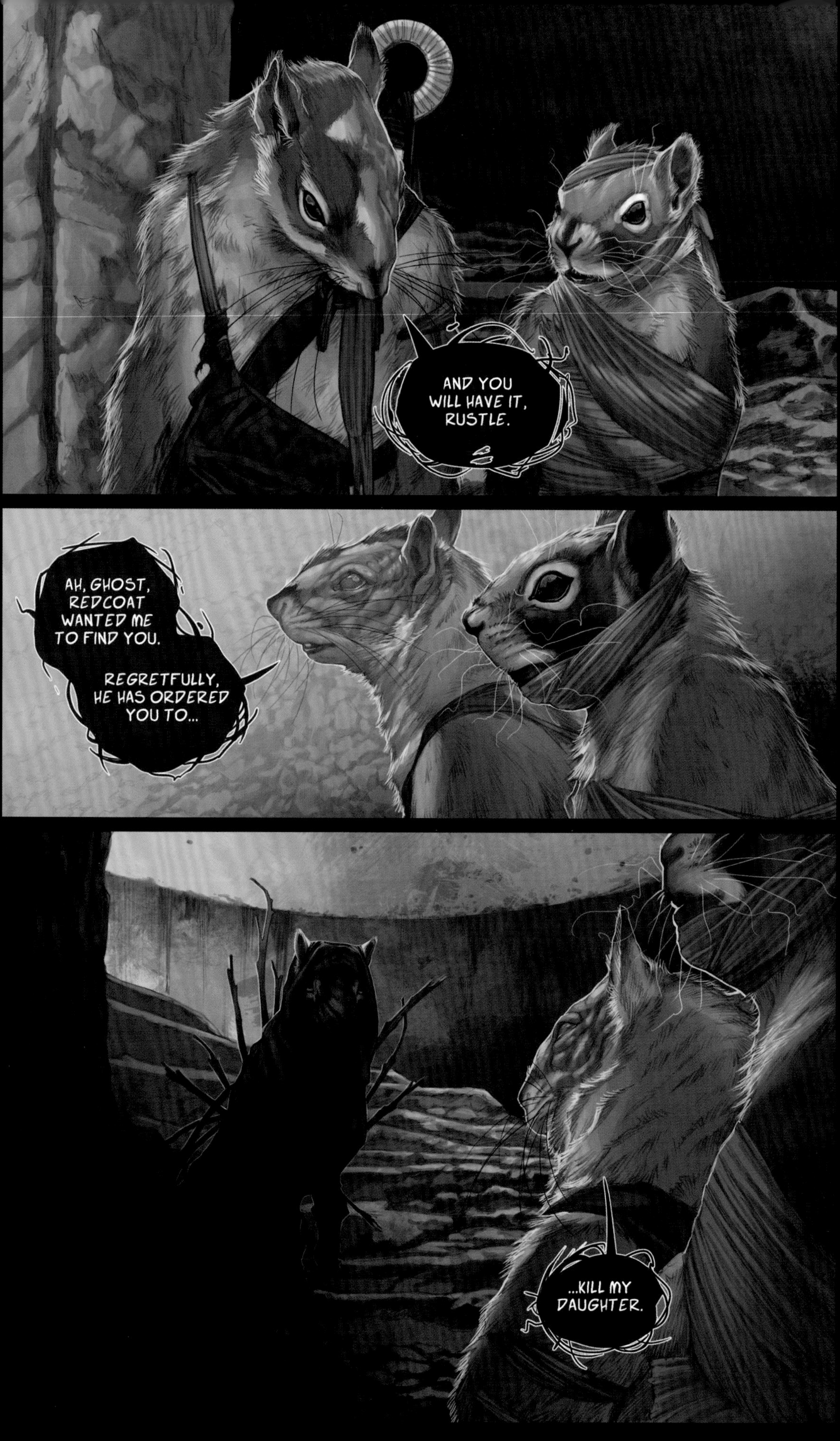
AND YOU WILL HAVE IT, RUSTLE.
AH, GHOST, REDCOAT WANTED ME TO FIND YOU.
REGRETFULLY, HE HAS ORDERED YOU TO...
...KILL MY DAUGHTER.

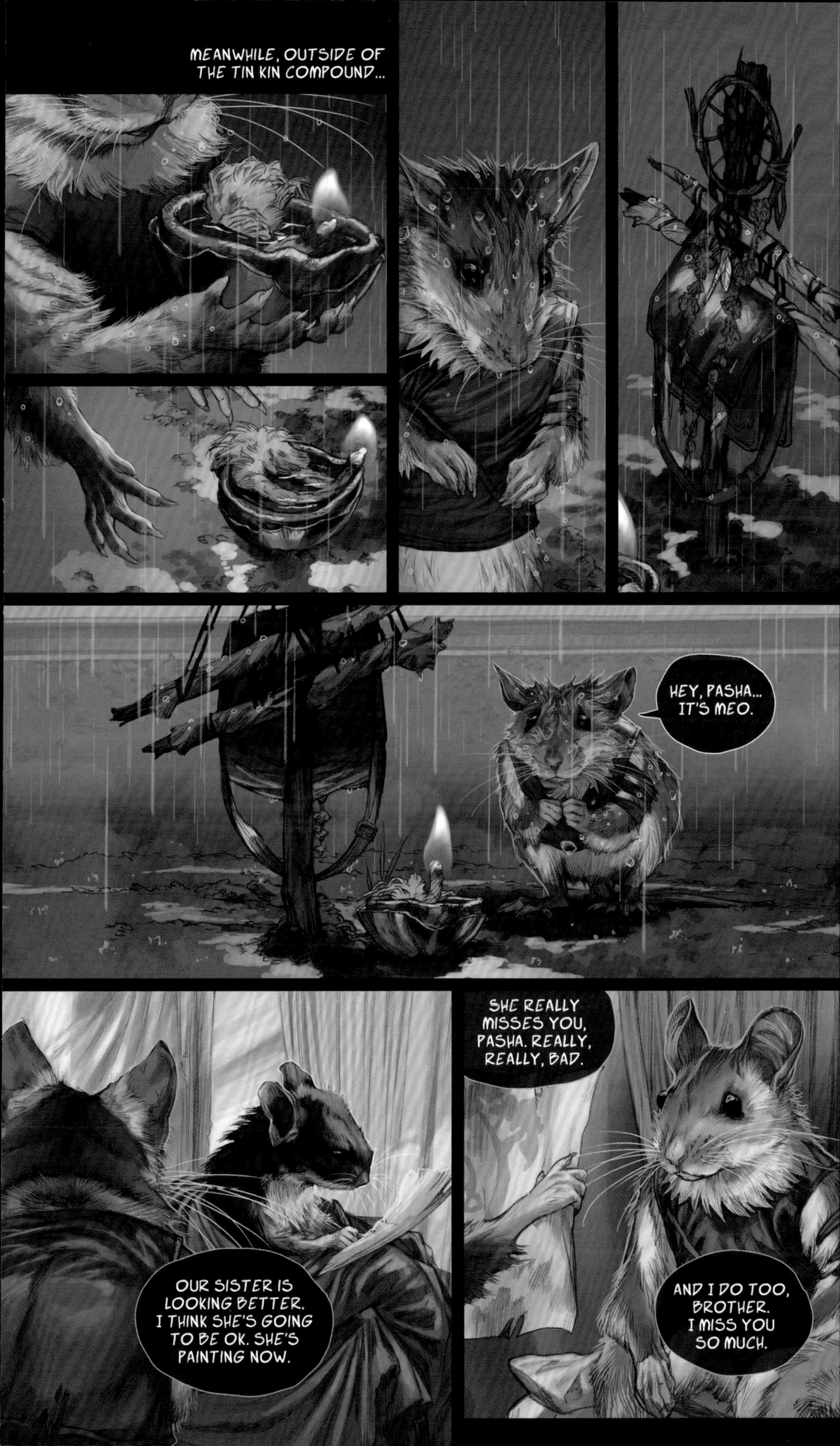
MEANWHILE, OUTSIDE OF THE TIN KIN COMPOUND...
HEY, PASHA... IT'S MEO.
OUR SISTER IS LOOKING BETTER. I THINK SHE'S GOING TO BE OK. SHE'S PAINTING NOW.
SHE REALLY MISSES YOU, PASHA. REALLY, REALLY, BAD.
AND I DO TOO, BROTHER. I MISS YOU SO MUCH.

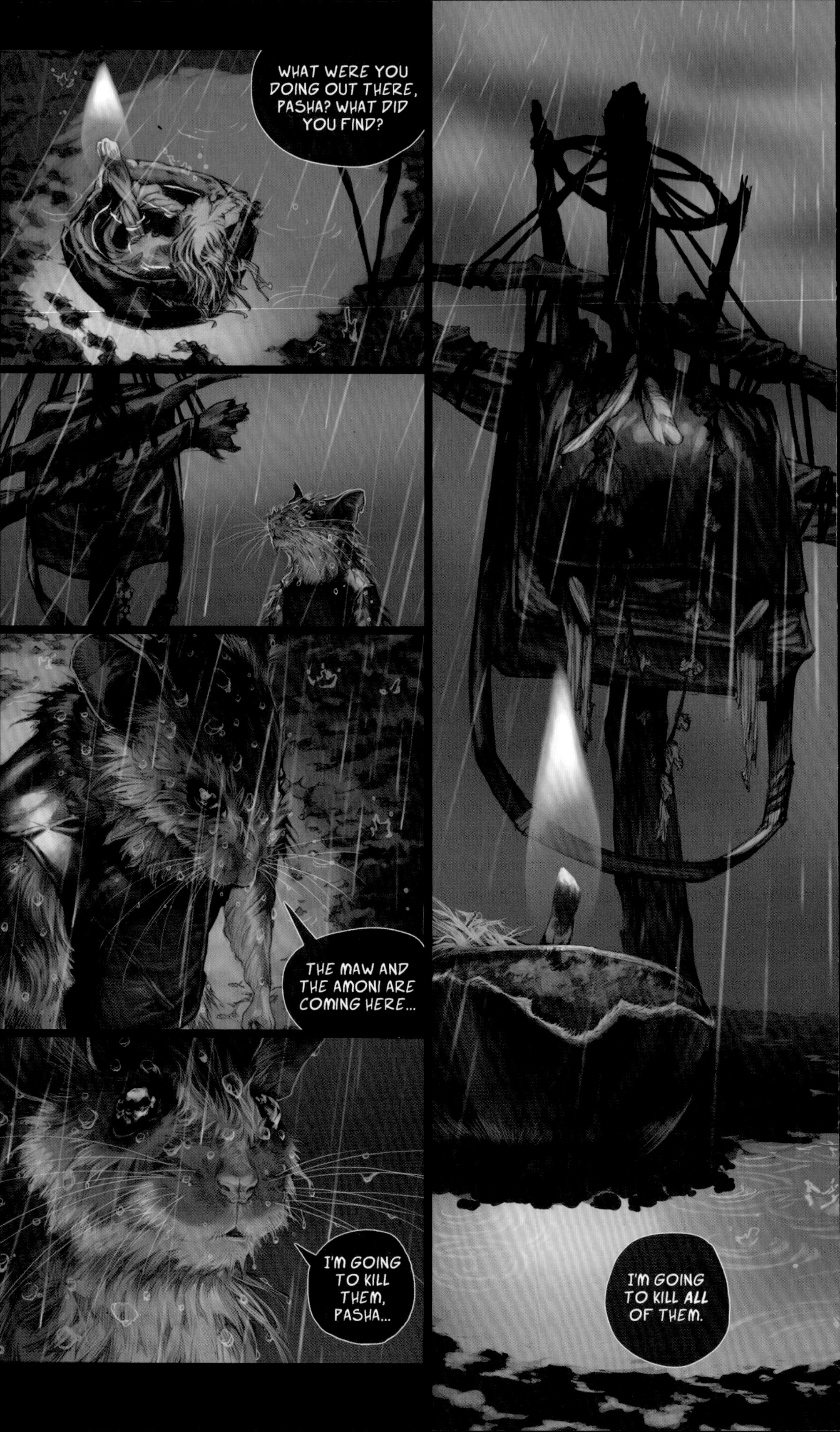
WHAT WERE YOU DOING OUT THERE, PASHA? WHAT DID YOU FIND?
THE MAW AND THE AMONI ARE COMING HERE...
I'M GOING TO KILL THEM, PASHA...
I'M GOING TO KILL ALL OF THEM.

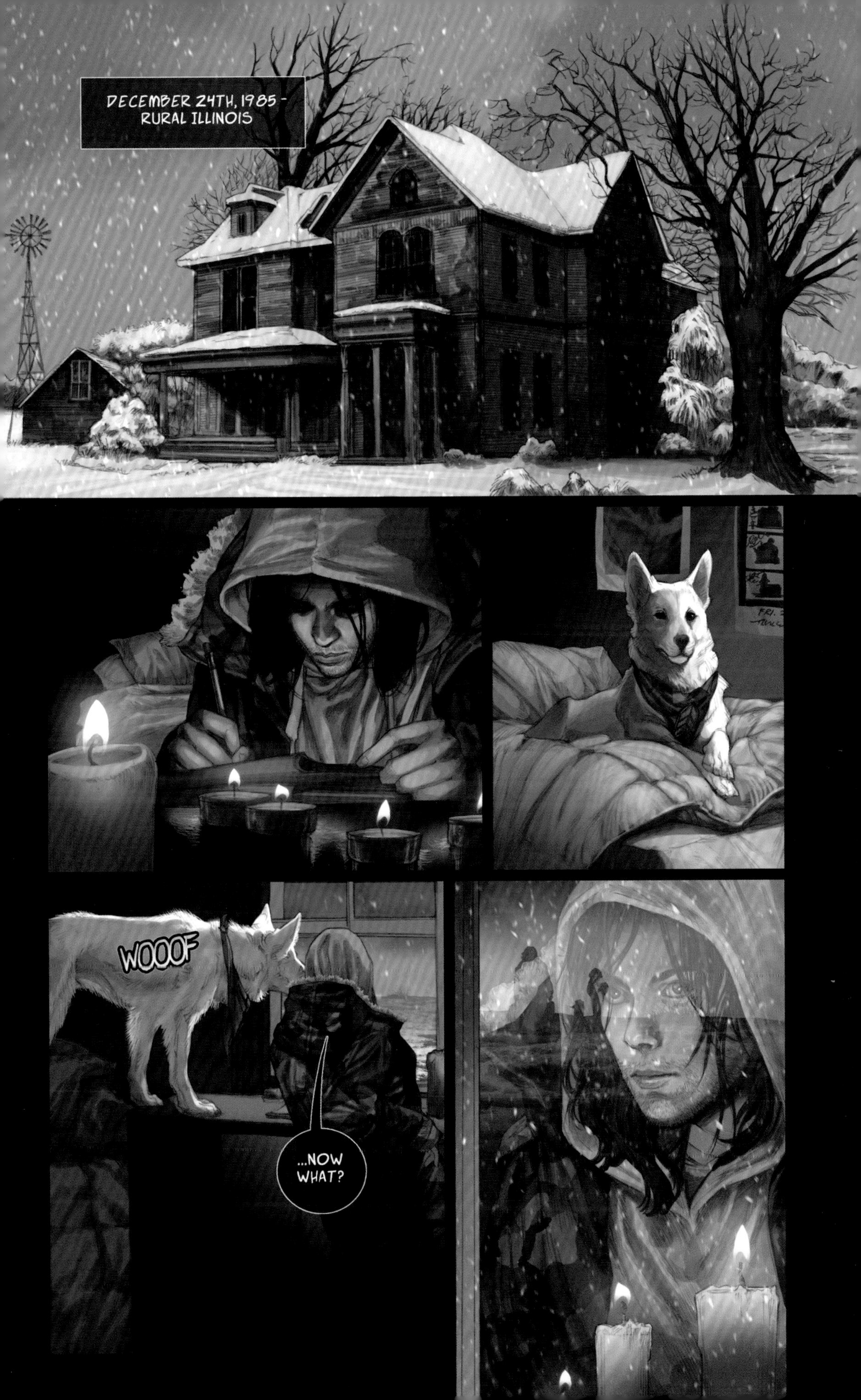

DECEMBER 24TH, 1985 -
RURAL ILLINOIS
WOOOF
...NOW WHAT?

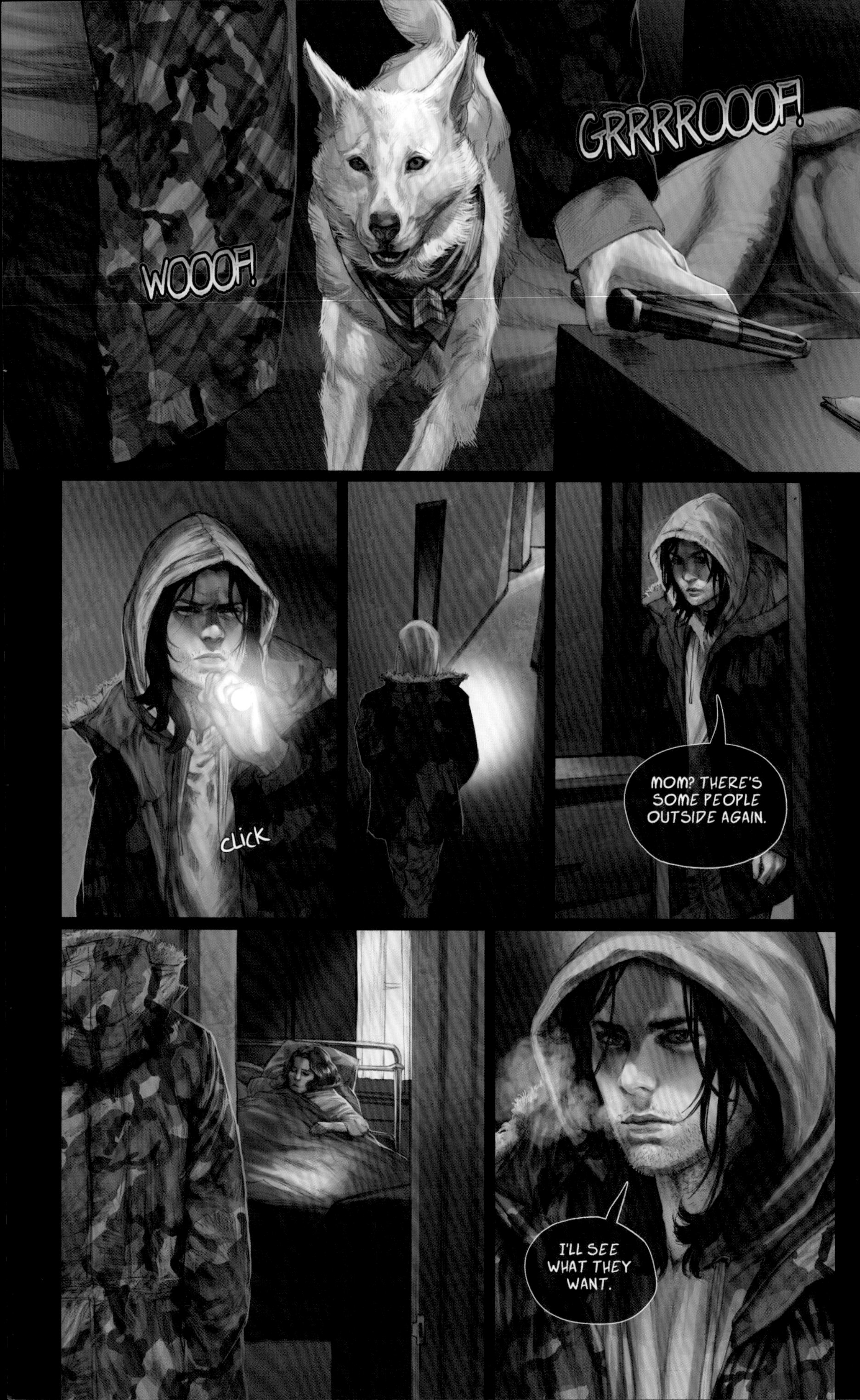
WOOOF!
GRRRROOOF!
CLICK
MOM? THERE'S SOME PEOPLE OUTSIDE AGAIN.
I'LL SEE WHAT THEY WANT.

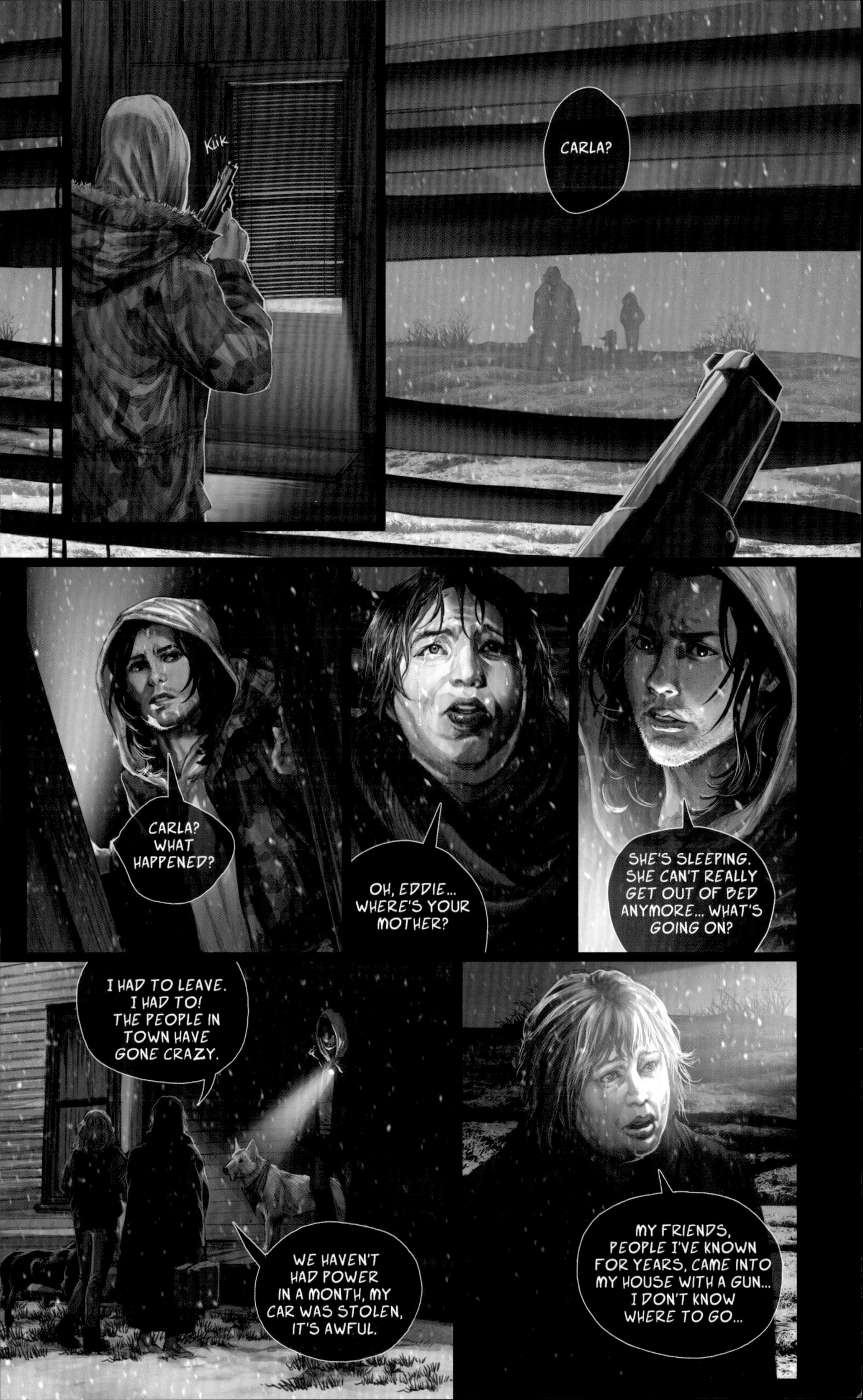
KLIK
CARLA?
CARLA? WHAT HAPPENED?
OH, EDDIE... WHERE'S YOUR MOTHER?
SHE'S SLEEPING. SHE CAN'T REALLY GET OUT OF BED ANYMORE... WHAT'S GOING ON?
I HAD TO LEAVE. I HAD TO! THE PEOPLE IN TOWN HAVE GONE CRAZY.
WE HAVEN'T HAD POWER IN A MONTH, MY CAR WAS STOLEN, IT'S AWFUL.
MY FRIENDS, PEOPLE I'VE KNOWN FOR YEARS, CAME INTO MY HOUSE WITH A GUN... I DON'T KNOW WHERE TO GO...

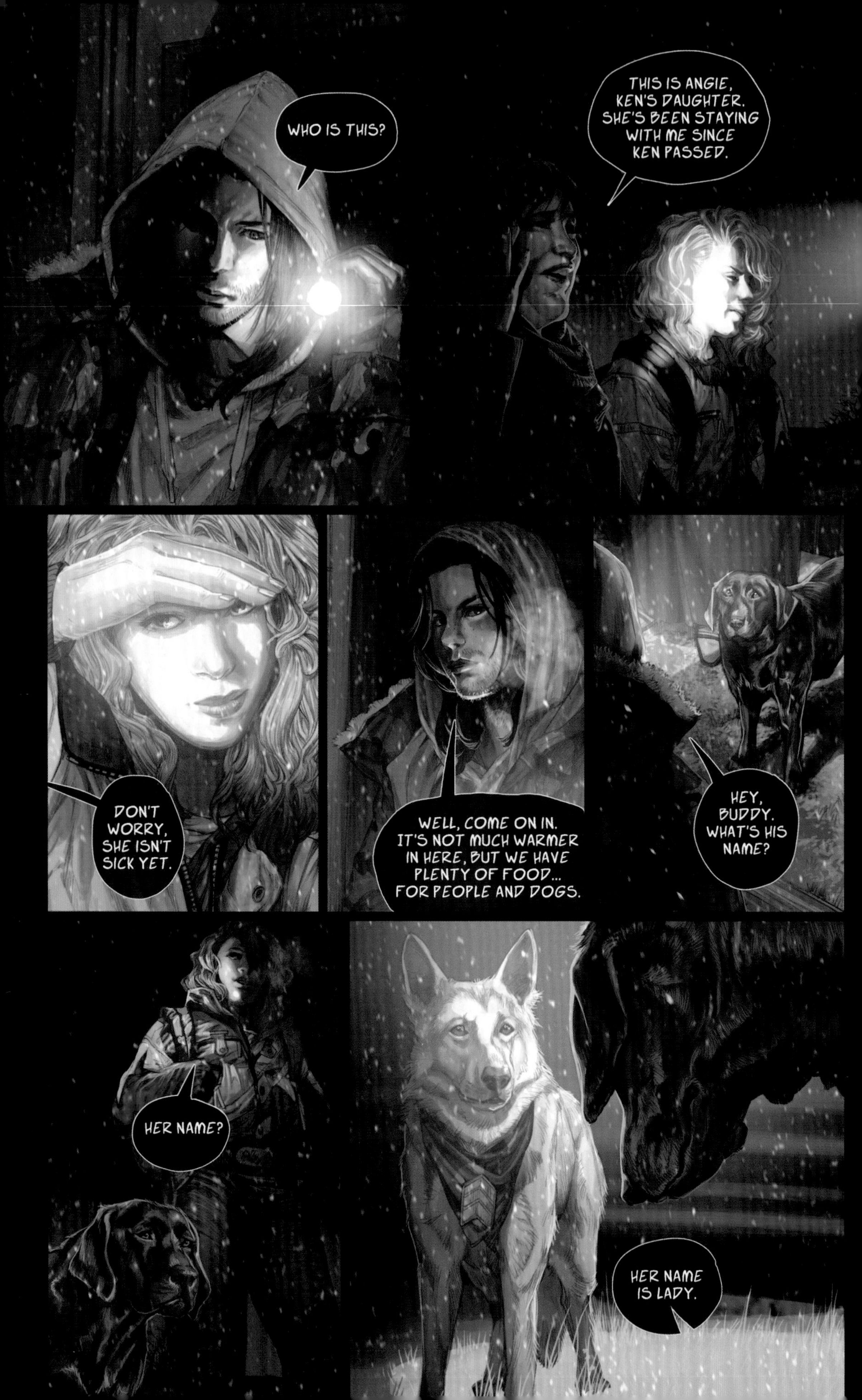
WHO IS THIS?
THIS IS ANGIE, KEN'S DAUGHTER. SHE'S BEEN STAYING WITH ME SINCE KEN PASSED.
DON'T WORRY, SHE ISN'T SICK YET.
WELL, COME ON IN. IT'S NOT MUCH WARMER IN HERE, BUT WE HAVE PLENTY OF FOOD... FOR PEOPLE AND DOGS.
HEY, BUDDY. WHAT'S HIS NAME?
HER NAME?
HER NAME IS LADY.

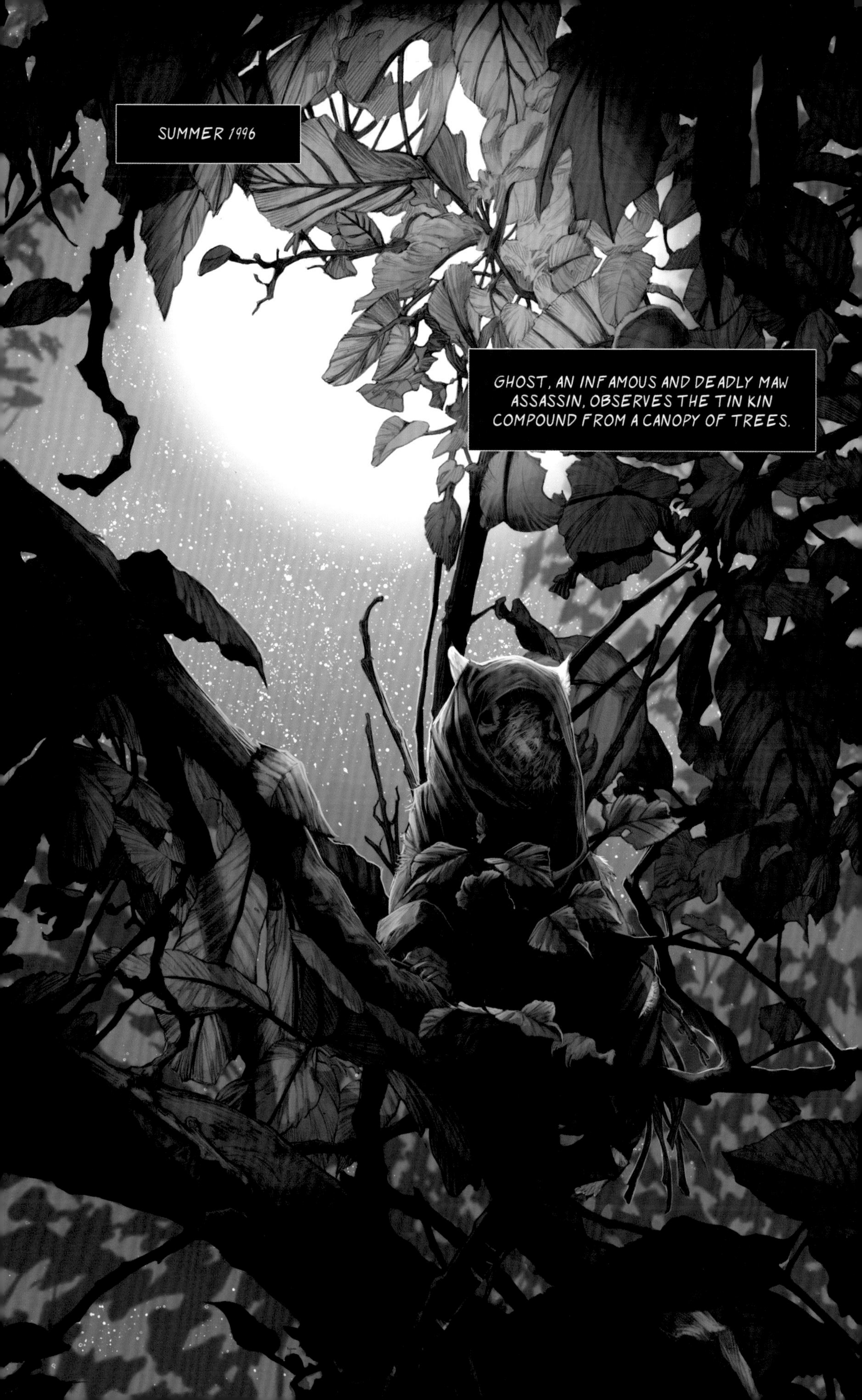
SUMMER 1996
GHOST, AN INFAMOUS AND DEADLY MAW ASSASSIN, OBSERVES THE TIN KIN COMPOUND FROM A CANOPY OF TREES.

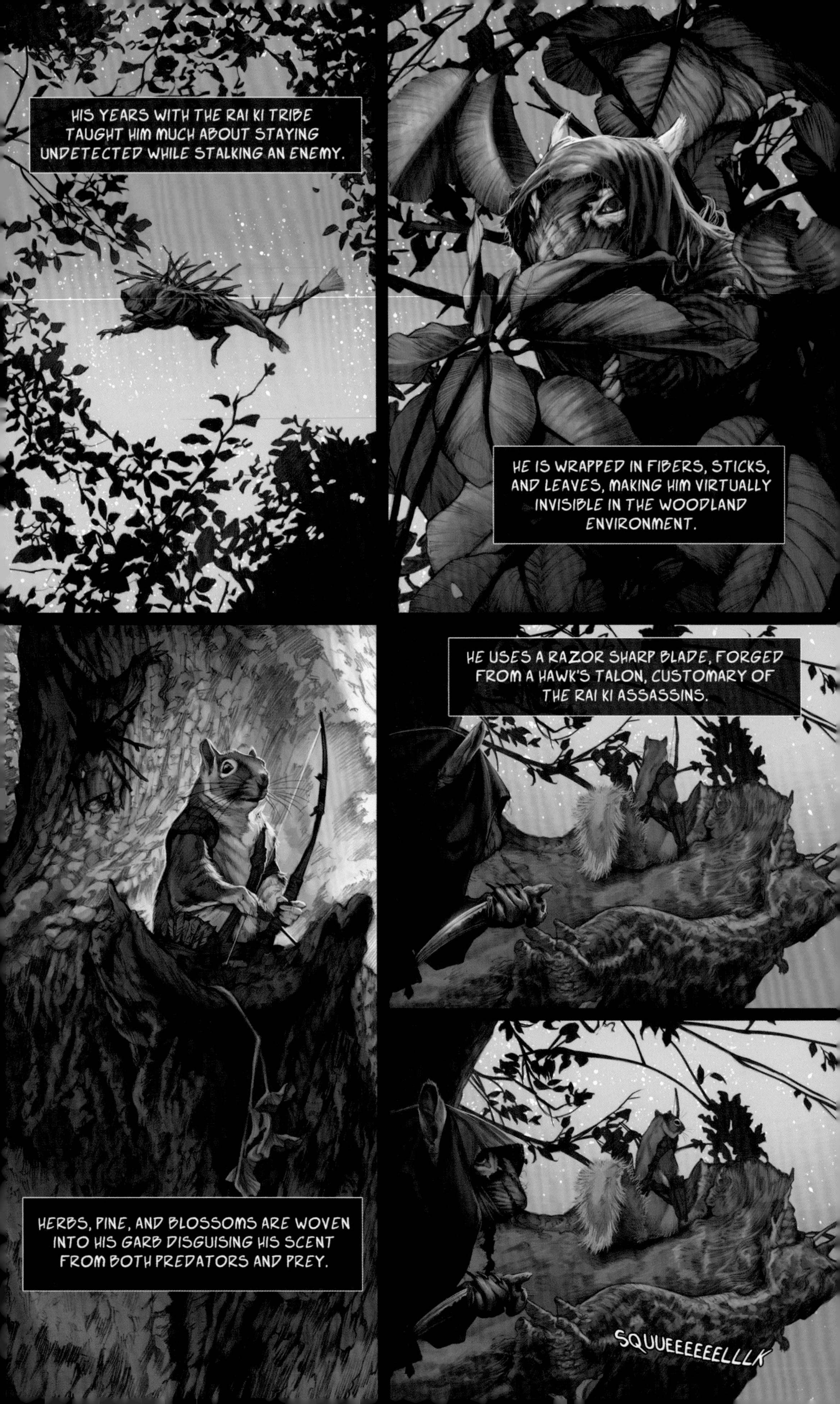
HIS YEARS WITH THE RAI KI TRIBE TAUGHT HIM MUCH ABOUT STAYING UNDETECTED WHILE STALKING AN ENEMY.
HE IS WRAPPED IN FIBERS, STICKS, AND LEAVES, MAKING HIM VIRTUALLY INVISIBLE IN THE WOODLAND ENVIRONMENT.
HERBS, PINE, AND BLOSSOMS ARE WOVEN INTO HIS GARB DISGUISING HIS SCENT FROM BOTH PREDATORS AND PREY.
HE USES A RAZOR SHARP BLADE, FORGED FROM A HAWK'S TALON, CUSTOMARY OF THE RAI KI ASSASSINS.
SQUUEEEEEELLLK

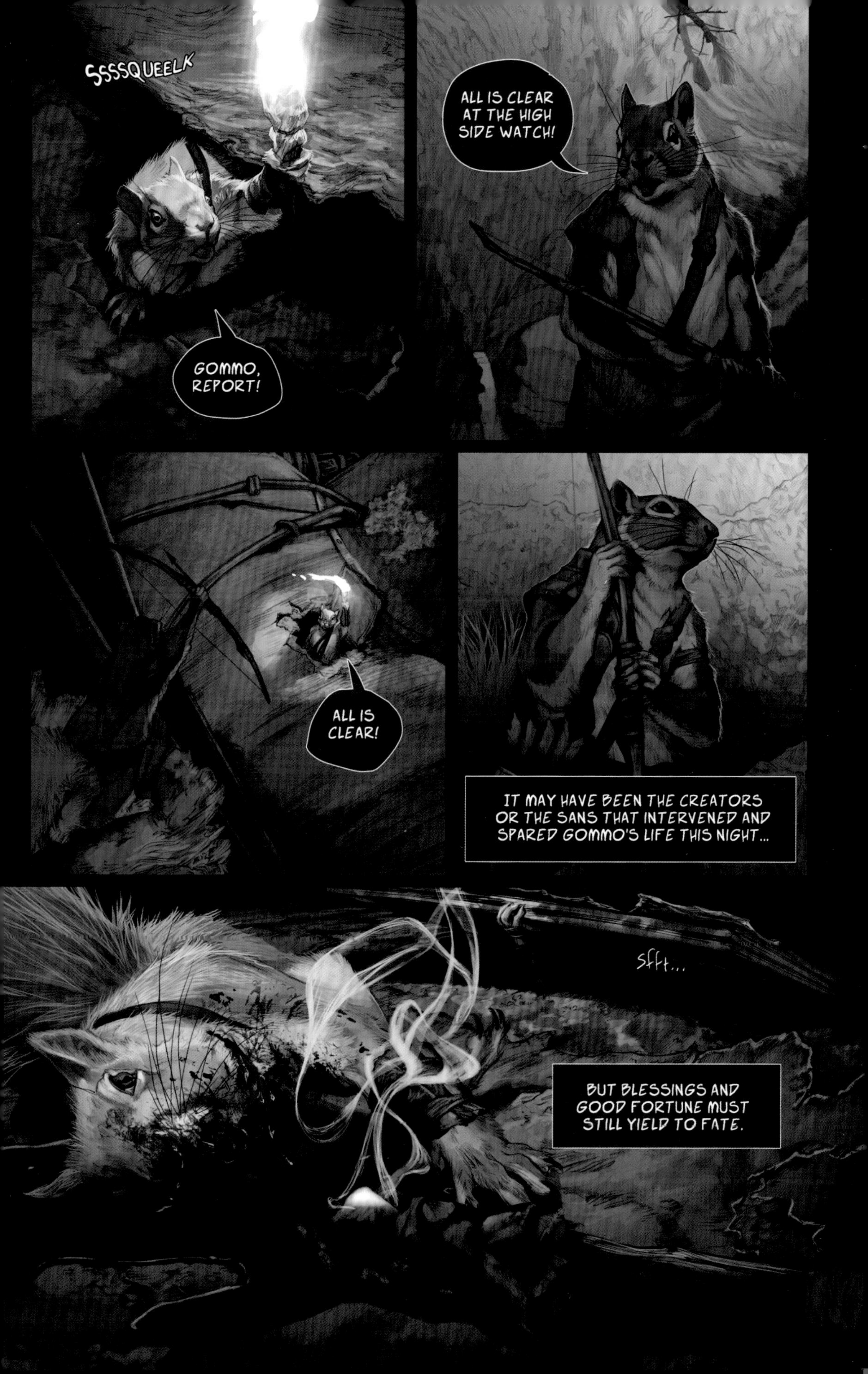
SSSSQUEELK
GOMMO, REPORT!
ALL IS CLEAR AT THE HIGH SIDE WATCH!
ALL IS CLEAR!
IT MAY HAVE BEEN THE CREATORS OR THE SANS THAT INTERVENED AND SPARED GOMMO'S LIFE THIS NIGHT...
Sfft...
BUT BLESSINGS AND GOOD FORTUNE MUST STILL YIELD TO FATE.

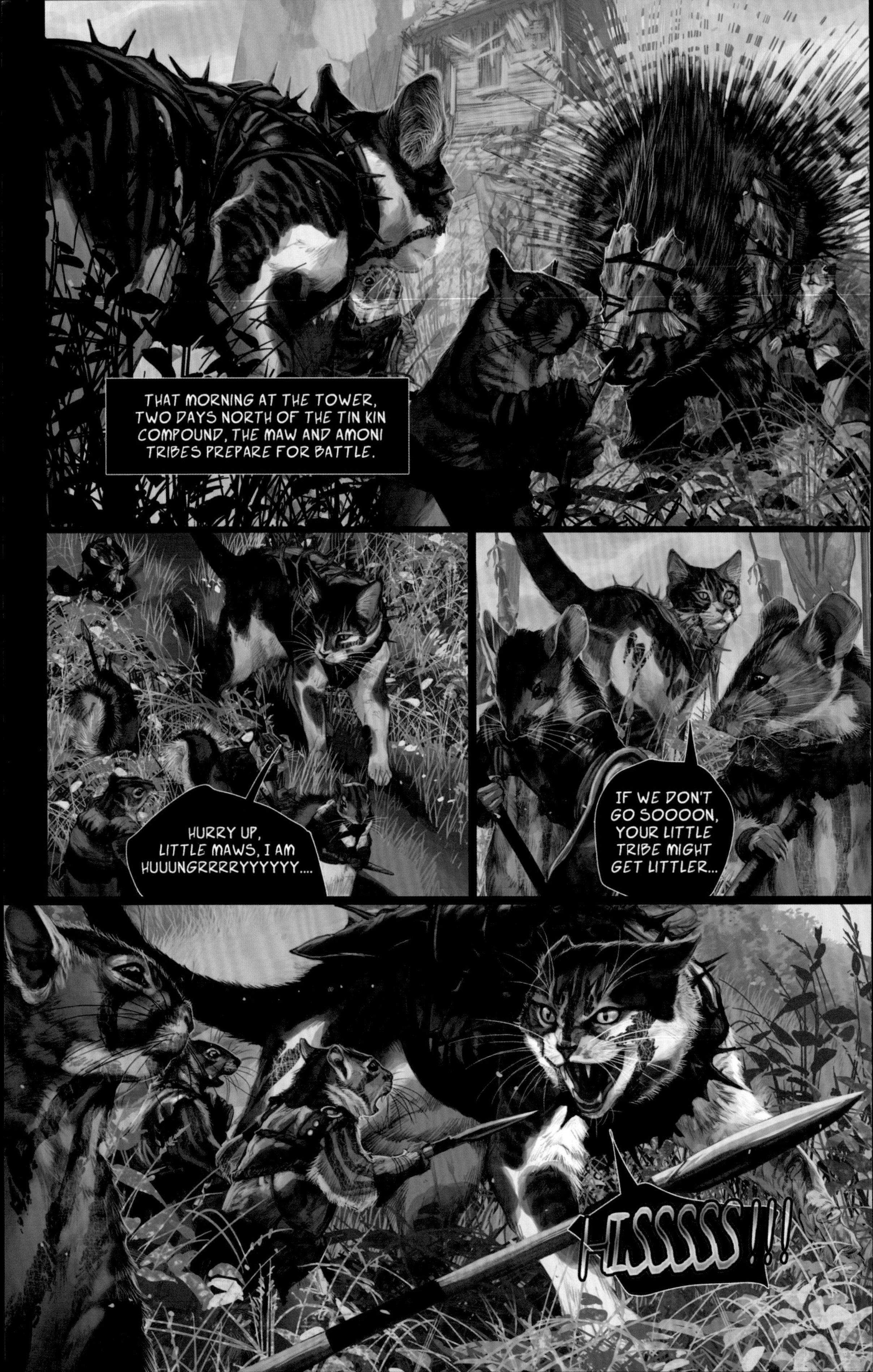
THAT MORNING AT THE TOWER, TWO DAYS NORTH OF THE TIN KIN COMPOUND, THE MAW AND AMONI TRIBES PREPARE FOR BATTLE.
HURRY UP, LITTLE MAWS, I AM HUUUNGRRRRYYYYYY....
IF WE DON'T GO SOOOON, YOUR LITTLE TRIBE MIGHT GET LITTLER...
HISSSSS!!!

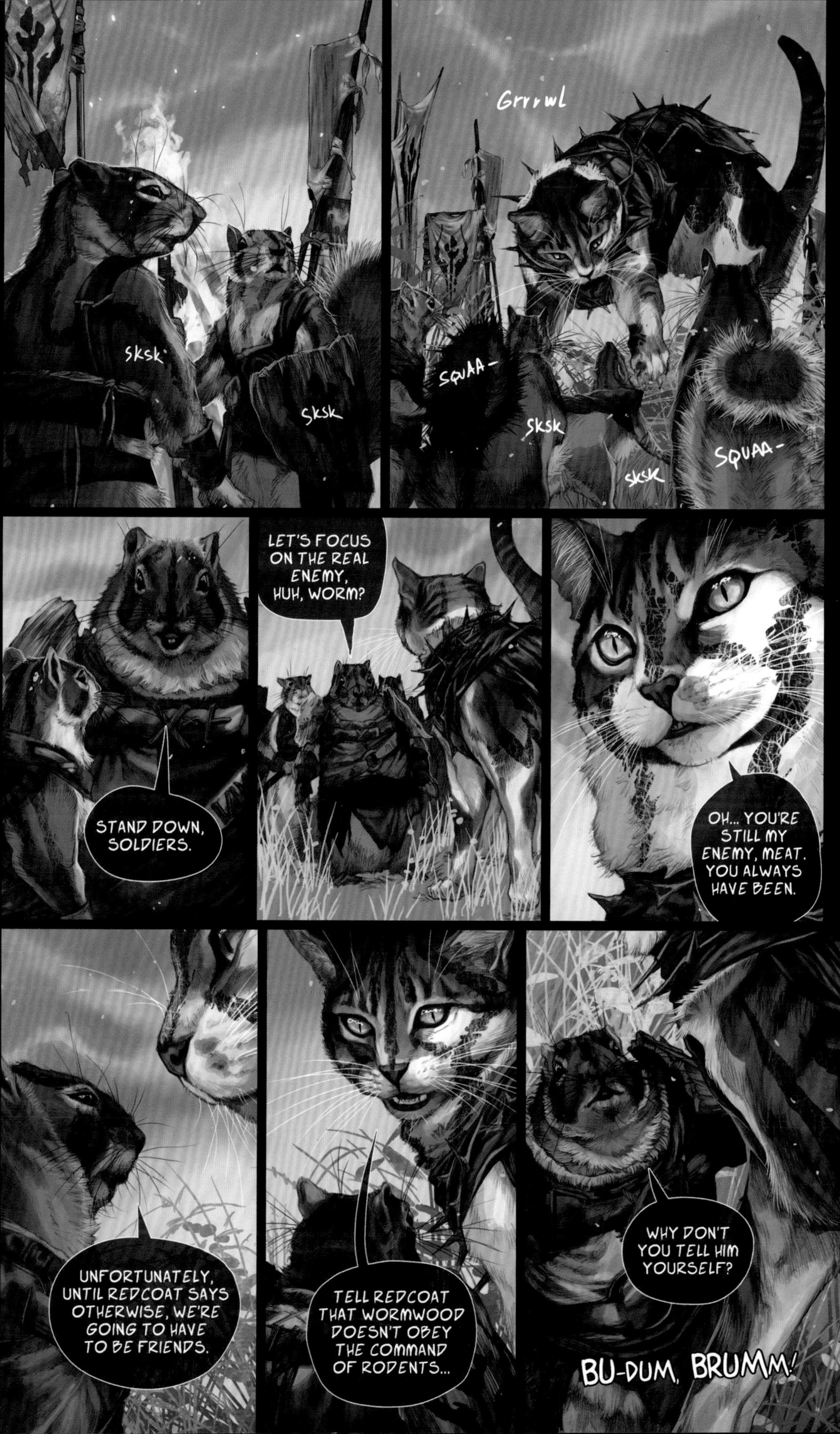
Sksk
Sksk
Grrrwl
SQUAA-
Sksk
Sksk
SQUAA-
STAND DOWN, SOLDIERS.
LET'S FOCUS ON THE REAL ENEMY, HUH, WORM?
OH... YOU'RE STILL MY ENEMY, MEAT. YOU ALWAYS HAVE BEEN.
UNFORTUNATELY, UNTIL REDCOAT SAYS OTHERWISE, WE'RE GOING TO HAVE TO BE FRIENDS.
TELL REDCOAT THAT WORMWOOD DOESN'T OBEY THE COMMAND OF RODENTS...
WHY DON'T YOU TELL HIM YOURSELF?
BU-DUM, BRUMM!

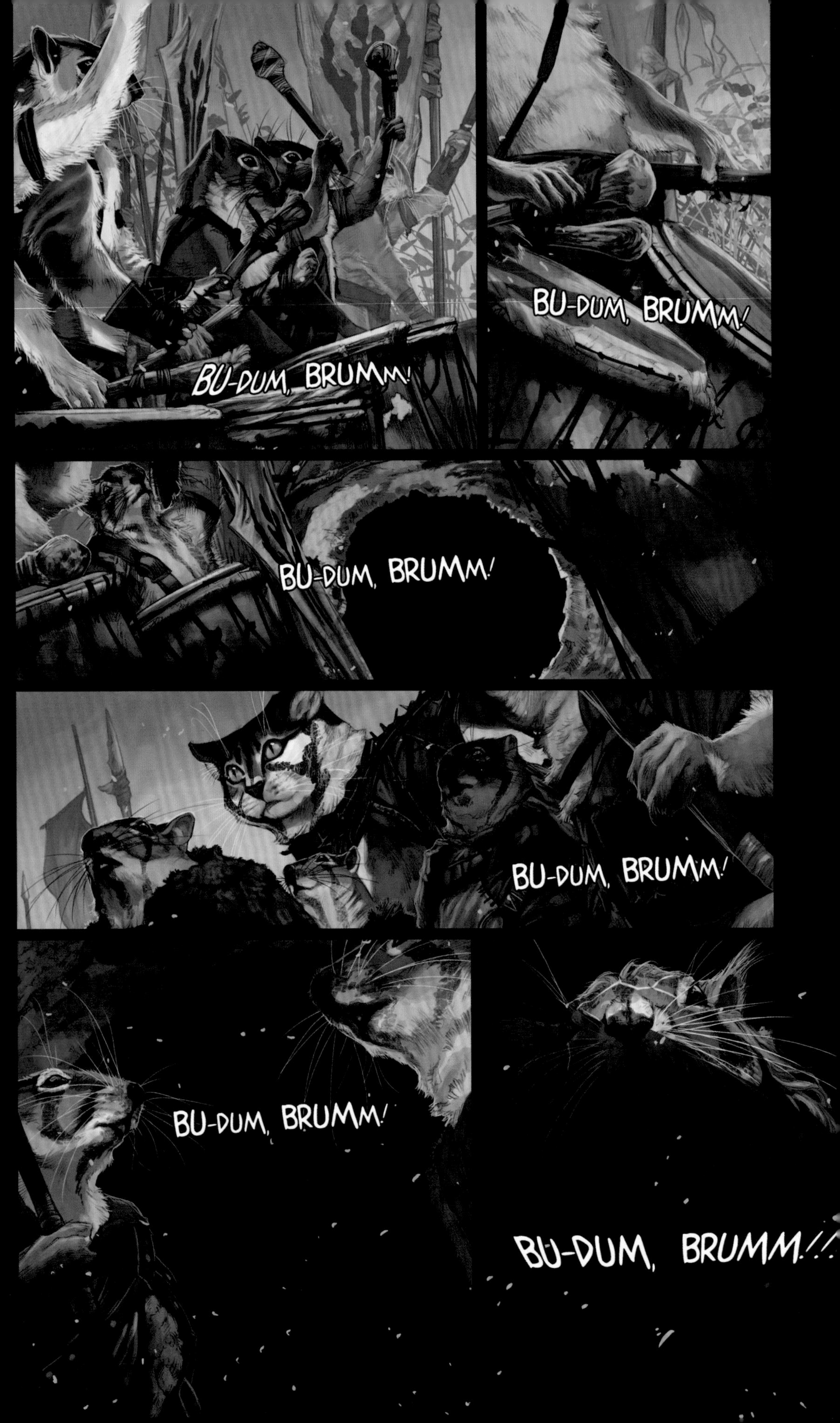
BU-DUM, BRUMM!
BU-DUM, BRUMM!
BU-DUM, BRUMM!
BU-DUM, BRUMM!
BU-DUM, BRUMM!
BU-DUM, BRUMM!!!

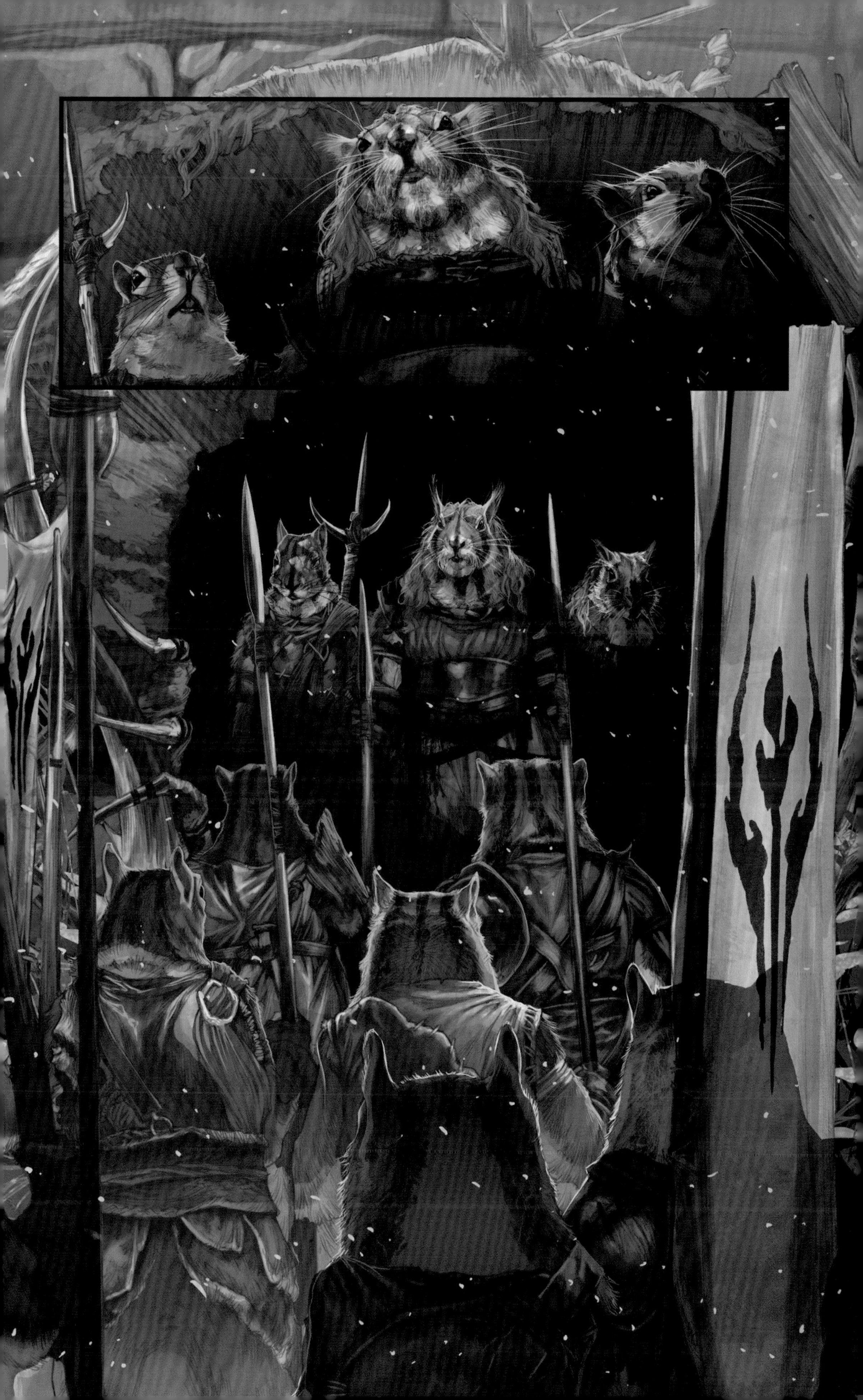

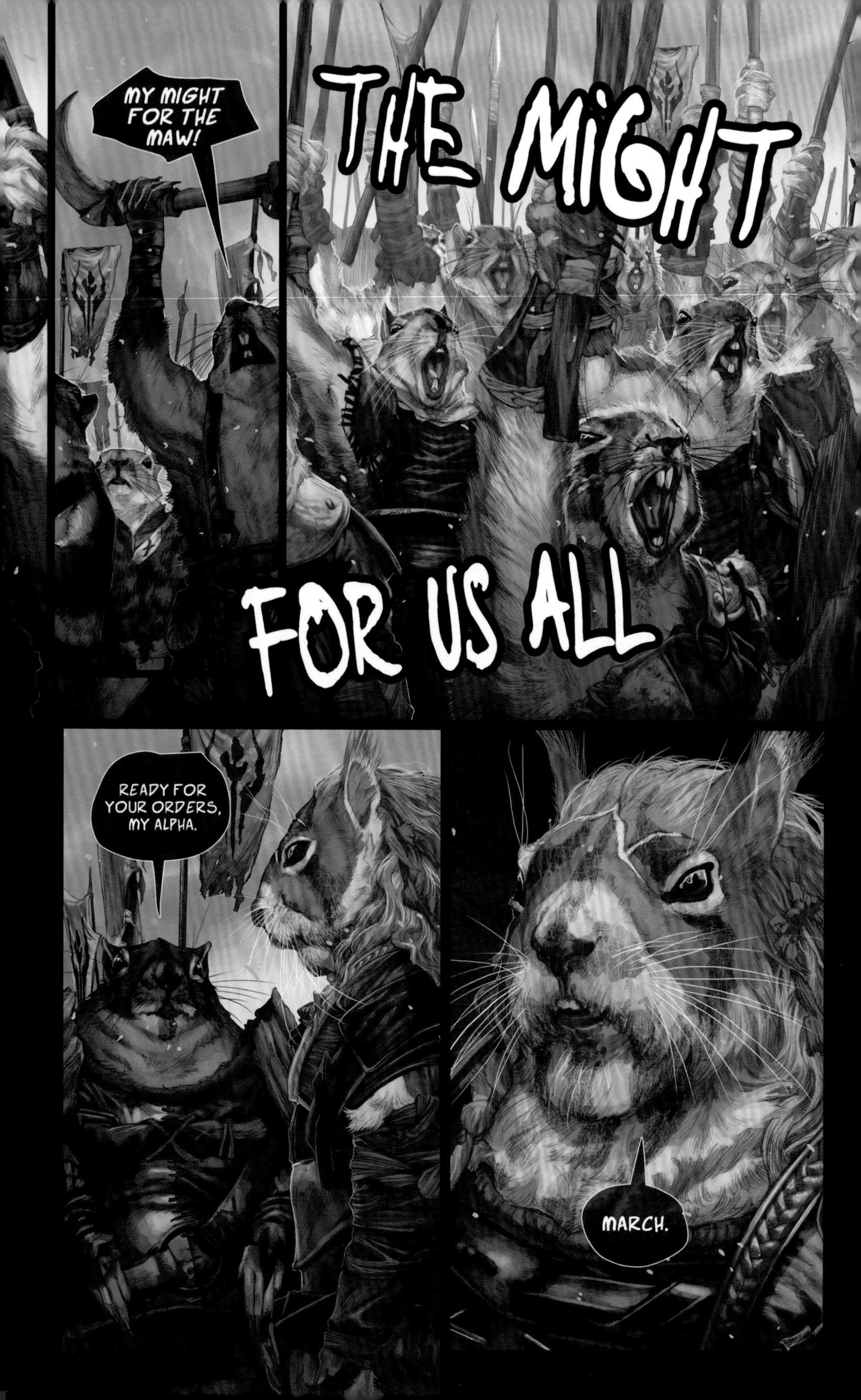
MY MIGHT FOR THE MAW!
THE MIGHT
FOR US ALL
READY FOR YOUR ORDERS, MY ALPHA.
MARCH.

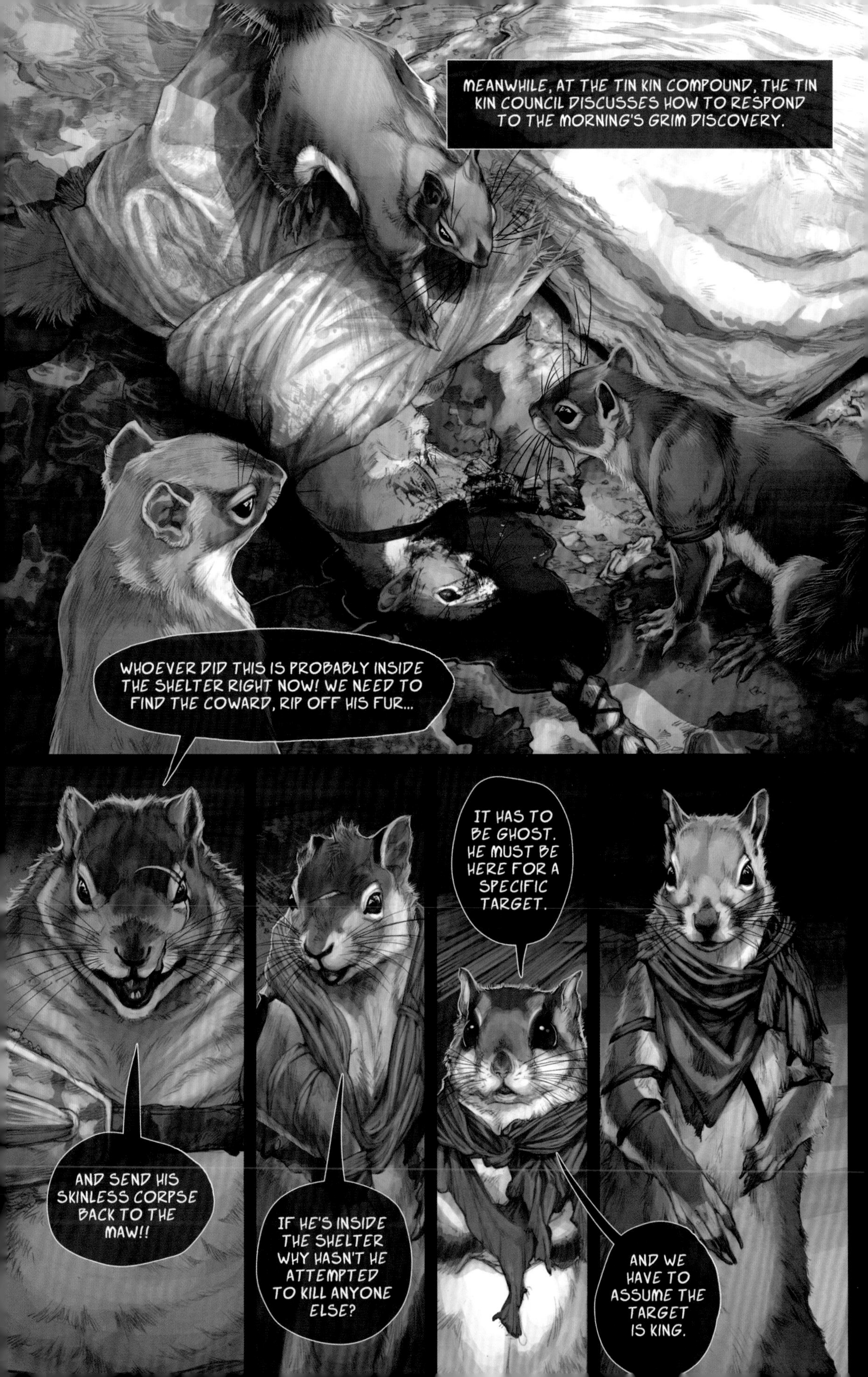
MEANWHILE, AT THE TIN KIN COMPOUND, THE TIN KIN COUNCIL DISCUSSES HOW TO RESPOND TO THE MORNING'S GRIM DISCOVERY.
WHOEVER DID THIS IS PROBABLY INSIDE THE SHELTER RIGHT NOW! WE NEED TO FIND THE COWARD, RIP OFF HIS FUR...
AND SEND HIS SKINLESS CORPSE BACK TO THE MAW!!
IF HE'S INSIDE THE SHELTER WHY HASN'T HE ATTEMPTED TO KILL ANYONE ELSE?
IT HAS TO BE GHOST. HE MUST BE HERE FOR A SPECIFIC TARGET.
AND WE HAVE TO ASSUME THE TARGET IS KING.

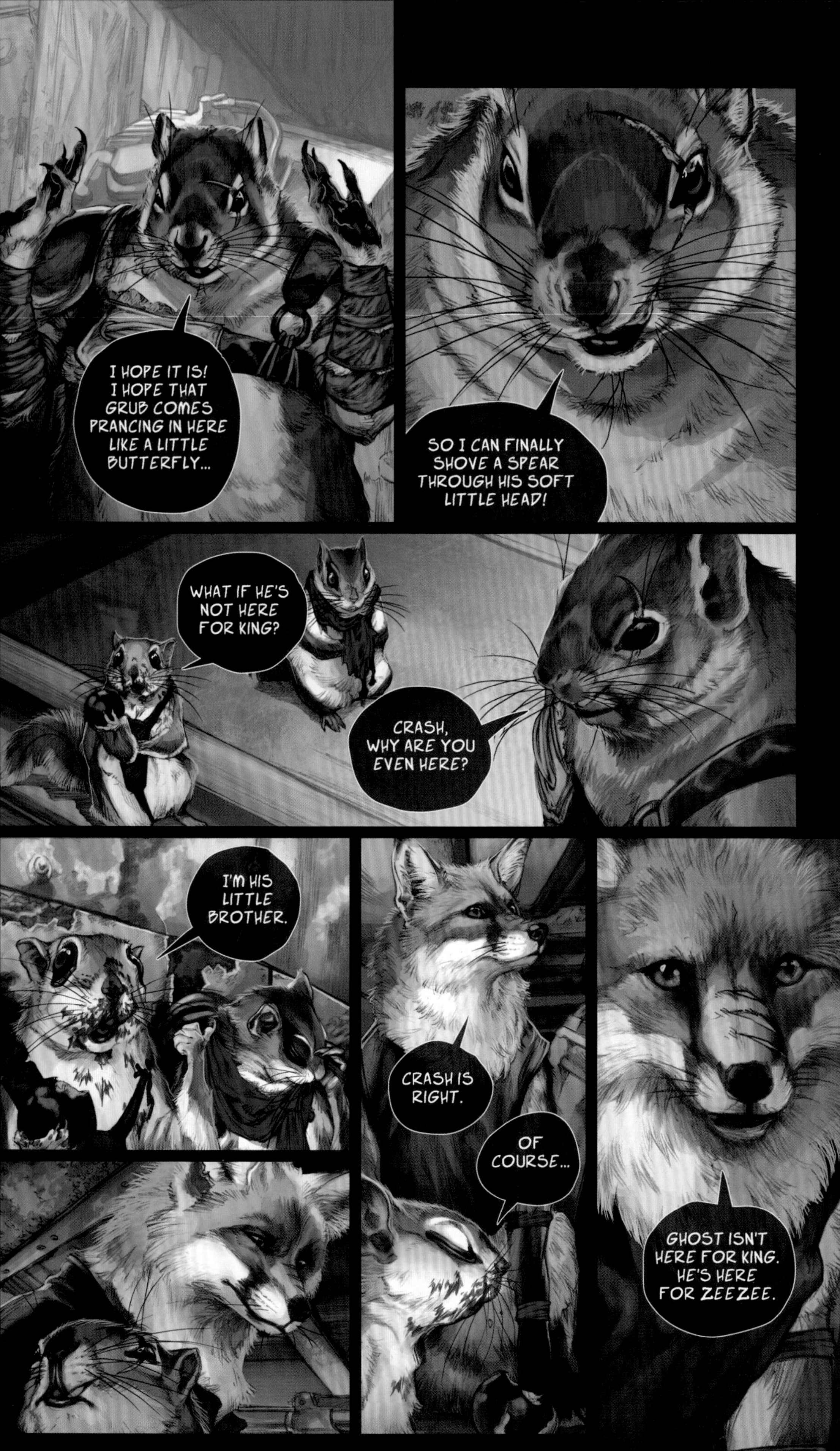
I HOPE IT IS! I HOPE THAT GRUB COMES PRANCING IN HERE LIKE A LITTLE BUTTERFLY...
SO I CAN FINALLY SHOVE A SPEAR THROUGH HIS SOFT LITTLE HEAD!
WHAT IF HE'S NOT HERE FOR KING?
CRASH, WHY ARE YOU EVEN HERE?
I'M HIS LITTLE BROTHER.
CRASH IS RIGHT.
OF COURSE...
GHOST ISN'T HERE FOR KING. HE'S HERE FOR ZEEZEE.

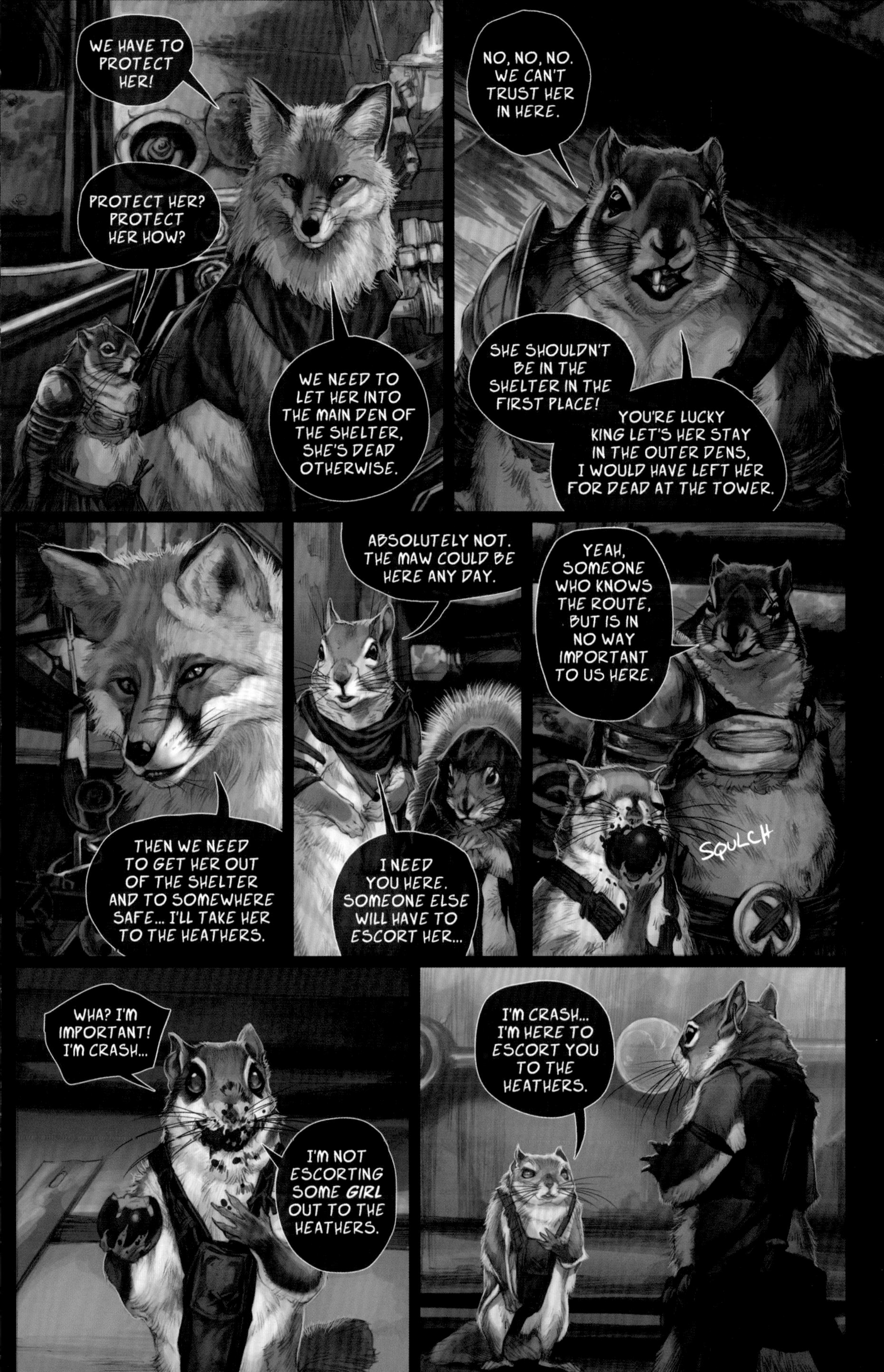
WE HAVE TO PROTECT HER!
PROTECT HER? PROTECT HER HOW?
WE NEED TO LET HER INTO THE MAIN DEN OF THE SHELTER, SHE'S DEAD OTHERWISE.
NO, NO, NO. WE CAN'T TRUST HER IN HERE.
SHE SHOULDN'T BE IN THE SHELTER IN THE FIRST PLACE!
YOU'RE LUCKY KING LET'S HER STAY IN THE OUTER DENS, I WOULD HAVE LEFT HER FOR DEAD AT THE TOWER.
THEN WE NEED TO GET HER OUT OF THE SHELTER AND TO SOMEWHERE SAFE... I'LL TAKE HER TO THE HEATHERS.
ABSOLUTELY NOT. THE MAW COULD BE HERE ANY DAY.
I NEED YOU HERE. SOMEONE ELSE WILL HAVE TO ESCORT HER...
YEAH, SOMEONE WHO KNOWS THE ROUTE, BUT IS IN NO WAY IMPORTANT TO US HERE.
SQULCH
WHA? I'M IMPORTANT! I'M CRASH...
I'M NOT ESCORTING SOME GIRL OUT TO THE HEATHERS.
I'M CRASH... I'M HERE TO ESCORT YOU TO THE HEATHERS.

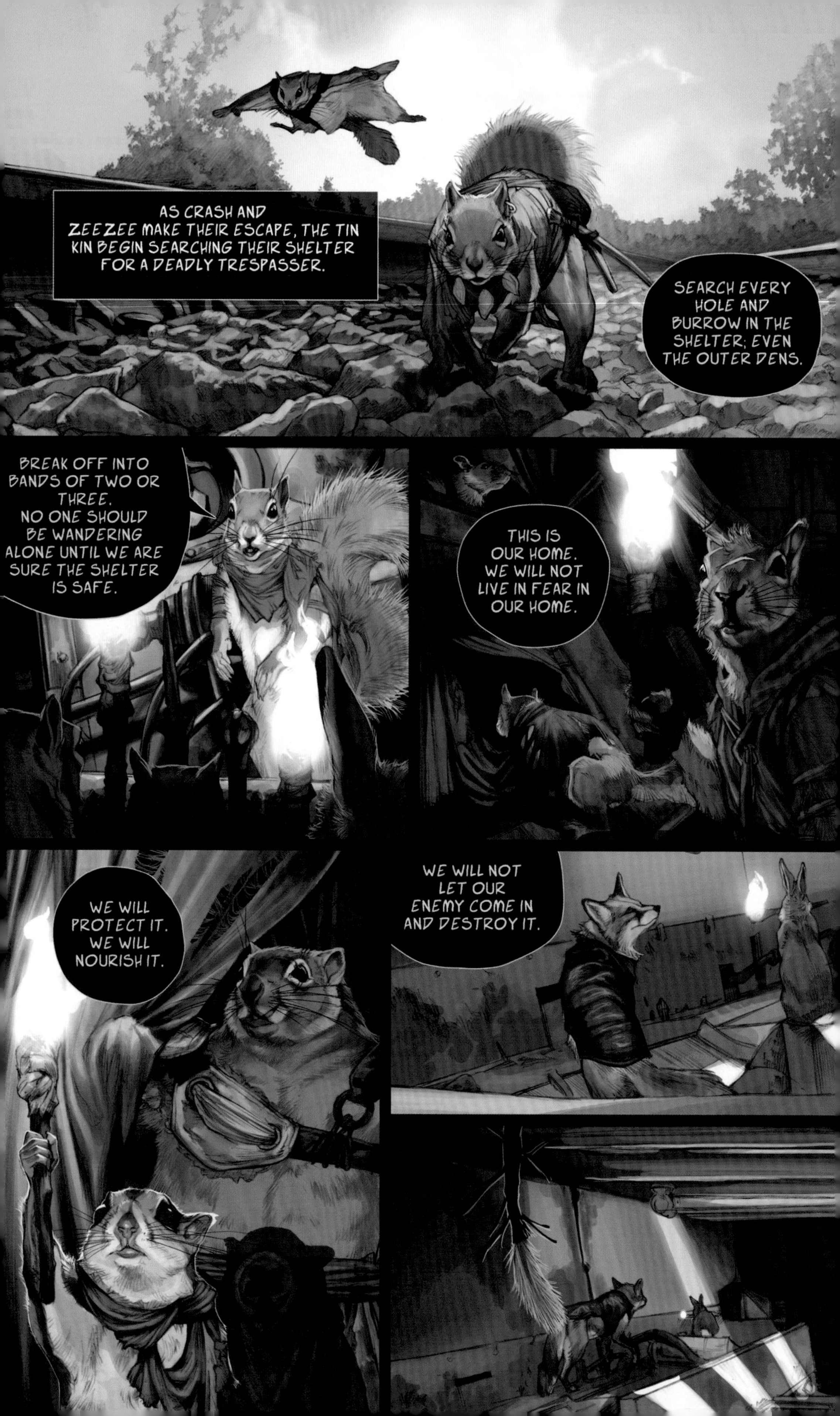
AS CRASH AND ZEEZEE MAKE THEIR ESCAPE, THE TIN KIN BEGIN SEARCHING THEIR SHELTER FOR A DEADLY TRESPASSER.
SEARCH EVERY HOLE AND BURROW IN THE SHELTER; EVEN THE OUTER DENS.
BREAK OFF INTO BANDS OF TWO OR THREE. NO ONE SHOULD BE WANDERING ALONE UNTIL WE ARE SURE THE SHELTER IS SAFE.
THIS IS OUR HOME. WE WILL NOT LIVE IN FEAR IN OUR HOME.
WE WILL PROTECT IT. WE WILL NOURISH IT.
WE WILL NOT LET OUR ENEMY COME IN AND DESTROY IT.

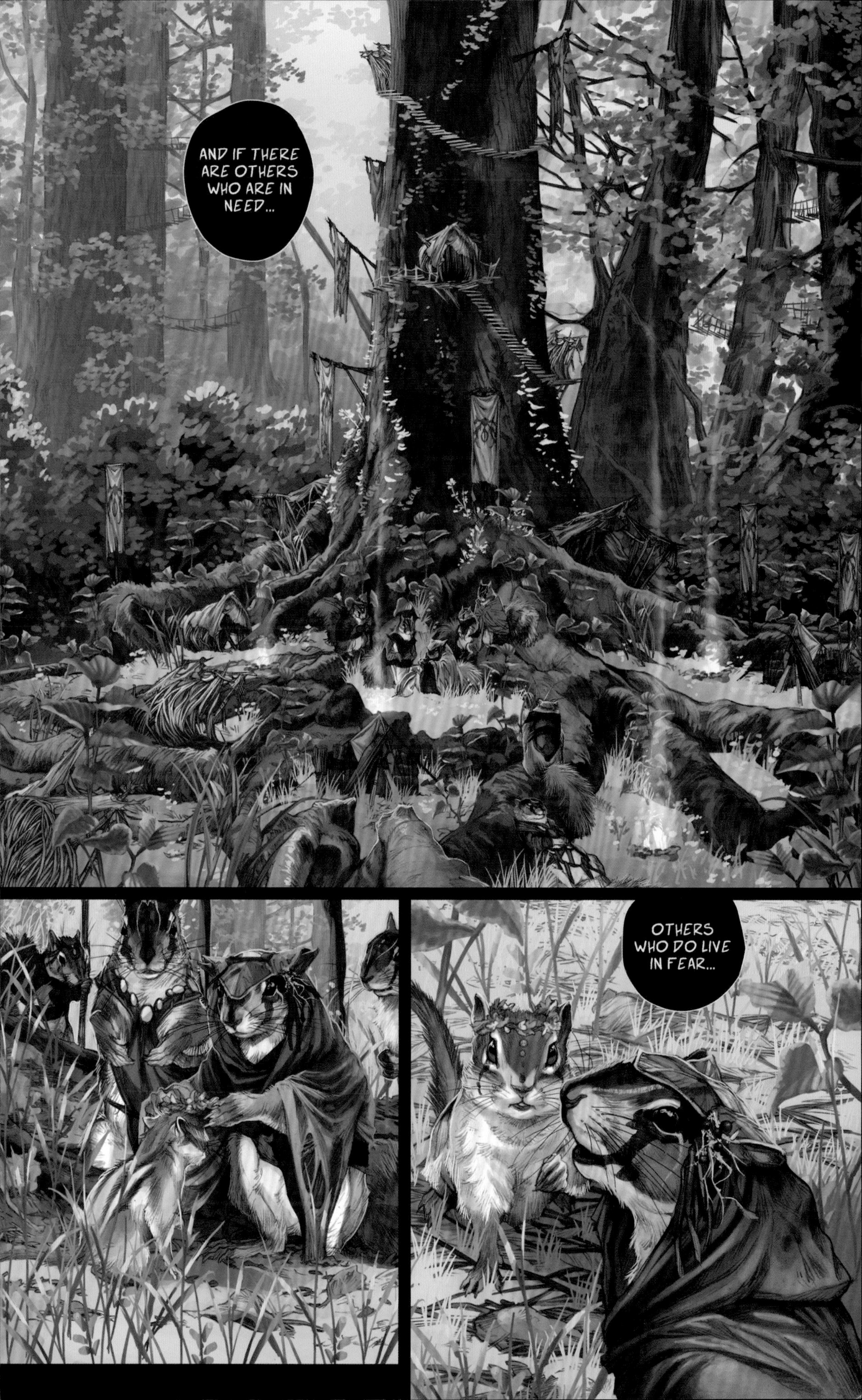
AND IF THERE ARE OTHERS WHO ARE IN NEED...
OTHERS WHO DO LIVE IN FEAR...

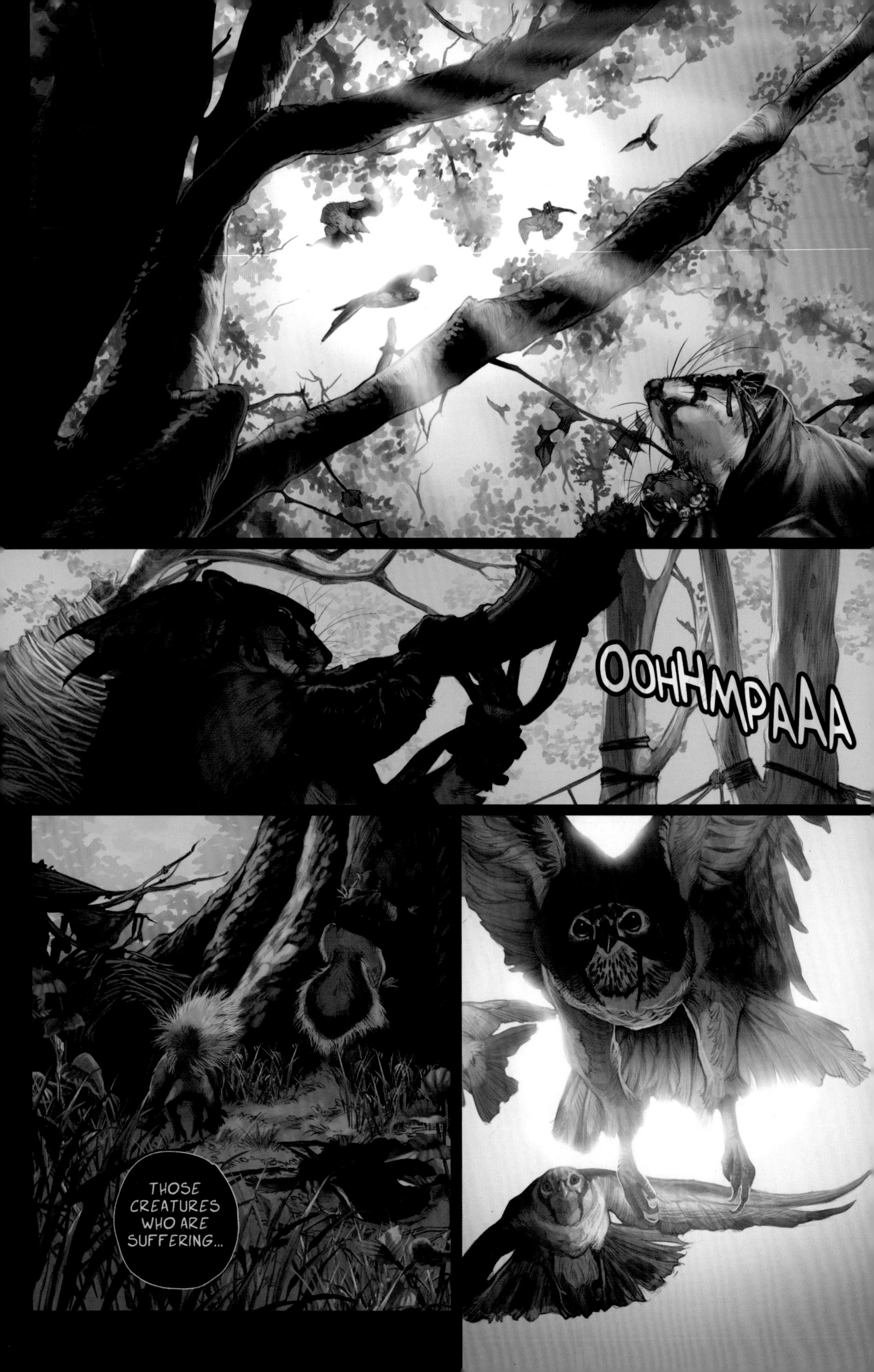
OOHHMPAAA
THOSE CREATURES WHO ARE SUFFERING...

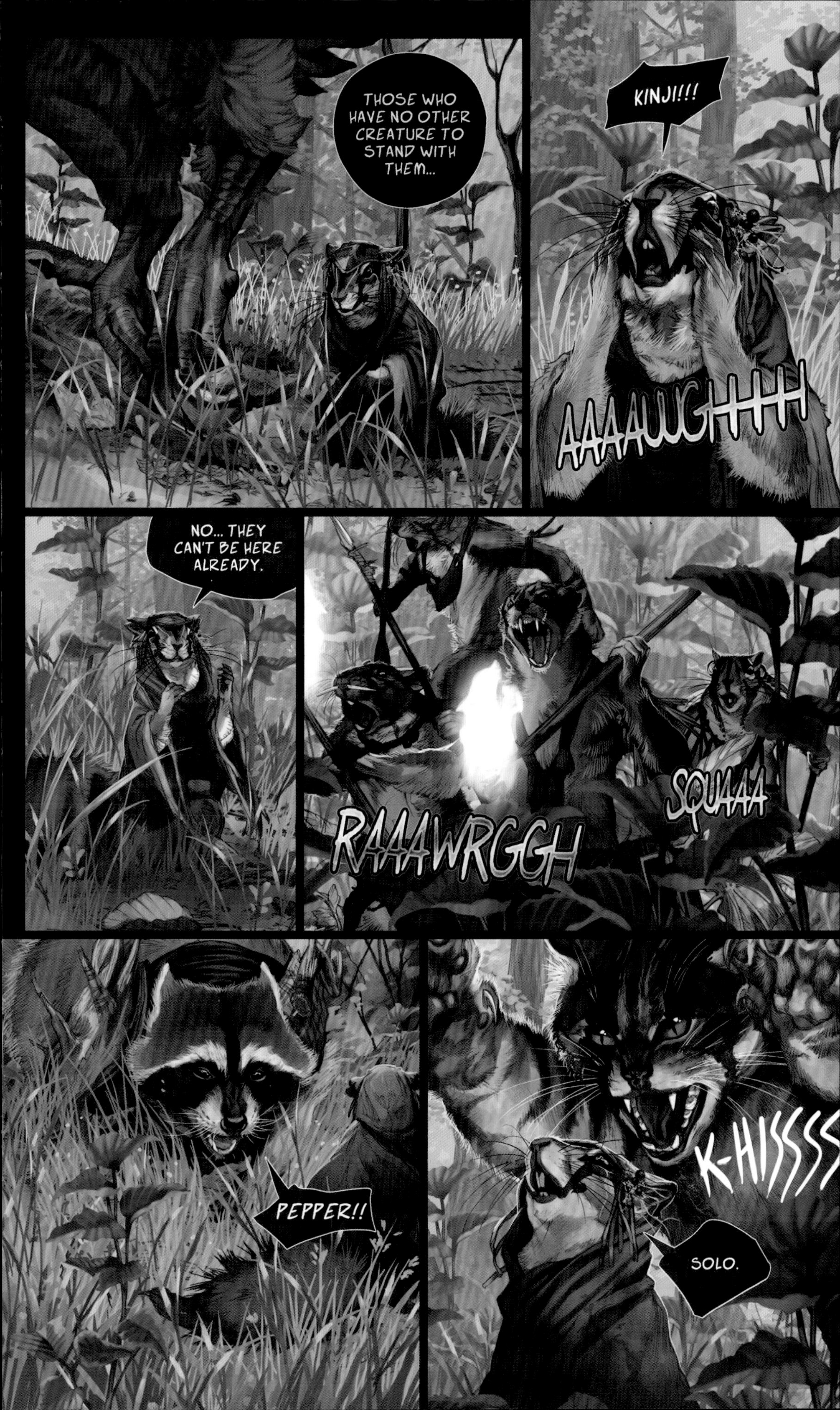

THOSE WHO HAVE NO OTHER CREATURE TO STAND WITH THEM...
KINJI!!!
AAAAUUGHHHH
NO... THEY CAN'T BE HERE ALREADY.
RAAAWRGGH
SQUAAA
PEPPER!!
K-HISSSS
SOLO.

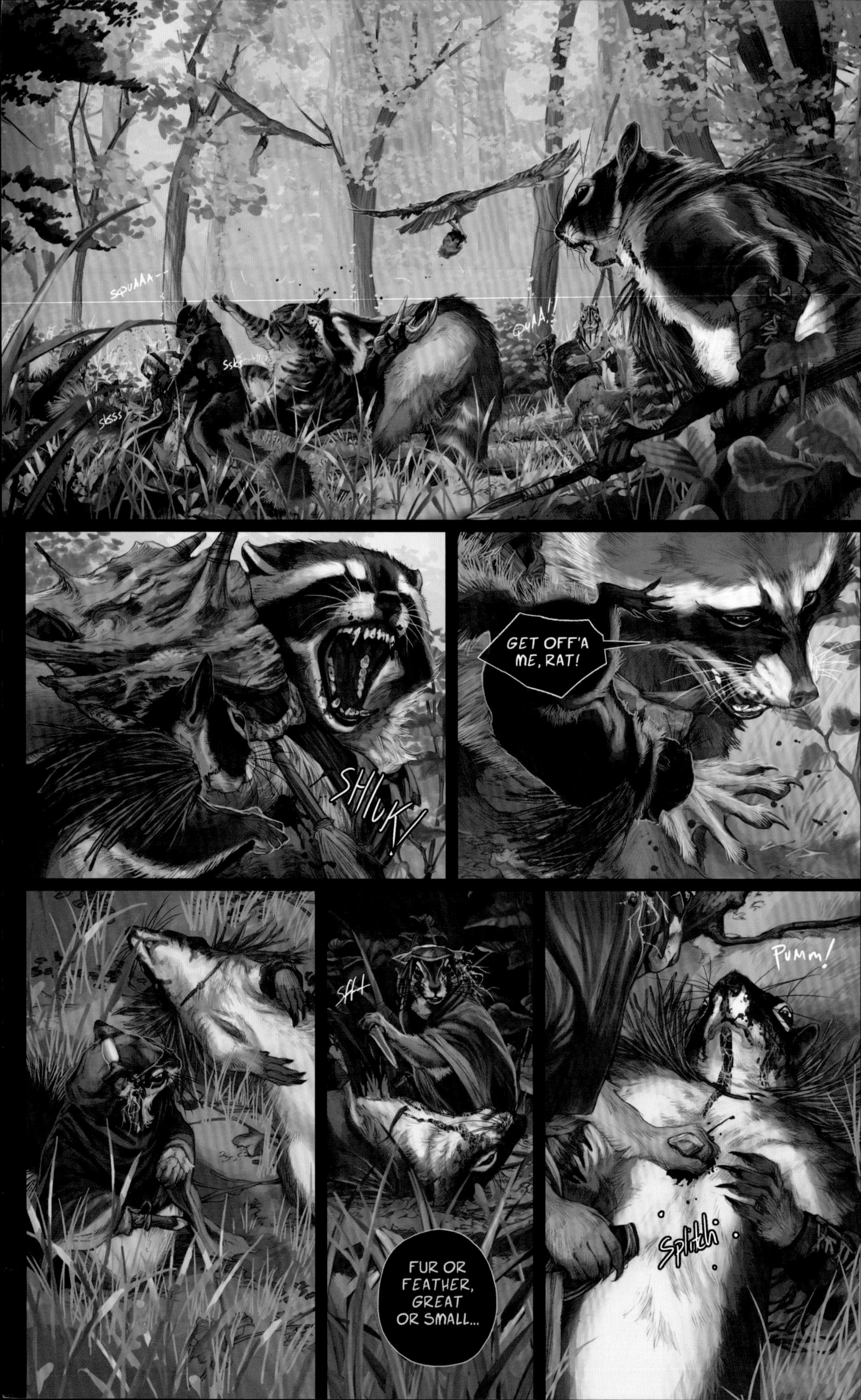
SQUAAA--
QUAA!!
SHLUK!
GET OFF'A ME, RAT!
FUR OR FEATHER, GREAT OR SMALL...
PUMM!
Splitch

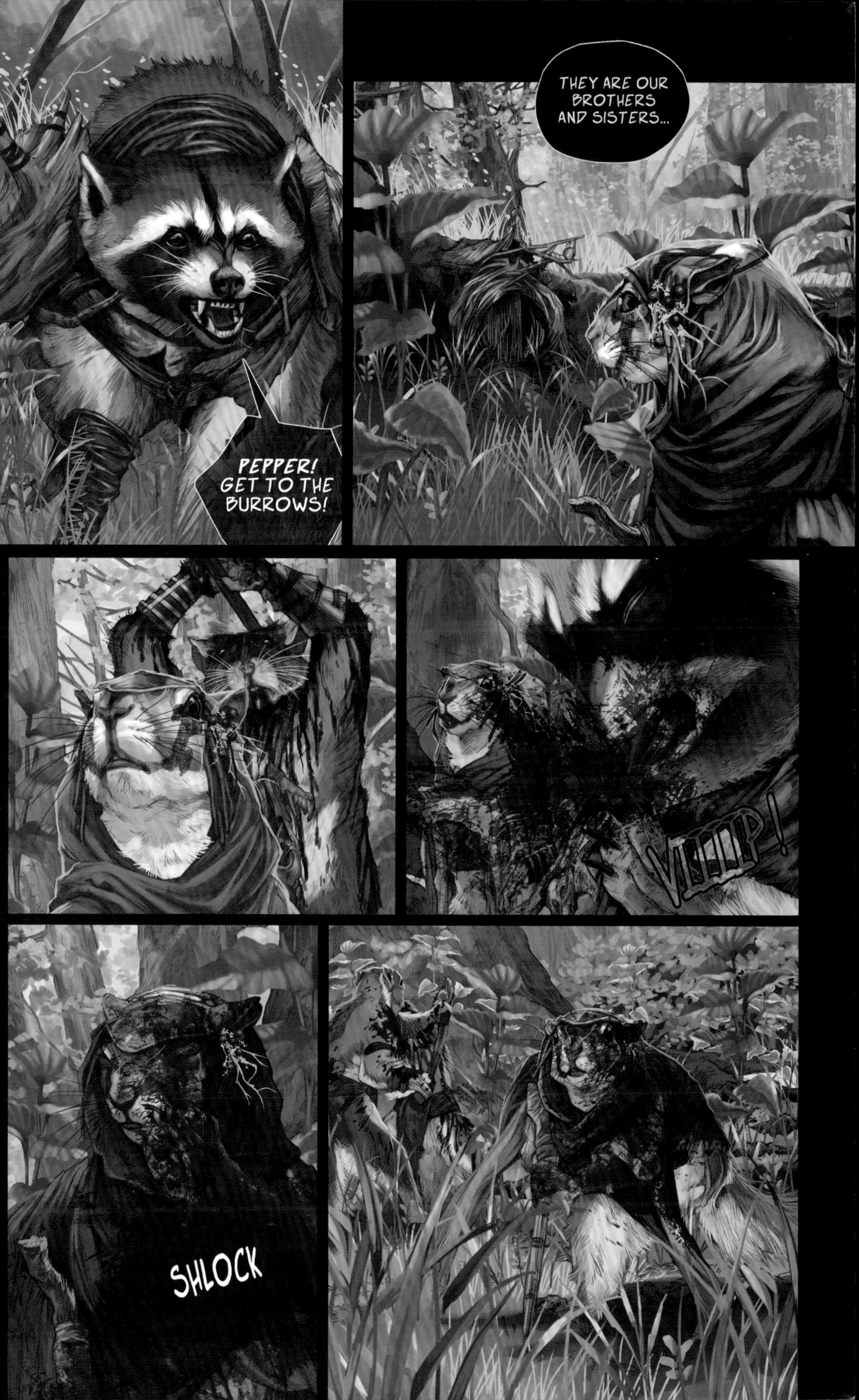
PEPPER! GET TO THE BURROWS!
THEY ARE OUR BROTHERS AND SISTERS...
VIIIIP!
SHLOCK

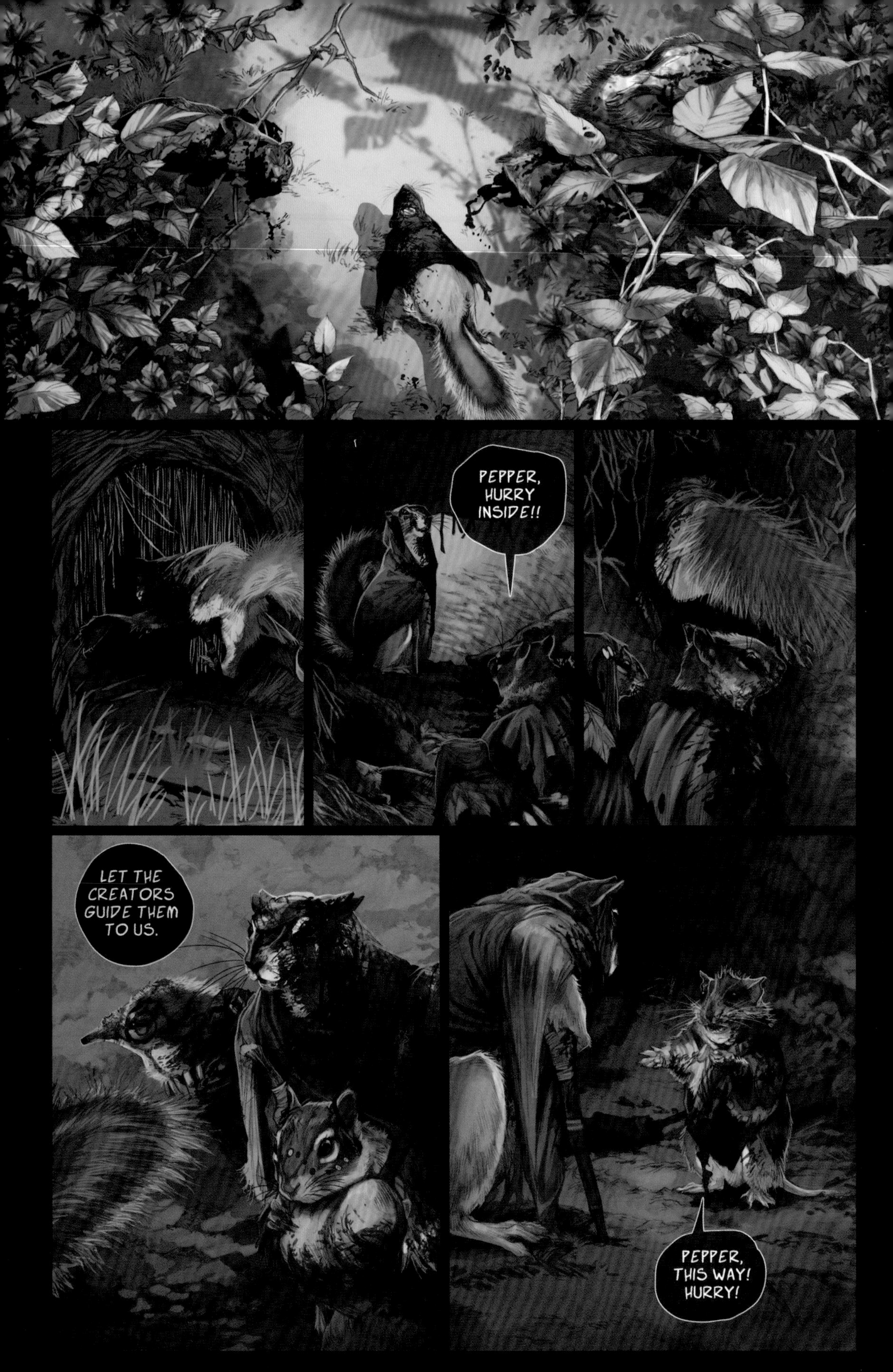
PEPPER, HURRY INSIDE!!
LET THE CREATORS GUIDE THEM TO US.
PEPPER, THIS WAY! HURRY!

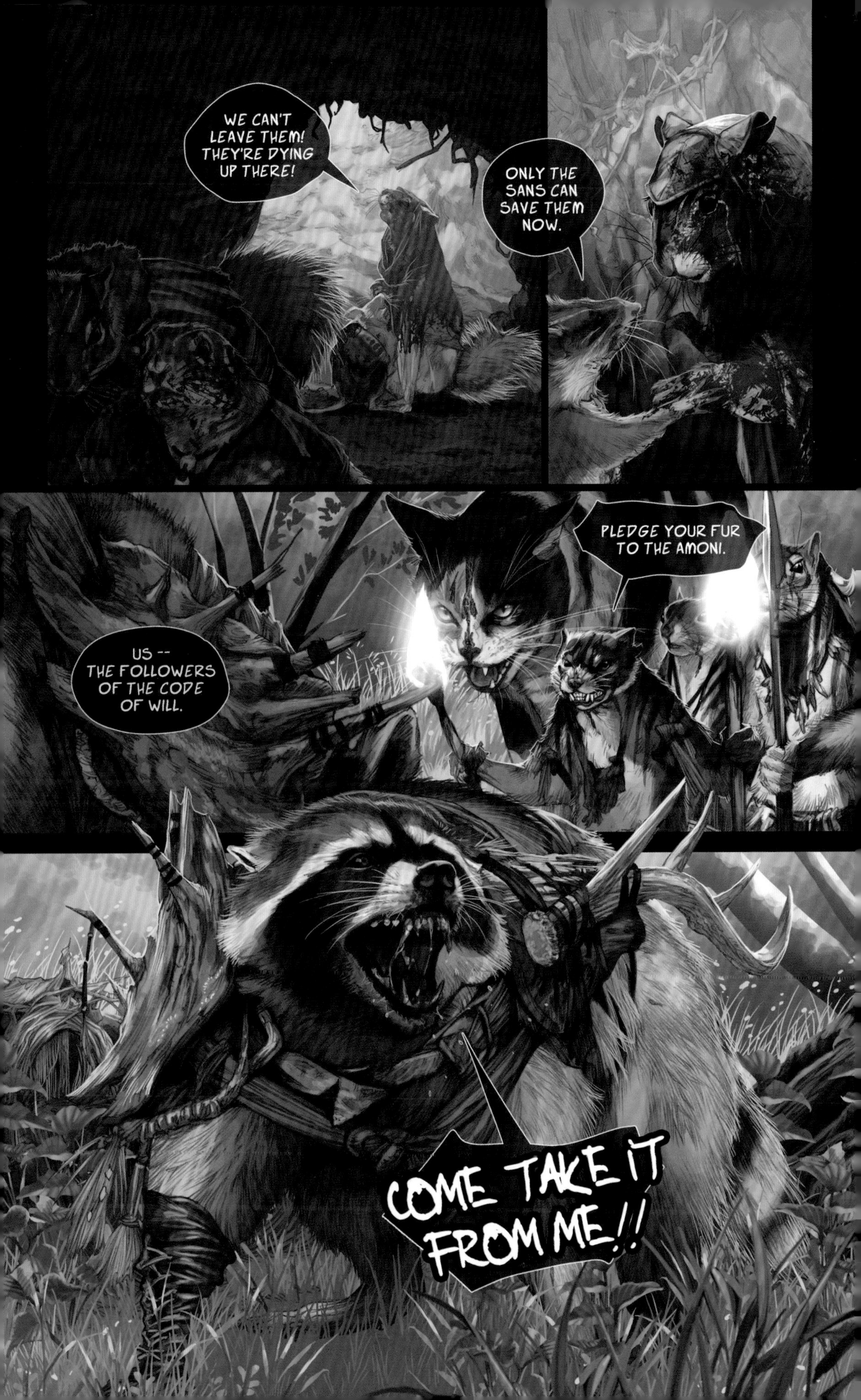
WE CAN'T LEAVE THEM! THEY'RE DYING UP THERE!
ONLY THE SANS CAN SAVE THEM NOW.
PLEDGE YOUR FUR TO THE AMONI.
US -- THE FOLLOWERS OF THE CODE OF WILL.
COME TAKE IT FROM ME!!

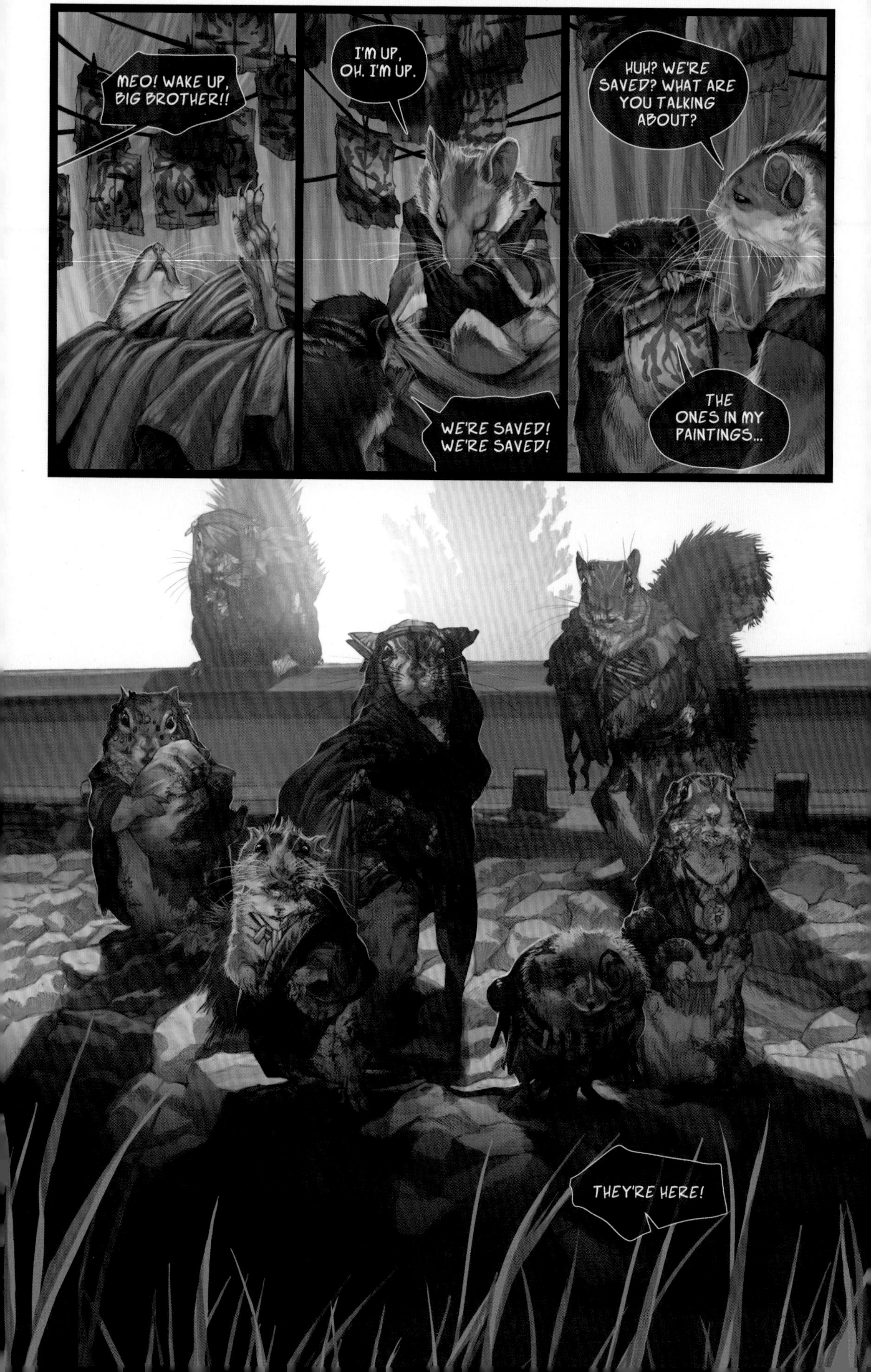
MEO! WAKE UP, BIG BROTHER!!
I'M UP, OH. I'M UP.
WE'RE SAVED! WE'RE SAVED!
HUH? WE'RE SAVED? WHAT ARE YOU TALKING ABOUT?
THE ONES IN MY PAINTINGS...
THEY'RE HERE!

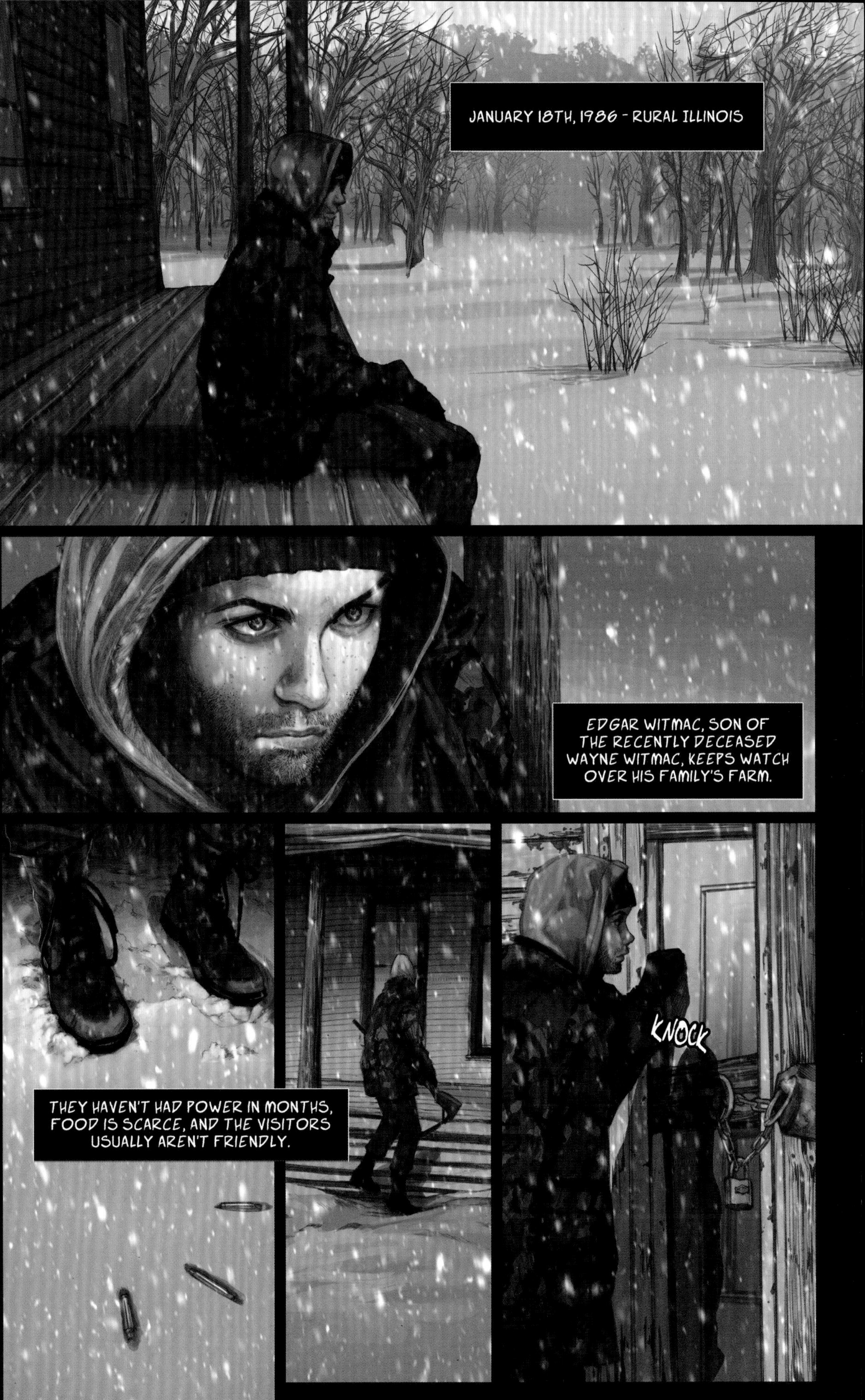
JANUARY 18TH, 1986 - RURAL ILLINOIS
EDGAR WITMAC, SON OF THE RECENTLY DECEASED WAYNE WITMAC, KEEPS WATCH OVER HIS FAMILY'S FARM.
THEY HAVEN'T HAD POWER IN MONTHS, FOOD IS SCARCE, AND THE VISITORS USUALLY AREN'T FRIENDLY.
KNOCK

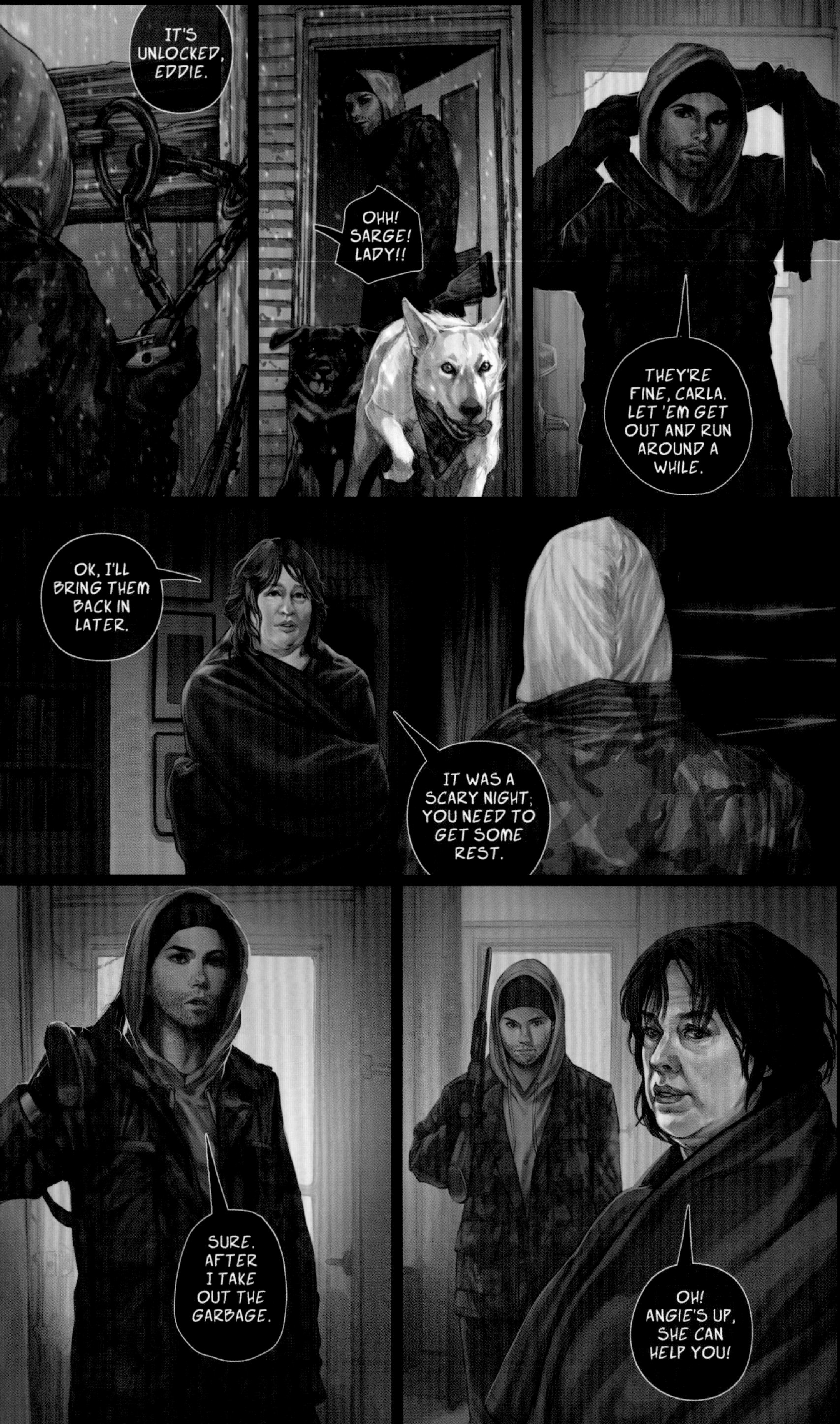
IT'S UNLOCKED, EDDIE.
OHH! SARGE! LADY!!
THEY'RE FINE, CARLA. LET 'EM GET OUT AND RUN AROUND A WHILE.
OK, I'LL BRING THEM BACK IN LATER.
IT WAS A SCARY NIGHT; YOU NEED TO GET SOME REST.
SURE. AFTER I TAKE OUT THE GARBAGE.
OH! ANGIE'S UP, SHE CAN HELP YOU!

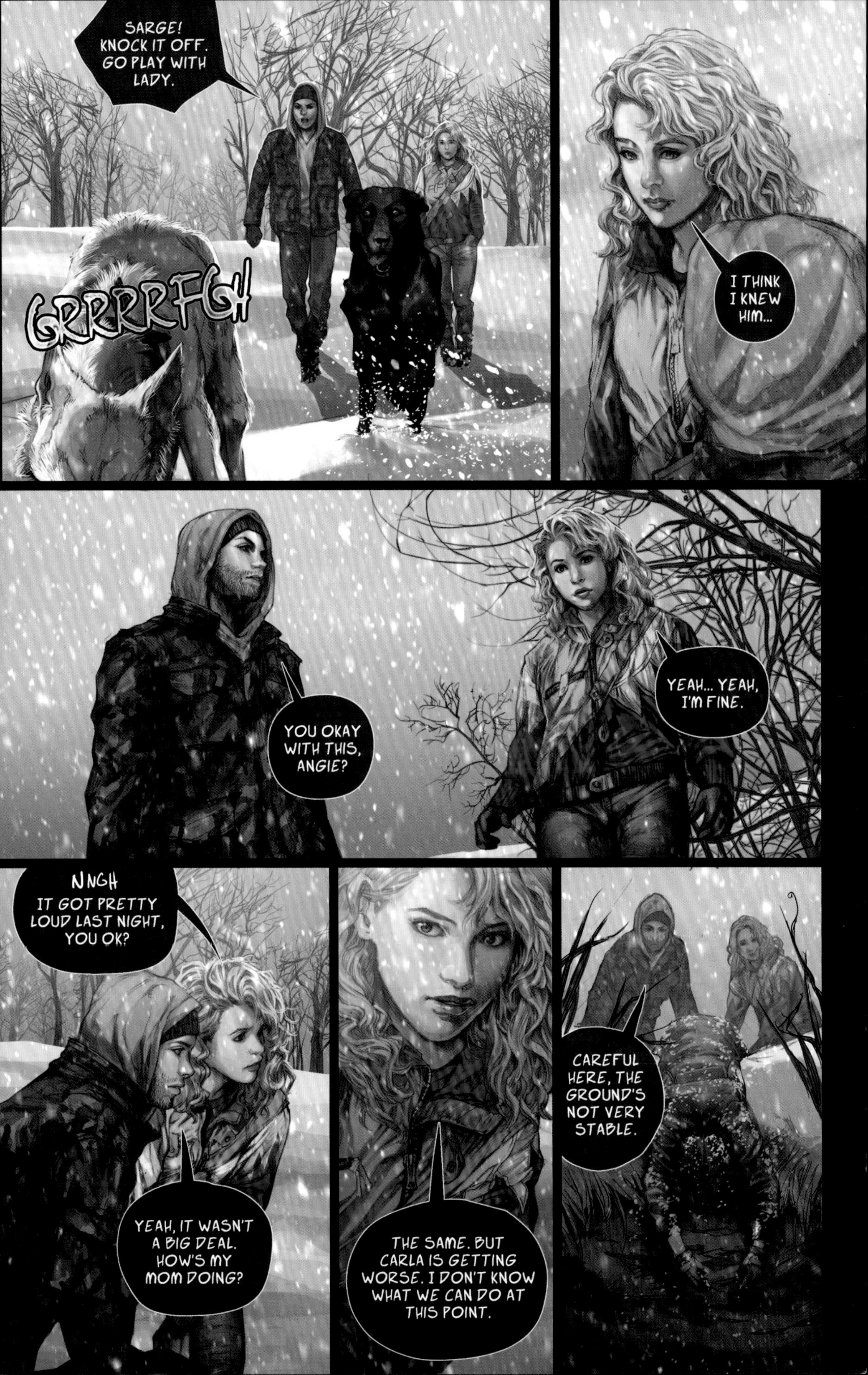
SARGE! KNOCK IT OFF. GO PLAY WITH LADY.
GRRRRFGH
I THINK I KNEW HIM...
YOU OKAY WITH THIS, ANGIE?
YEAH... YEAH, I'M FINE.
NNGH
IT GOT PRETTY LOUD LAST NIGHT, YOU OK?
YEAH, IT WASN'T A BIG DEAL. HOW'S MY MOM DOING?
THE SAME. BUT CARLA IS GETTING WORSE. I DON'T KNOW WHAT WE CAN DO AT THIS POINT.
CAREFUL HERE, THE GROUND'S NOT VERY STABLE.

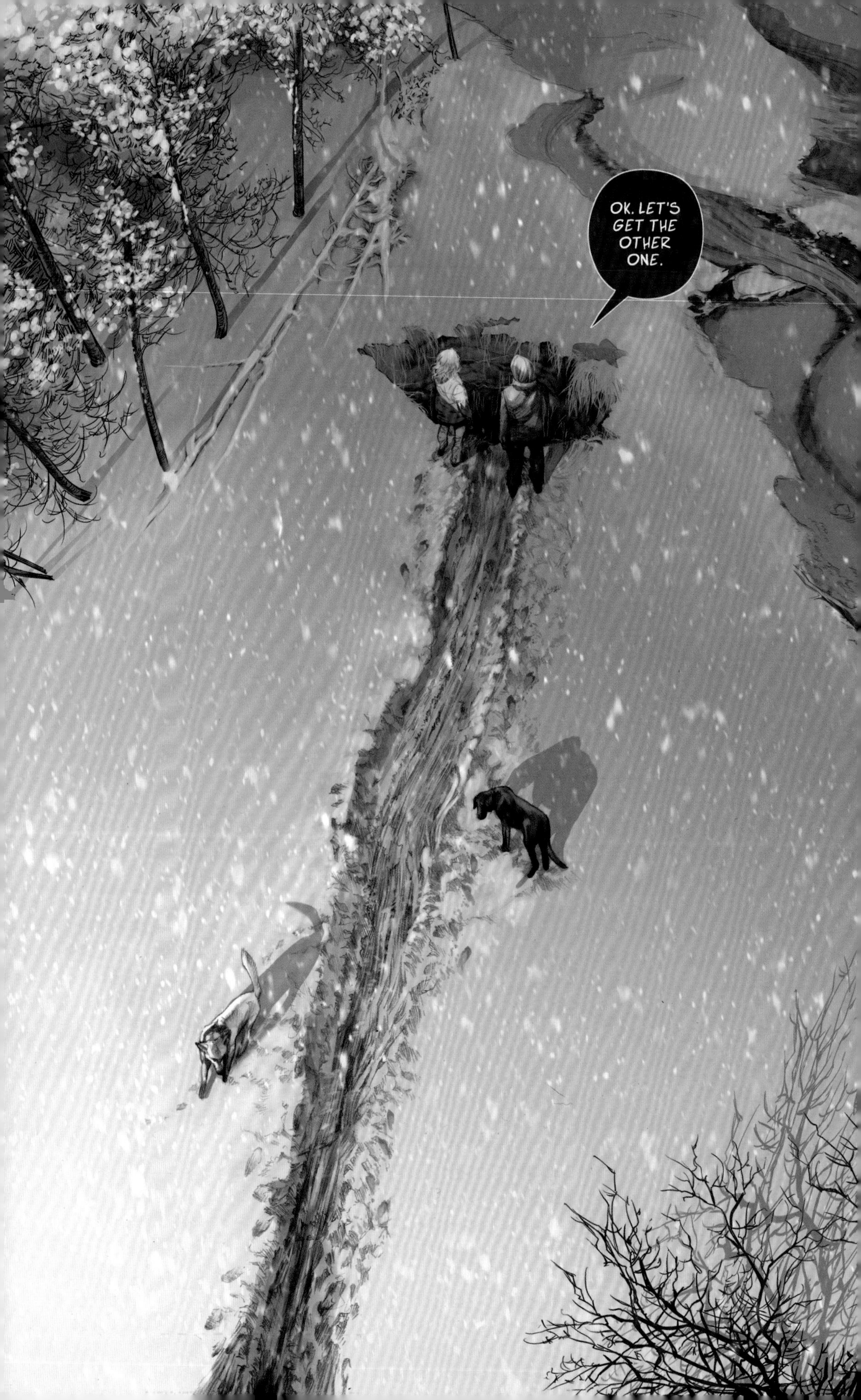
OK. LET'S GET THE OTHER ONE.

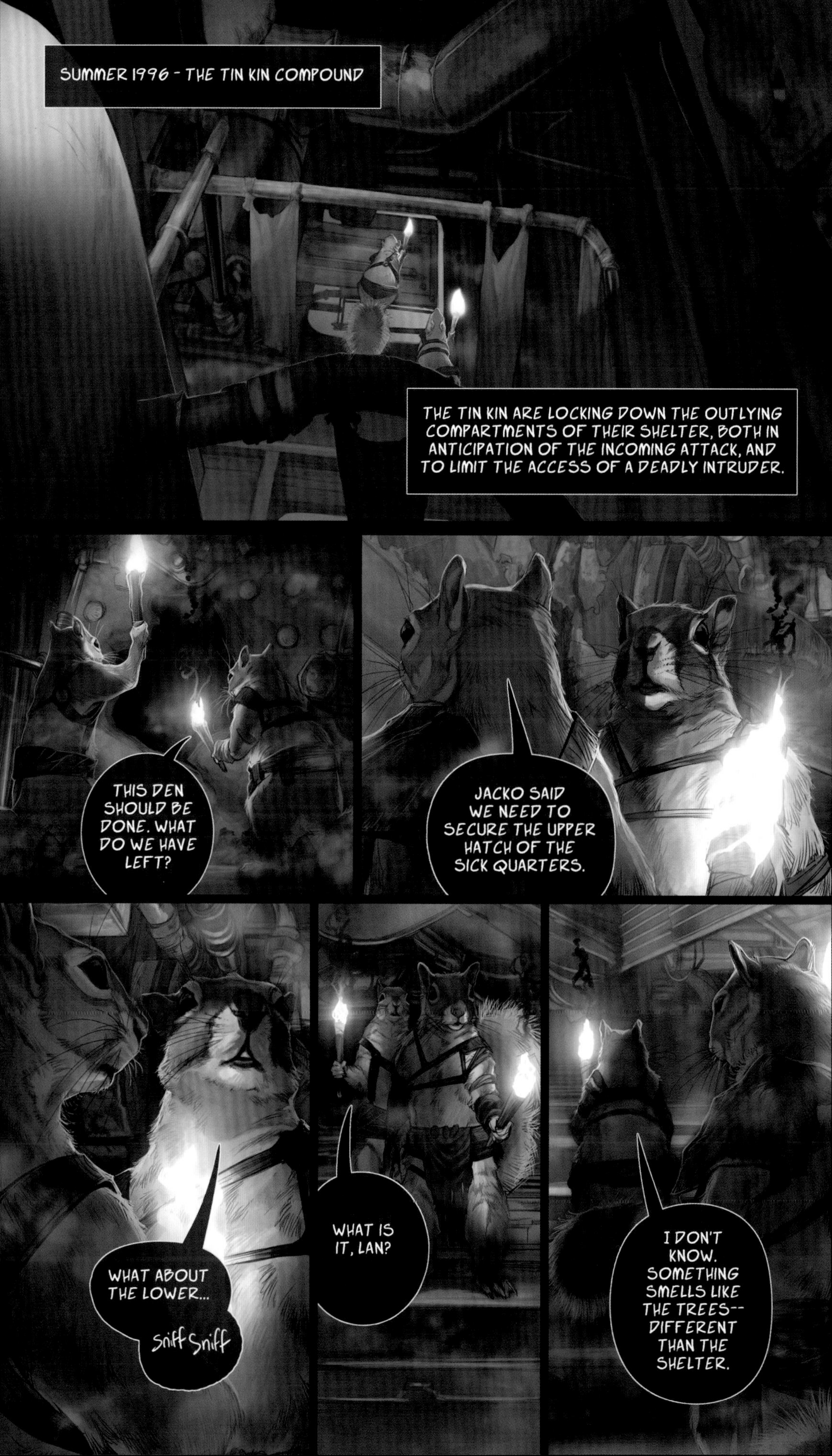
SUMMER 1996 - THE TIN KIN COMPOUND
THE TIN KIN ARE LOCKING DOWN THE OUTLYING COMPARTMENTS OF THEIR SHELTER, BOTH IN ANTICIPATION OF THE INCOMING ATTACK, AND TO LIMIT THE ACCESS OF A DEADLY INTRUDER.
THIS DEN SHOULD BE DONE. WHAT DO WE HAVE LEFT?
JACKO SAID WE NEED TO SECURE THE UPPER HATCH OF THE SICK QUARTERS.
WHAT ABOUT THE LOWER...
Sniff Sniff
WHAT IS IT, LAN?
I DON'T KNOW. SOMETHING SMELLS LIKE THE TREES-- DIFFERENT THAN THE SHELTER.

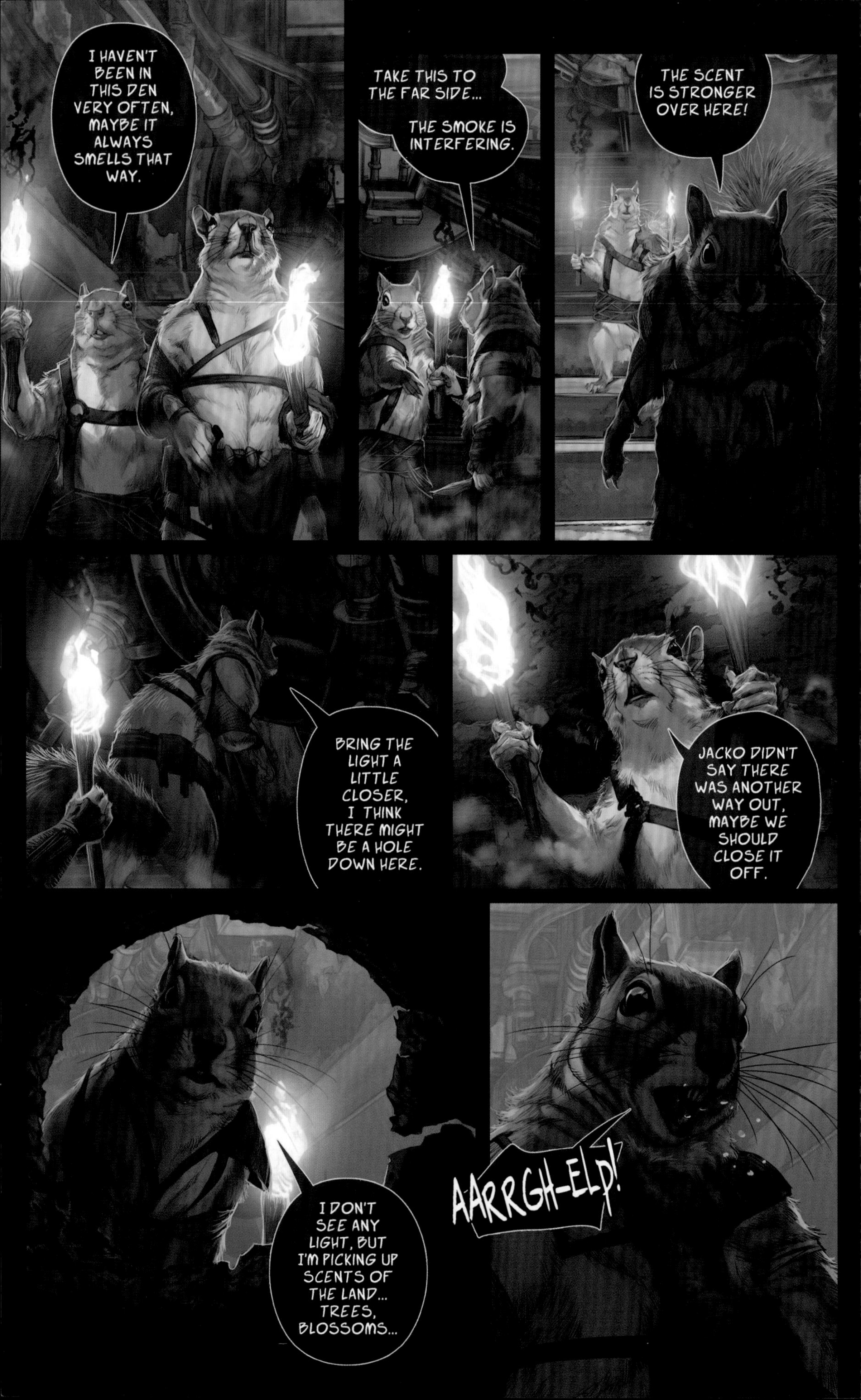

I HAVEN'T BEEN IN THIS DEN VERY OFTEN, MAYBE IT ALWAYS SMELLS THAT WAY.
TAKE THIS TO THE FAR SIDE...
THE SMOKE IS INTERFERING.
THE SCENT IS STRONGER OVER HERE!
BRING THE LIGHT A LITTLE CLOSER, I THINK THERE MIGHT BE A HOLE DOWN HERE.
JACKO DIDN'T SAY THERE WAS ANOTHER WAY OUT, MAYBE WE SHOULD CLOSE IT OFF.
I DON'T SEE ANY LIGHT, BUT I'M PICKING UP SCENTS OF THE LAND... TREES, BLOSSOMS...
AARRGH-ELP!

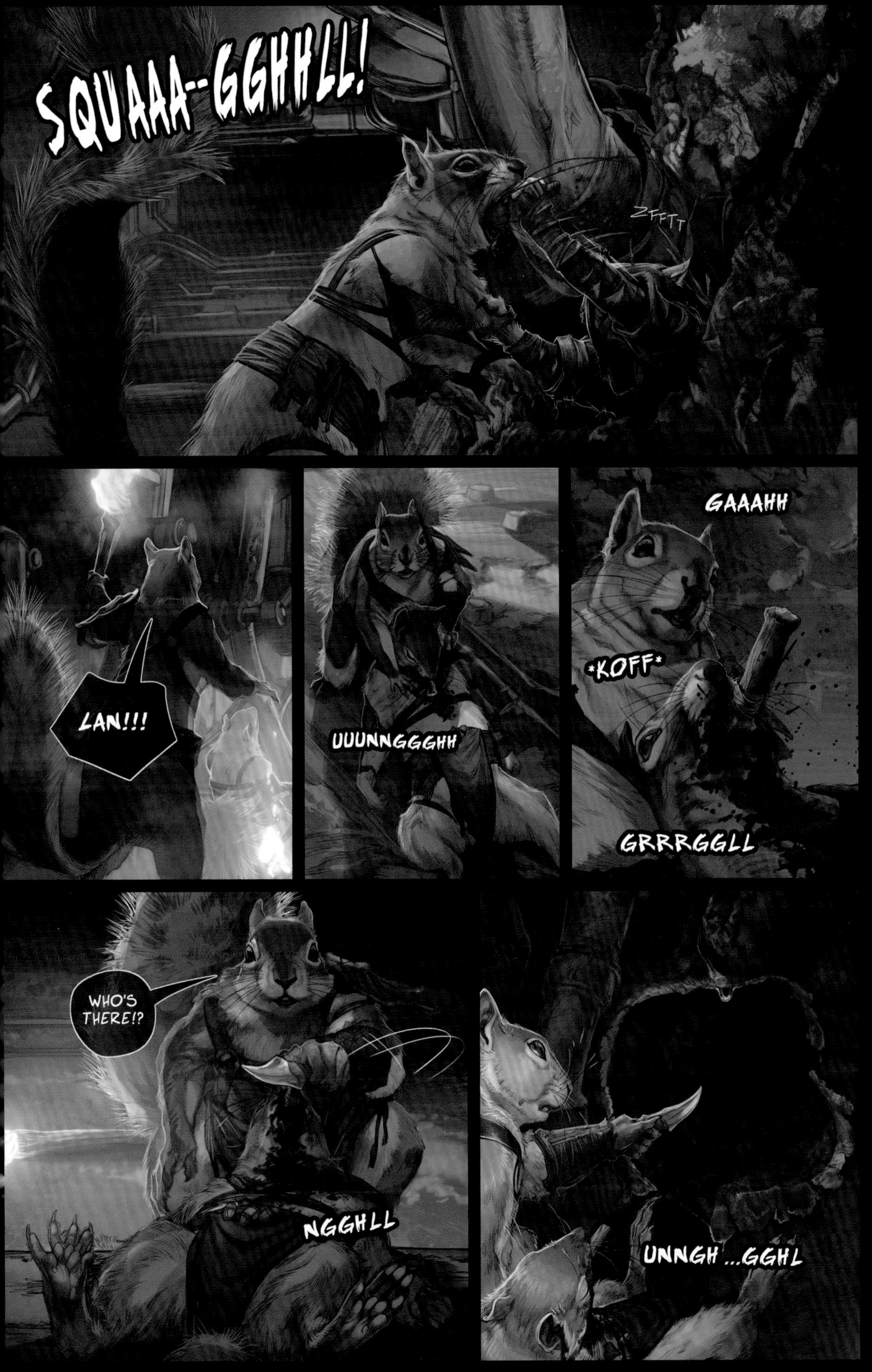
SQUAAA--GGHHLL!
ZFFTT
LAN!!!
UUUNNGGGHH
GAAAHH
KOFF
GRRRGGLL
WHO'S THERE!?
NGGHLL
UNNGH ...GGHL

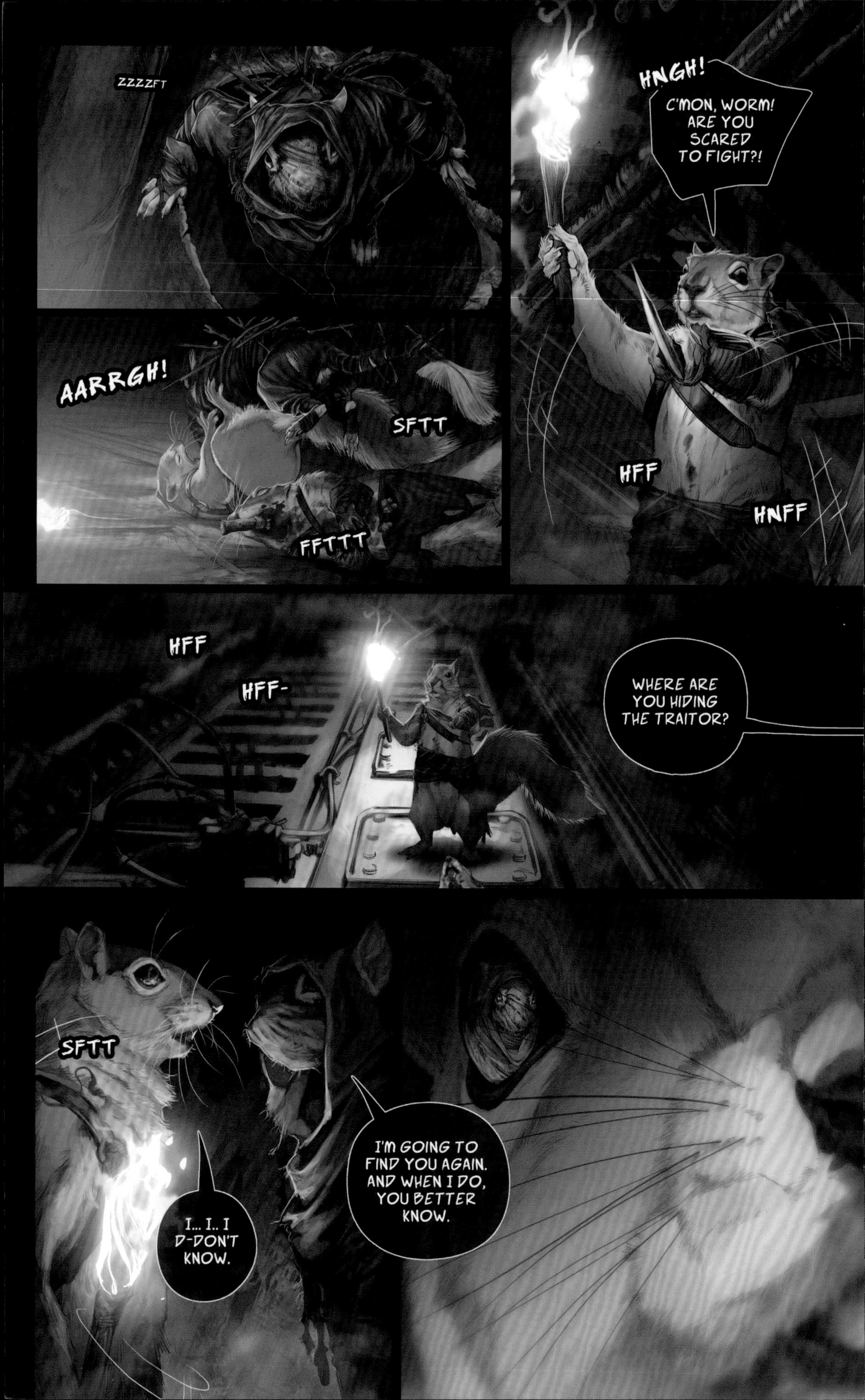
ZZZZFT
AARRGH!
SFTT
FFTTT
HNGH!
C'MON, WORM! ARE YOU SCARED TO FIGHT?!
HFF
HNFF
HFF
HFF-
WHERE ARE YOU HIDING THE TRAITOR?
SFTT
I... I.. I D-DON'T KNOW.
I'M GOING TO FIND YOU AGAIN. AND WHEN I DO, YOU BETTER KNOW.

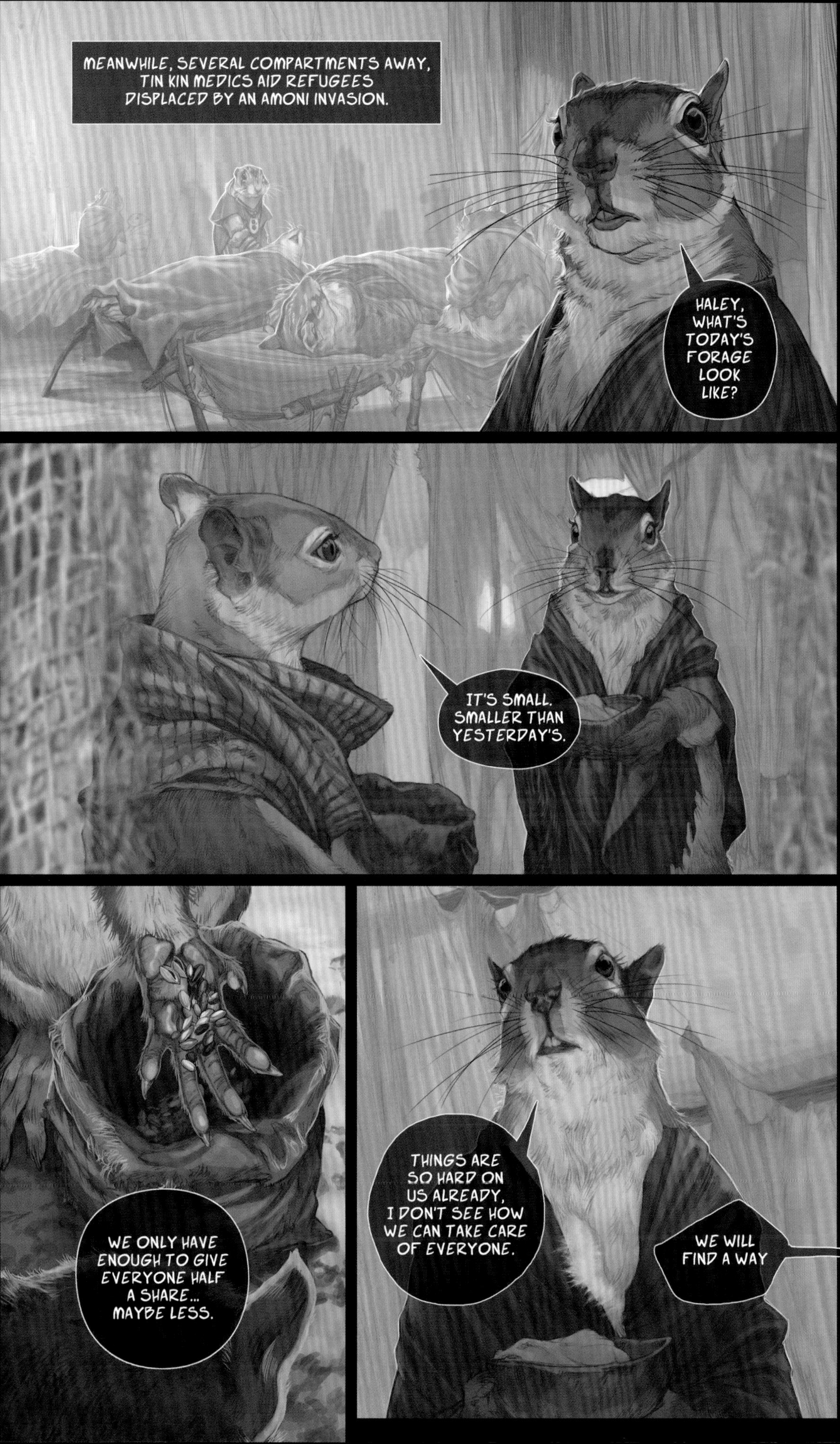
MEANWHILE, SEVERAL COMPARTMENTS AWAY, TIN KIN MEDICS AID REFUGEES DISPLACED BY AN AMONI INVASION.
HALEY, WHAT'S TODAY'S FORAGE LOOK LIKE?
IT'S SMALL. SMALLER THAN YESTERDAY'S.
WE ONLY HAVE ENOUGH TO GIVE EVERYONE HALF A SHARE... MAYBE LESS.
THINGS ARE SO HARD ON US ALREADY, I DON'T SEE HOW WE CAN TAKE CARE OF EVERYONE.
WE WILL FIND A WAY

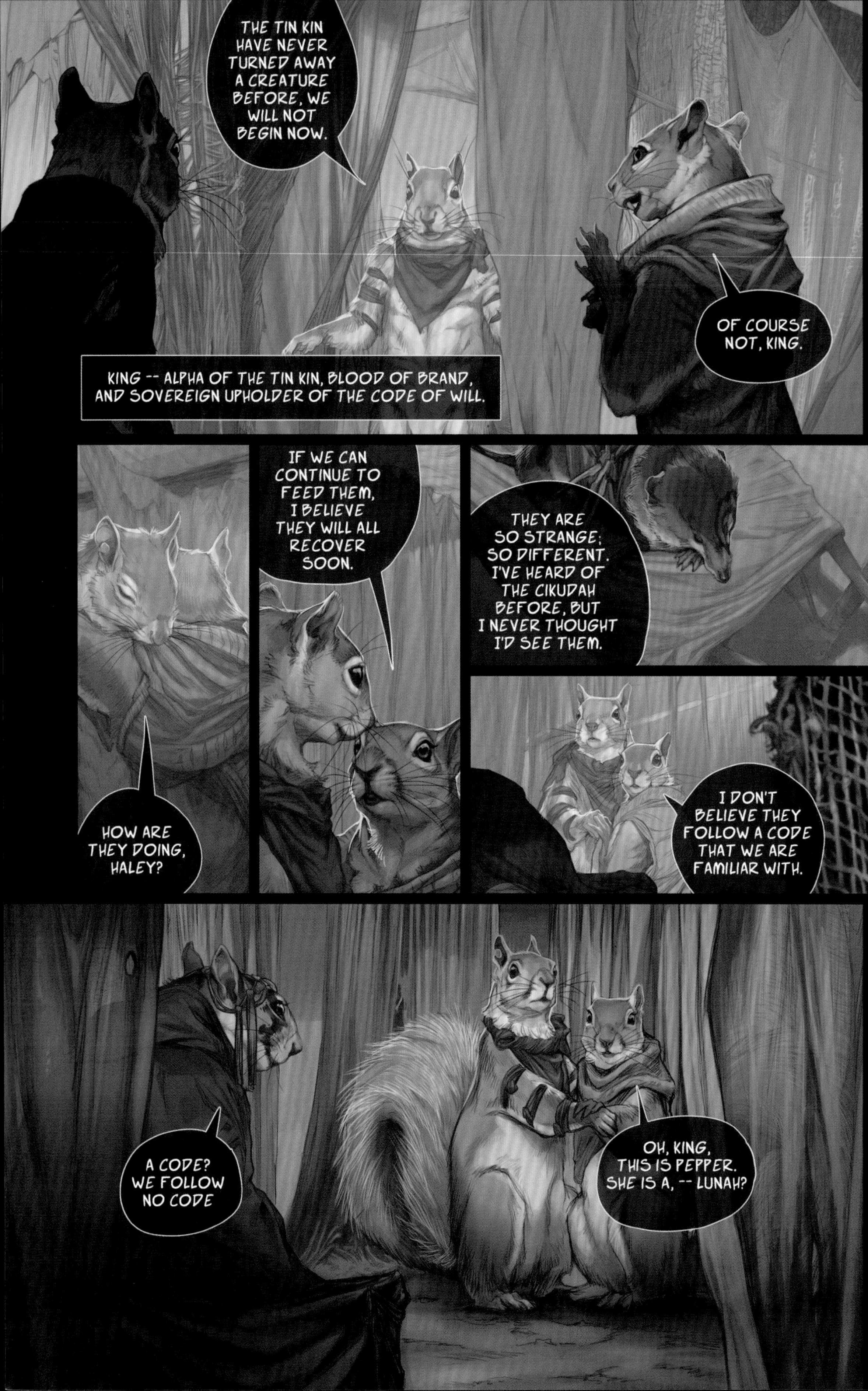
THE TIN KIN HAVE NEVER TURNED AWAY A CREATURE BEFORE, WE WILL NOT BEGIN NOW.
OF COURSE NOT, KING.
KING -- ALPHA OF THE TIN KIN, BLOOD OF BRAND, AND SOVEREIGN UPHOLDER OF THE CODE OF WILL.
HOW ARE THEY DOING, HALEY?
IF WE CAN CONTINUE TO FEED THEM, I BELIEVE THEY WILL ALL RECOVER SOON.
THEY ARE SO STRANGE; SO DIFFERENT. I'VE HEARD OF THE CIKUDAH BEFORE, BUT I NEVER THOUGHT I'D SEE THEM.
I DON'T BELIEVE THEY FOLLOW A CODE THAT WE ARE FAMILIAR WITH.
A CODE? WE FOLLOW NO CODE
OH, KING, THIS IS PEPPER. SHE IS A, -- LUNAH?

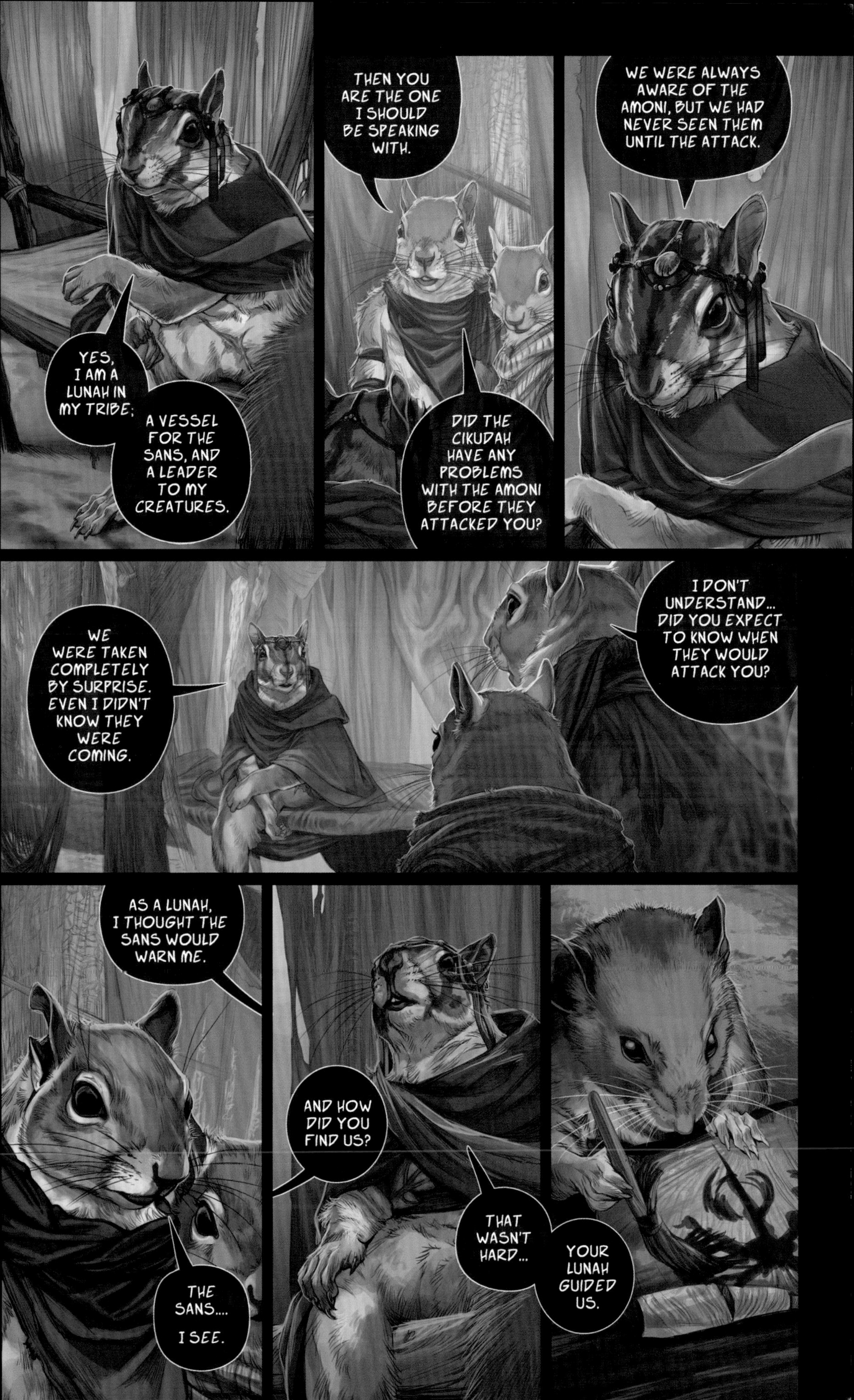
YES, I AM A LUNAH IN MY TRIBE;
A VESSEL FOR THE SANS, AND A LEADER TO MY CREATURES.
THEN YOU ARE THE ONE I SHOULD BE SPEAKING WITH.
DID THE CIKUDAH HAVE ANY PROBLEMS WITH THE AMONI BEFORE THEY ATTACKED YOU?
WE WERE ALWAYS AWARE OF THE AMONI, BUT WE HAD NEVER SEEN THEM UNTIL THE ATTACK.
WE WERE TAKEN COMPLETELY BY SURPRISE. EVEN I DIDN'T KNOW THEY WERE COMING.
I DON'T UNDERSTAND... DID YOU EXPECT TO KNOW WHEN THEY WOULD ATTACK YOU?
AS A LUNAH, I THOUGHT THE SANS WOULD WARN ME.
THE SANS....
I SEE.
AND HOW DID YOU FIND US?
THAT WASN'T HARD...
YOUR LUNAH GUIDED US.

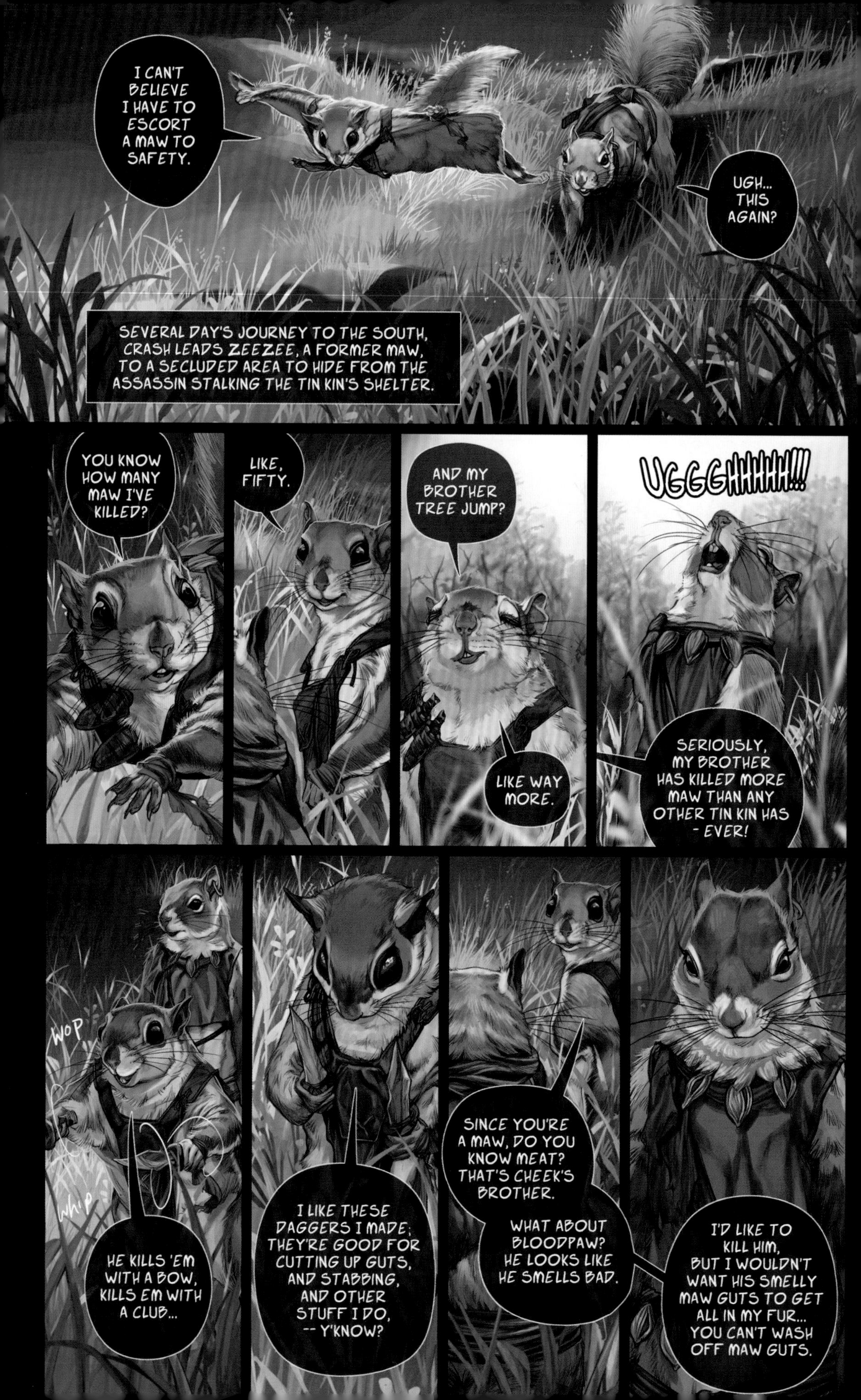
I CAN'T BELIEVE I HAVE TO ESCORT A MAW TO SAFETY.
UGH... THIS AGAIN?
SEVERAL DAY'S JOURNEY TO THE SOUTH, CRASH LEADS ZEEZEE, A FORMER MAW, TO A SECLUDED AREA TO HIDE FROM THE ASSASSIN STALKING THE TIN KIN'S SHELTER.
YOU KNOW HOW MANY MAW I'VE KILLED?
LIKE, FIFTY.
AND MY BROTHER TREE JUMP?
LIKE WAY MORE.
UGGGHHHHH!!!
SERIOUSLY, MY BROTHER HAS KILLED MORE MAW THAN ANY OTHER TIN KIN HAS - EVER!
WOP
WHIP
HE KILLS 'EM WITH A BOW, KILLS EM WITH A CLUB...
I LIKE THESE DAGGERS I MADE; THEY'RE GOOD FOR CUTTING UP GUTS, AND STABBING, AND OTHER STUFF I DO, -- Y'KNOW?
SINCE YOU'RE A MAW, DO YOU KNOW MEAT? THAT'S CHEEK'S BROTHER.
WHAT ABOUT BLOODPAW? HE LOOKS LIKE HE SMELLS BAD.
I'D LIKE TO KILL HIM, BUT I WOULDN'T WANT HIS SMELLY MAW GUTS TO GET ALL IN MY FUR... YOU CAN'T WASH OFF MAW GUTS.

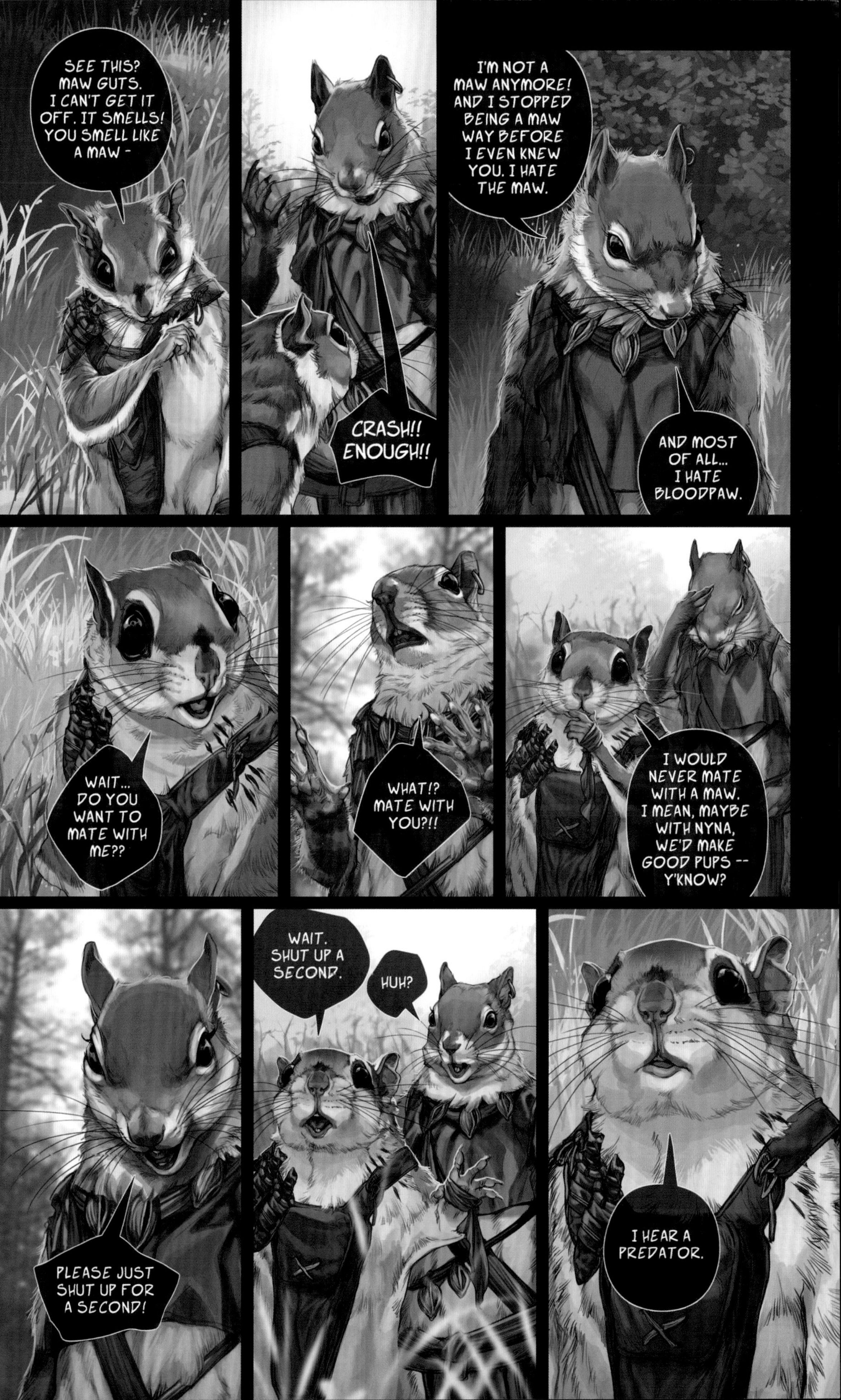
SEE THIS? MAW GUTS. I CAN'T GET IT OFF. IT SMELLS! YOU SMELL LIKE A MAW -
CRASH!! ENOUGH!!
I'M NOT A MAW ANYMORE! AND I STOPPED BEING A MAW WAY BEFORE I EVEN KNEW YOU. I HATE THE MAW.
AND MOST OF ALL... I HATE BLOODPAW.
WAIT... DO YOU WANT TO MATE WITH ME??
WHAT!? MATE WITH YOU?!!
I WOULD NEVER MATE WITH A MAW. I MEAN, MAYBE WITH NYNA, WE'D MAKE GOOD PUPS -- Y'KNOW?
PLEASE JUST SHUT UP FOR A SECOND!
WAIT. SHUT UP A SECOND.
HUH?
I HEAR A PREDATOR.

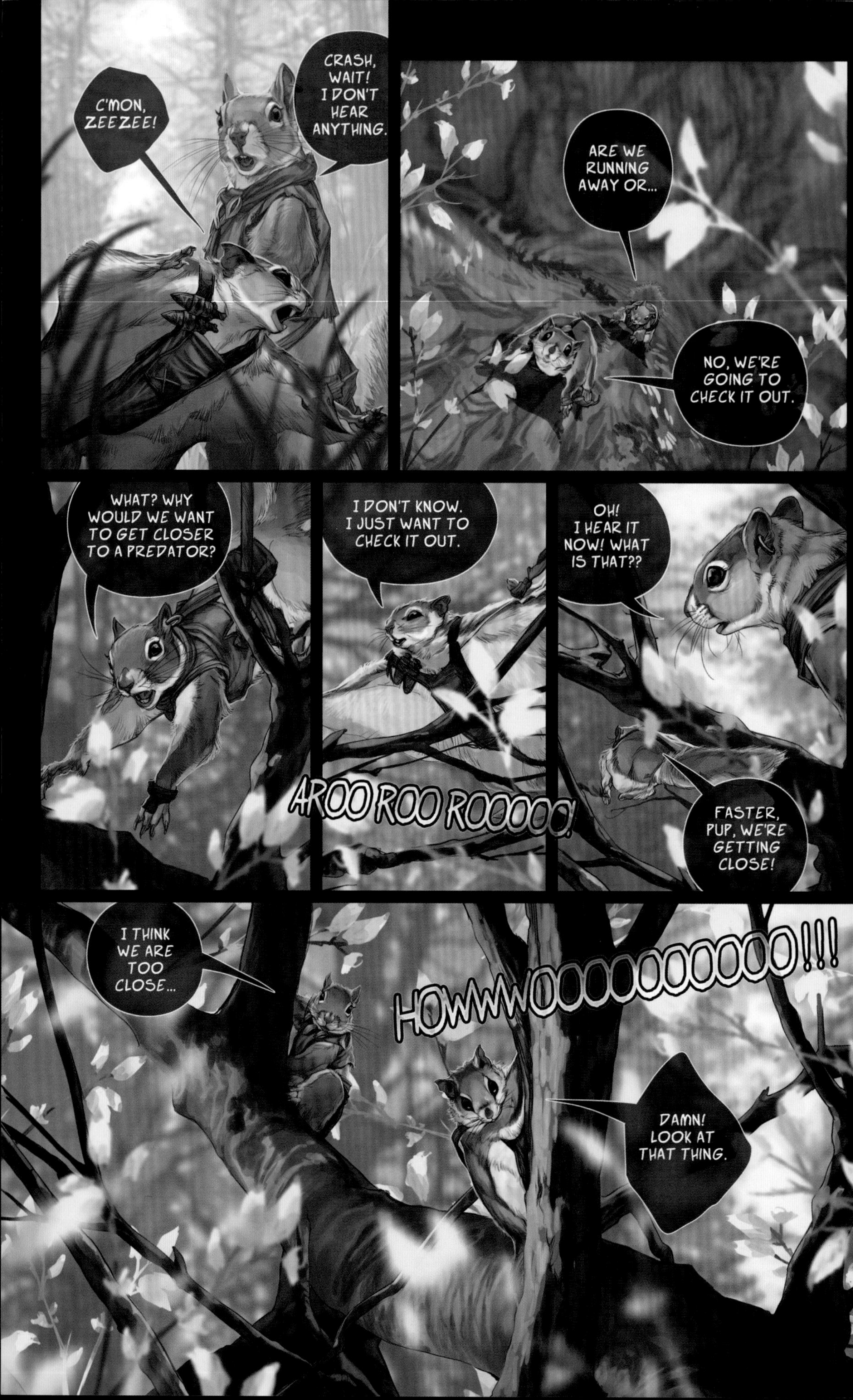
C'MON, ZEEZEE!
CRASH, WAIT! I DON'T HEAR ANYTHING.
ARE WE RUNNING AWAY OR...
NO, WE'RE GOING TO CHECK IT OUT.
WHAT? WHY WOULD WE WANT TO GET CLOSER TO A PREDATOR?
I DON'T KNOW. I JUST WANT TO CHECK IT OUT.
OH! I HEAR IT NOW! WHAT IS THAT??
AROO ROO ROOOOOO!
FASTER, PUP, WE'RE GETTING CLOSE!
I THINK WE ARE TOO CLOSE...
HOWWWOOOOOOOOOOOO!!!
DAMN! LOOK AT THAT THING.

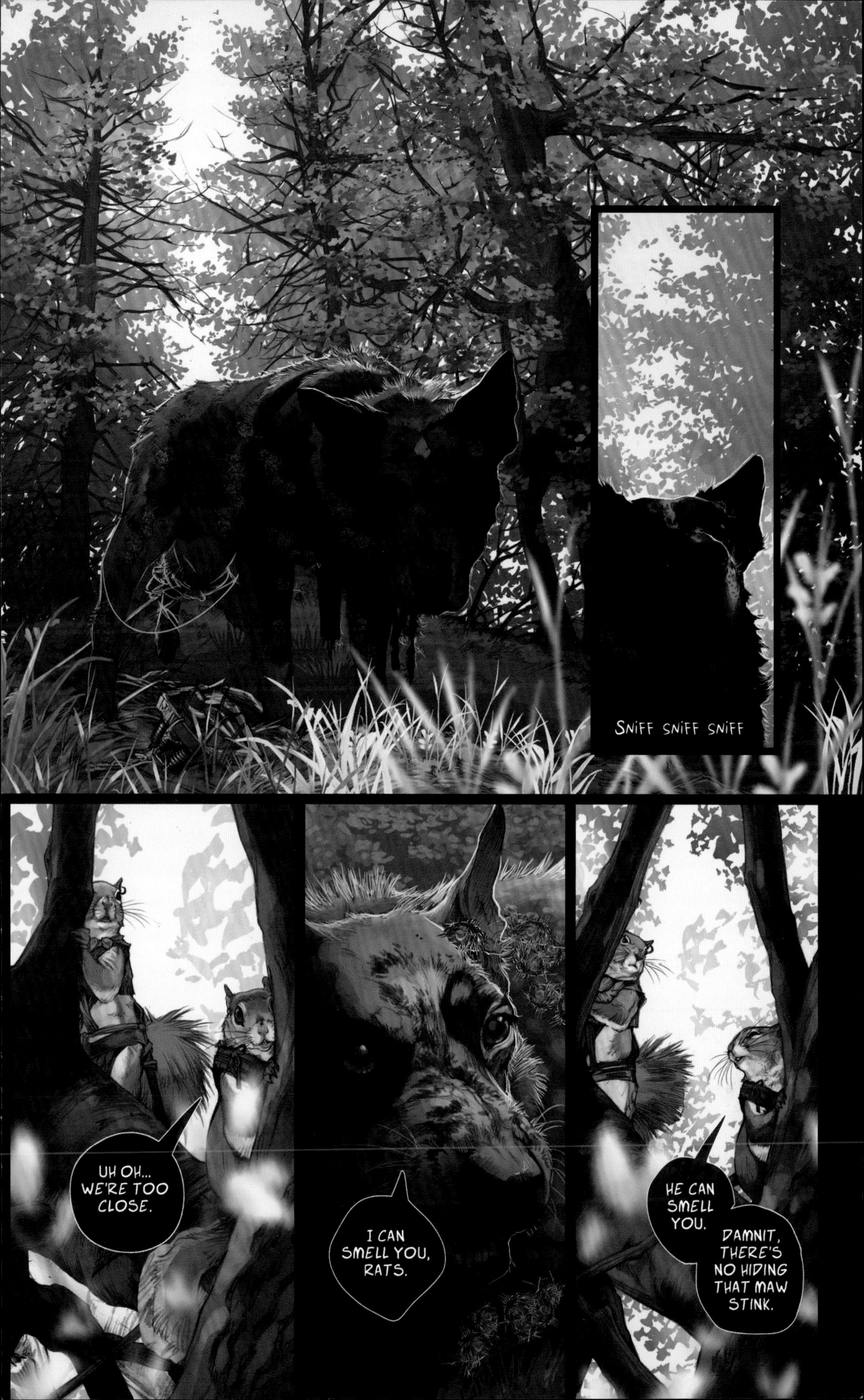
SNIFF SNIFF SNIFF
UH OH... WE'RE TOO CLOSE.
I CAN SMELL YOU, RATS.
HE CAN SMELL YOU.
DAMNIT, THERE'S NO HIDING THAT MAW STINK.

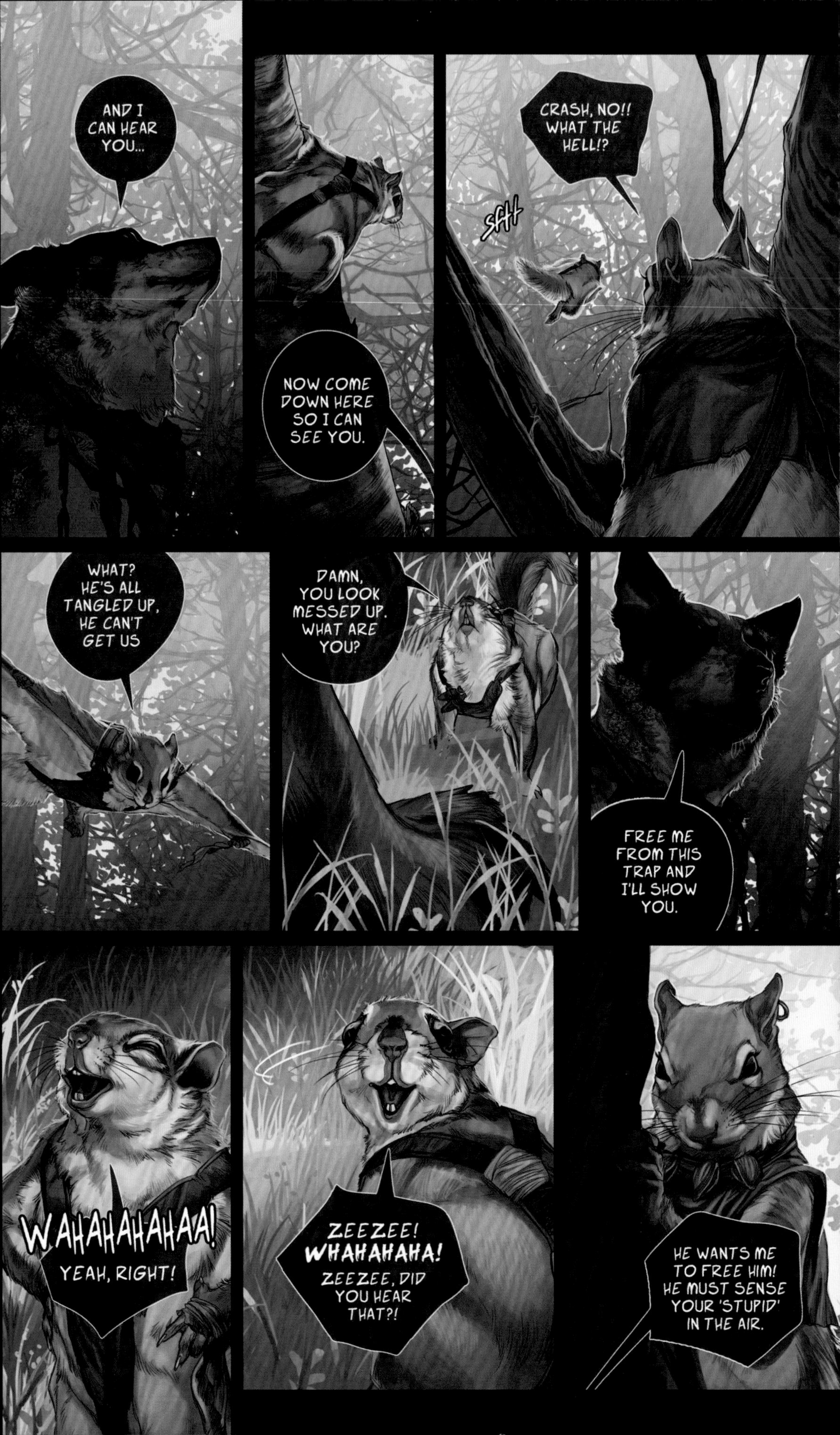
AND I CAN HEAR YOU...
NOW COME DOWN HERE SO I CAN SEE YOU.
CRASH, NO!! WHAT THE HELL!?
sfft
WHAT? HE'S ALL TANGLED UP, HE CAN'T GET US
DAMN, YOU LOOK MESSED UP. WHAT ARE YOU?
FREE ME FROM THIS TRAP AND I'LL SHOW YOU.
WAHAHAHAHAA!
YEAH, RIGHT!
ZEEZEE! WHAHAHAHA! ZEEZEE, DID YOU HEAR THAT?!
HE WANTS ME TO FREE HIM! HE MUST SENSE YOUR 'STUPID' IN THE AIR.

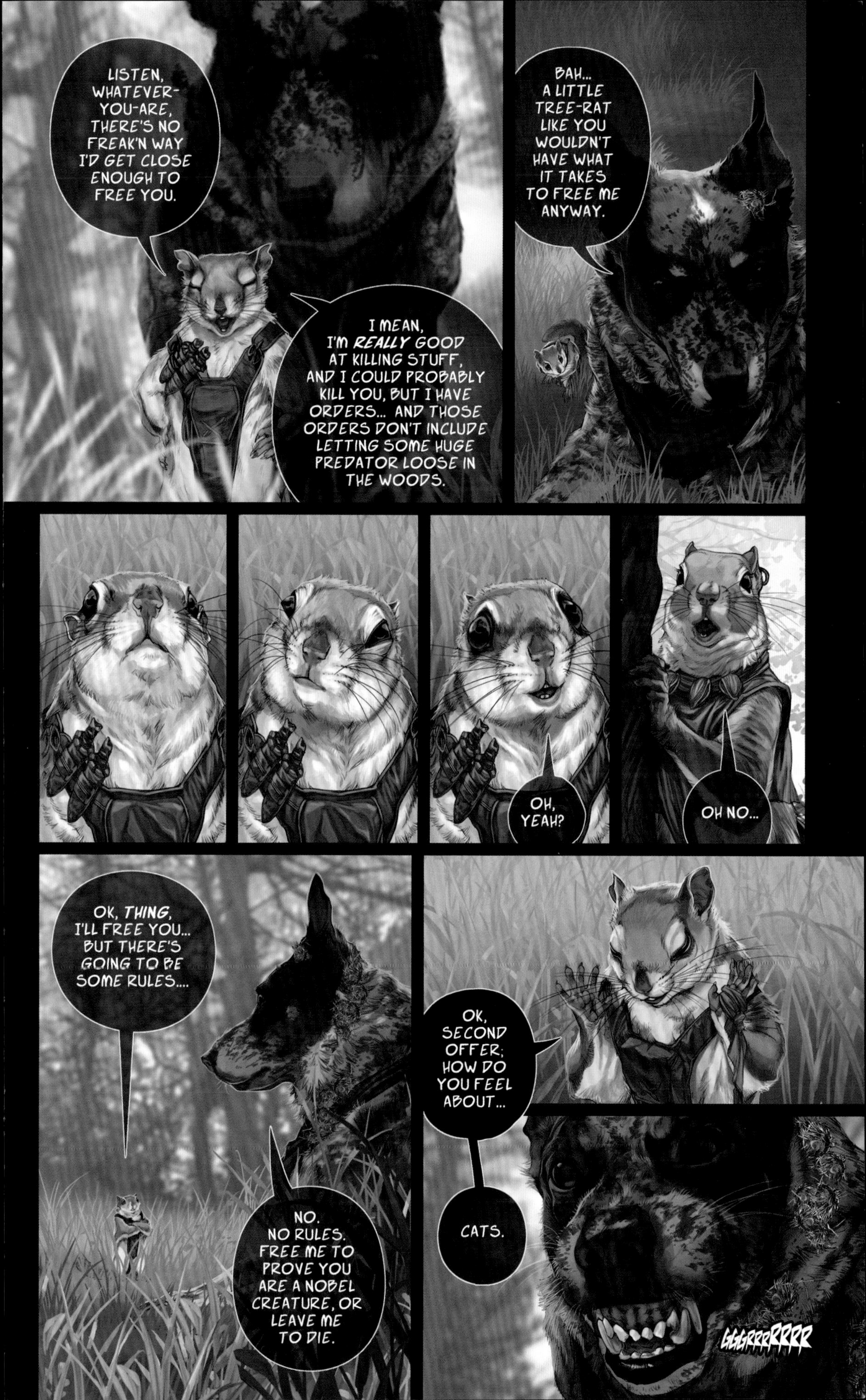
LISTEN, WHATEVER-YOU-ARE, THERE'S NO FREAK'N WAY I'D GET CLOSE ENOUGH TO FREE YOU.
I MEAN, I'M *REALLY* GOOD AT KILLING STUFF, AND I COULD PROBABLY KILL YOU, BUT I HAVE ORDERS... AND THOSE ORDERS DON'T INCLUDE LETTING SOME HUGE PREDATOR LOOSE IN THE WOODS.
BAH... A LITTLE TREE-RAT LIKE YOU WOULDN'T HAVE WHAT IT TAKES TO FREE ME ANYWAY.
OH, YEAH?
OH NO...
OK, *THING*, I'LL FREE YOU... BUT THERE'S GOING TO BE SOME RULES....
NO. NO RULES. FREE ME TO PROVE YOU ARE A NOBEL CREATURE, OR LEAVE ME TO DIE.
OK, SECOND OFFER; HOW DO YOU FEEL ABOUT...
CATS.
GGGGRRRRRRR

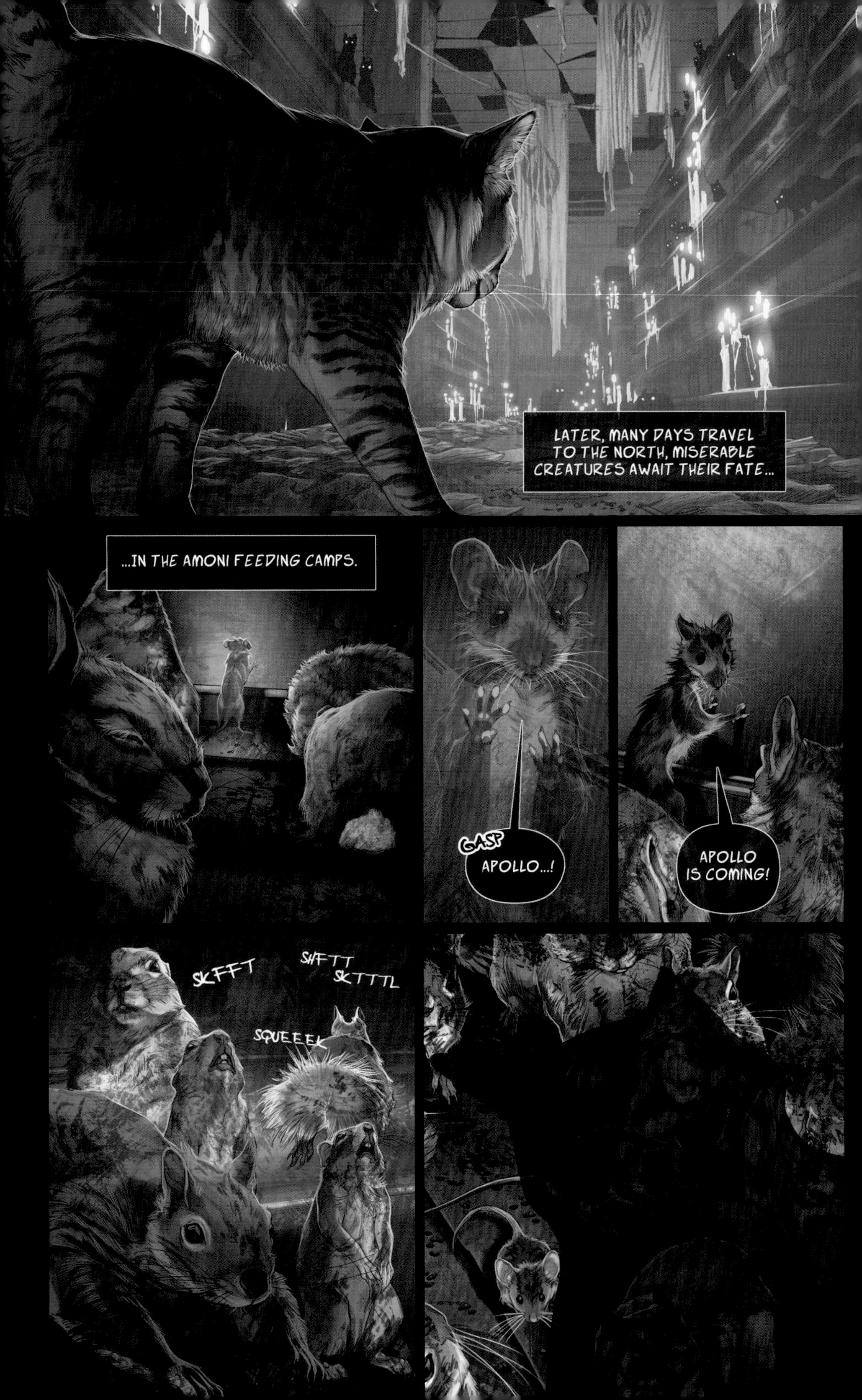
LATER, MANY DAYS TRAVEL TO THE NORTH, MISERABLE CREATURES AWAIT THEIR FATE...
...IN THE AMONI FEEDING CAMPS.
GASP
APOLLO...!
APOLLO IS COMING!
SKFFT
SHFTT
SKTTTL
SQUEEEK

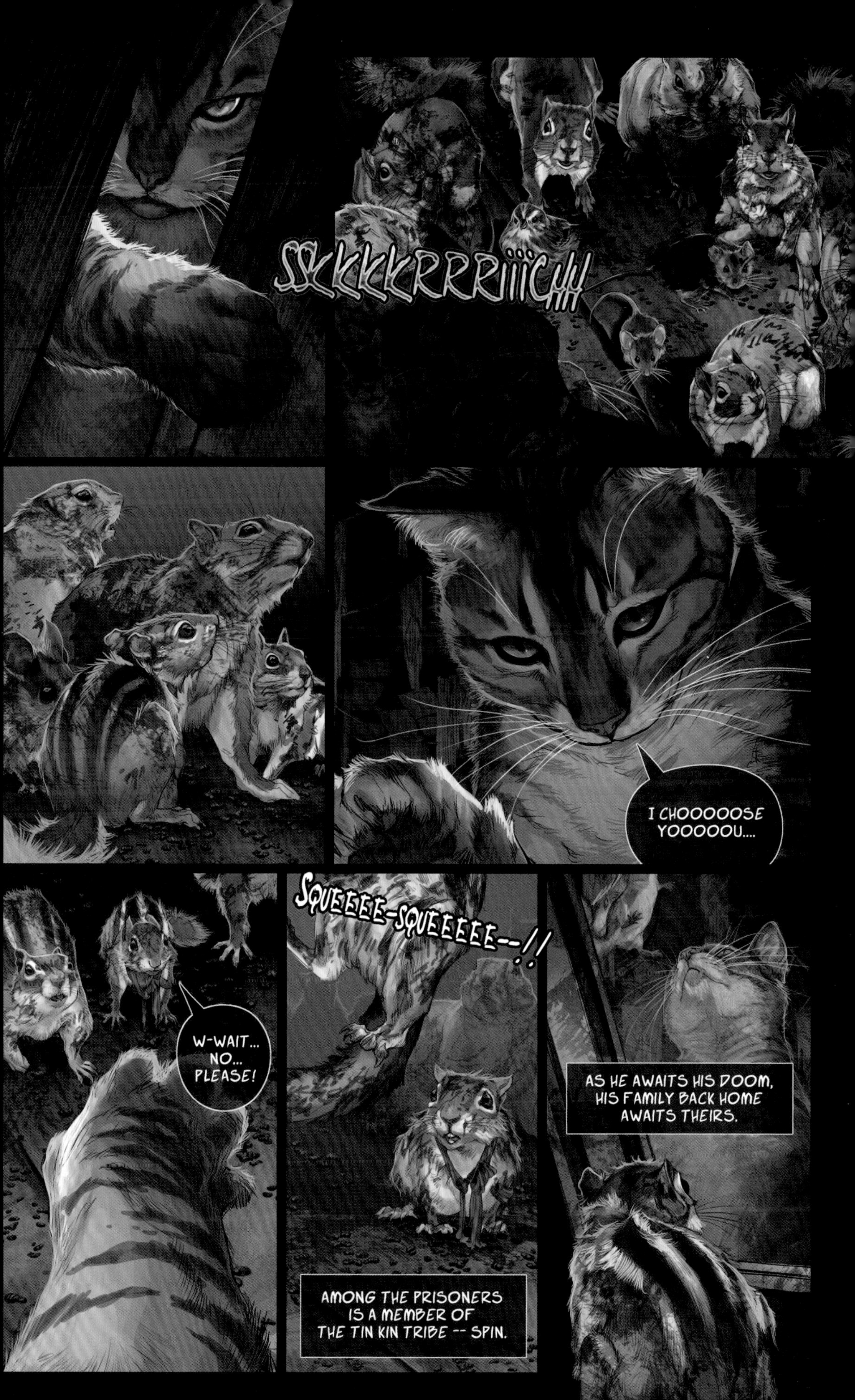
SSKKKKRRRRIIICHH
I CHOOOOOSE YOOOOOU....
W-WAIT... NO... PLEASE!
SQUEEEE-SQUEEEEEE--!!
AMONG THE PRISONERS IS A MEMBER OF THE TIN KIN TRIBE -- SPIN.
AS HE AWAITS HIS DOOM, HIS FAMILY BACK HOME AWAITS THEIRS.

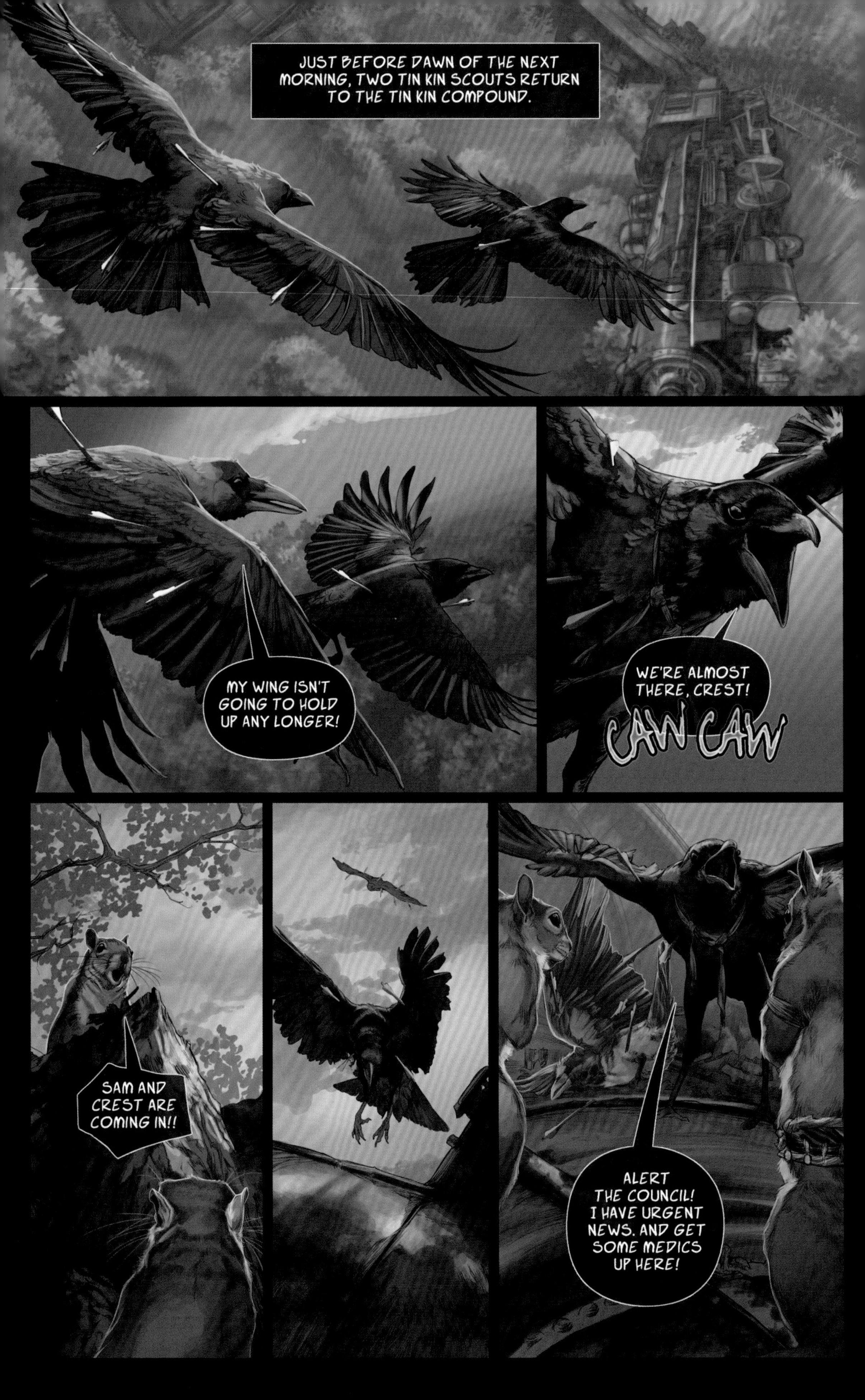
JUST BEFORE DAWN OF THE NEXT MORNING, TWO TIN KIN SCOUTS RETURN TO THE TIN KIN COMPOUND.
MY WING ISN'T GOING TO HOLD UP ANY LONGER!
WE'RE ALMOST THERE, CREST!
CAW CAW
SAM AND CREST ARE COMING IN!!
ALERT THE COUNCIL! I HAVE URGENT NEWS. AND GET SOME MEDICS UP HERE!

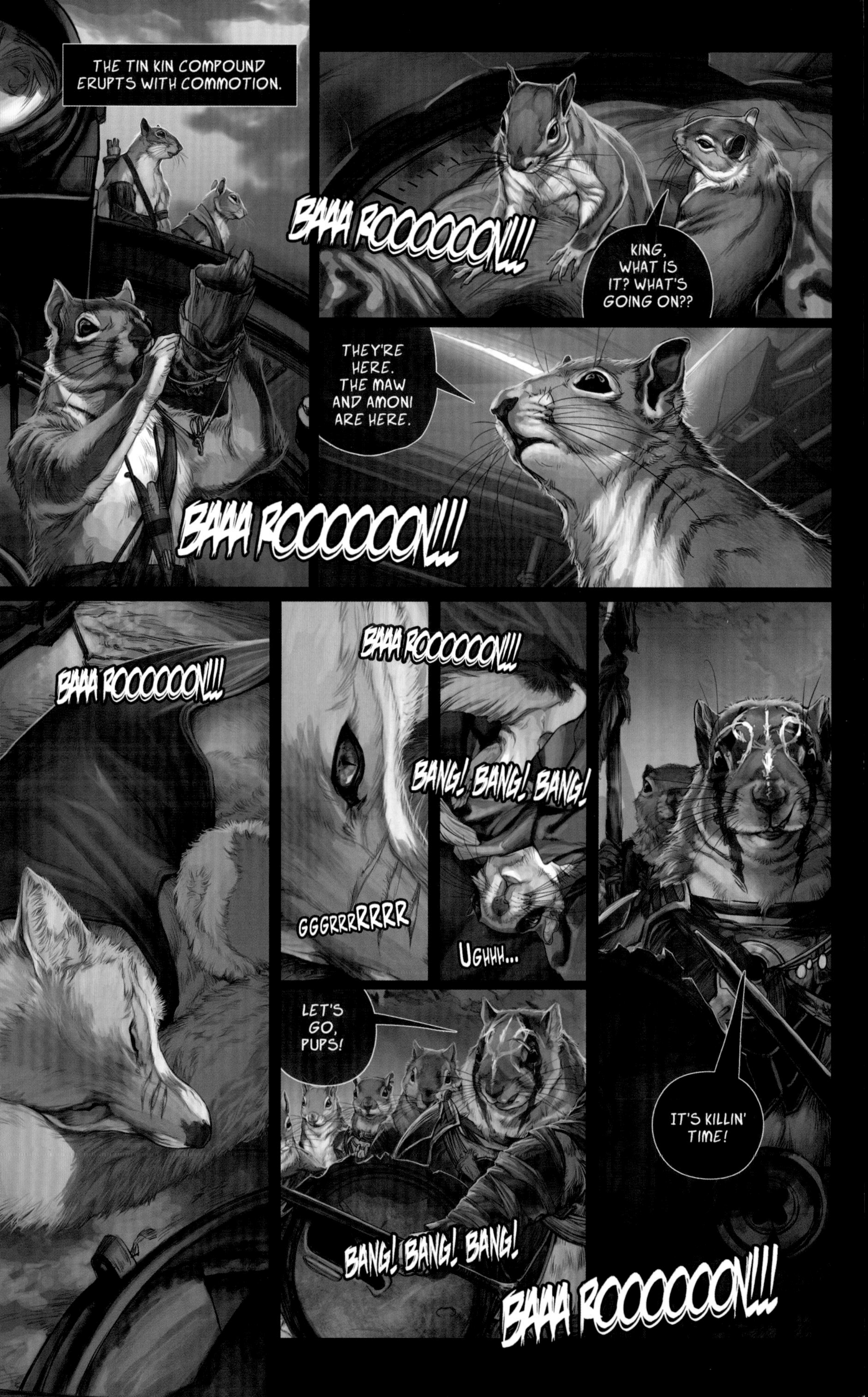
THE TIN KIN COMPOUND ERUPTS WITH COMMOTION.
BAAA ROOOOOON!!!
KING, WHAT IS IT? WHAT'S GOING ON??
THEY'RE HERE. THE MAW AND AMONI ARE HERE.
BAAA ROOOOOON!!!
BAAA ROOOOOON!!!
BAAA ROOOOOON!!!
GGGRRRRRR
BANG! BANG! BANG!
UGHHH...
LET'S GO, PUPS!
IT'S KILLIN' TIME!
BANG! BANG! BANG!
BAAA ROOOOOON!!!

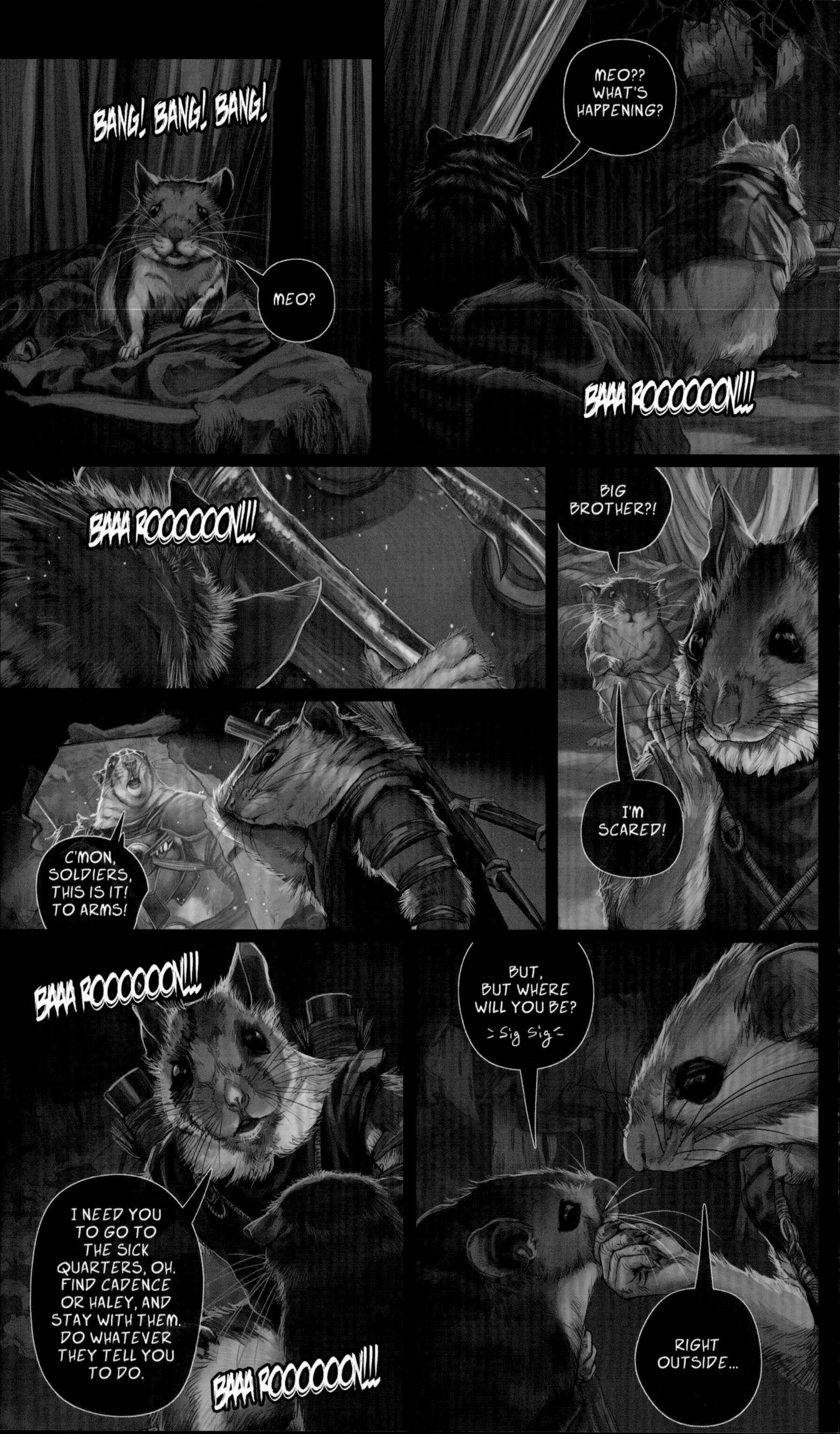

BANG! BANG! BANG!
MEO?
MEO?? WHAT'S HAPPENING?
BAAA ROOOOOON!!!
BAAA ROOOOOON!!!
BIG BROTHER?!
C'MON, SOLDIERS, THIS IS IT! TO ARMS!
I'M SCARED!
BAAA ROOOOOON!!!
I NEED YOU TO GO TO THE SICK QUARTERS, OH. FIND CADENCE OR HALEY, AND STAY WITH THEM. DO WHATEVER THEY TELL YOU TO DO.
BAAA ROOOOOON!!!
BUT, BUT WHERE WILL YOU BE?
> Sig Sig <
RIGHT OUTSIDE...

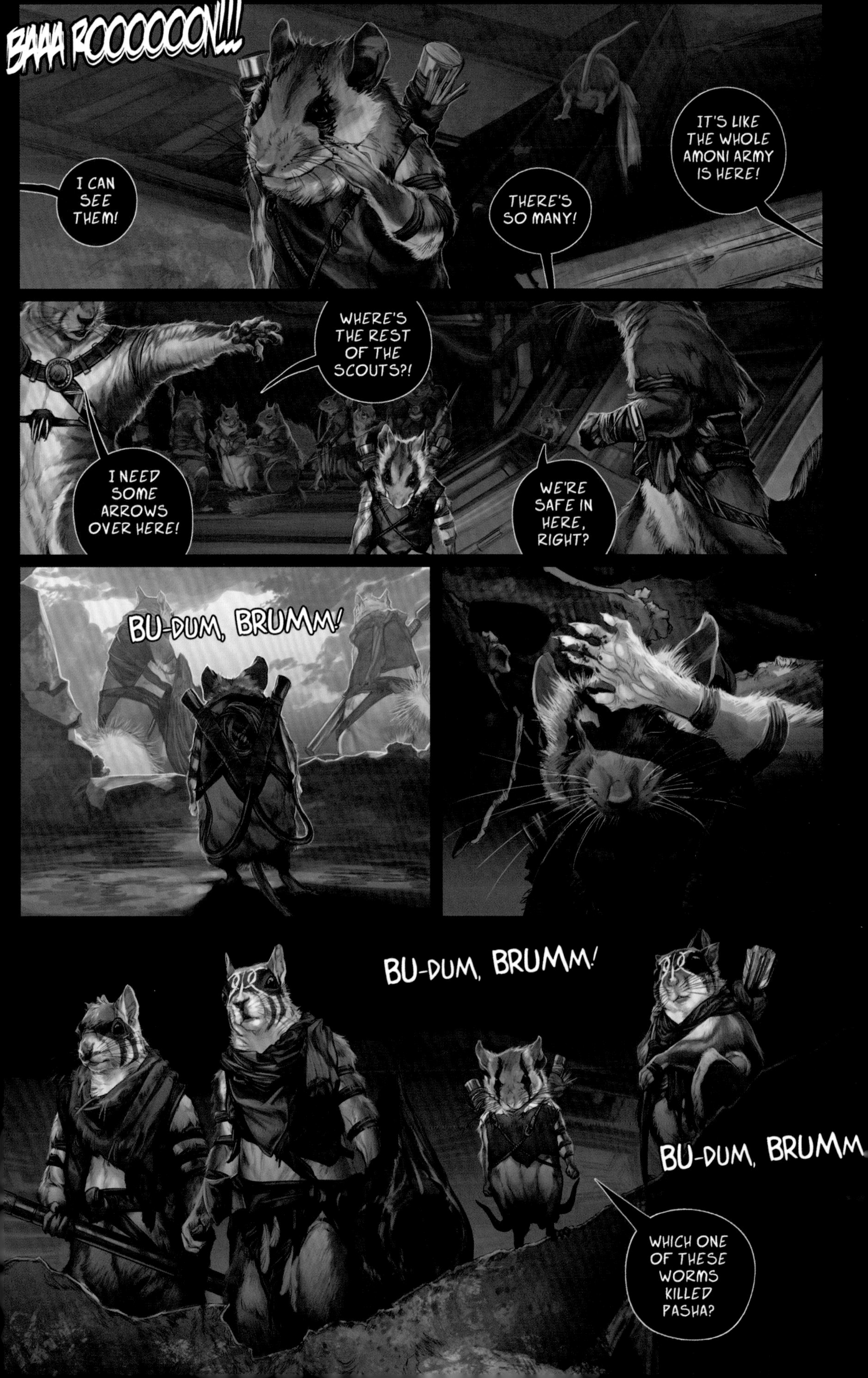
BAAA ROOOOOOON!!!
I CAN SEE THEM!
THERE'S SO MANY!
IT'S LIKE THE WHOLE AMONI ARMY IS HERE!
WHERE'S THE REST OF THE SCOUTS?!
I NEED SOME ARROWS OVER HERE!
WE'RE SAFE IN HERE, RIGHT?
BU-DUM, BRUMM!
BU-DUM, BRUMM!
BU-DUM, BRUMM
WHICH ONE OF THESE WORMS KILLED PASHA?

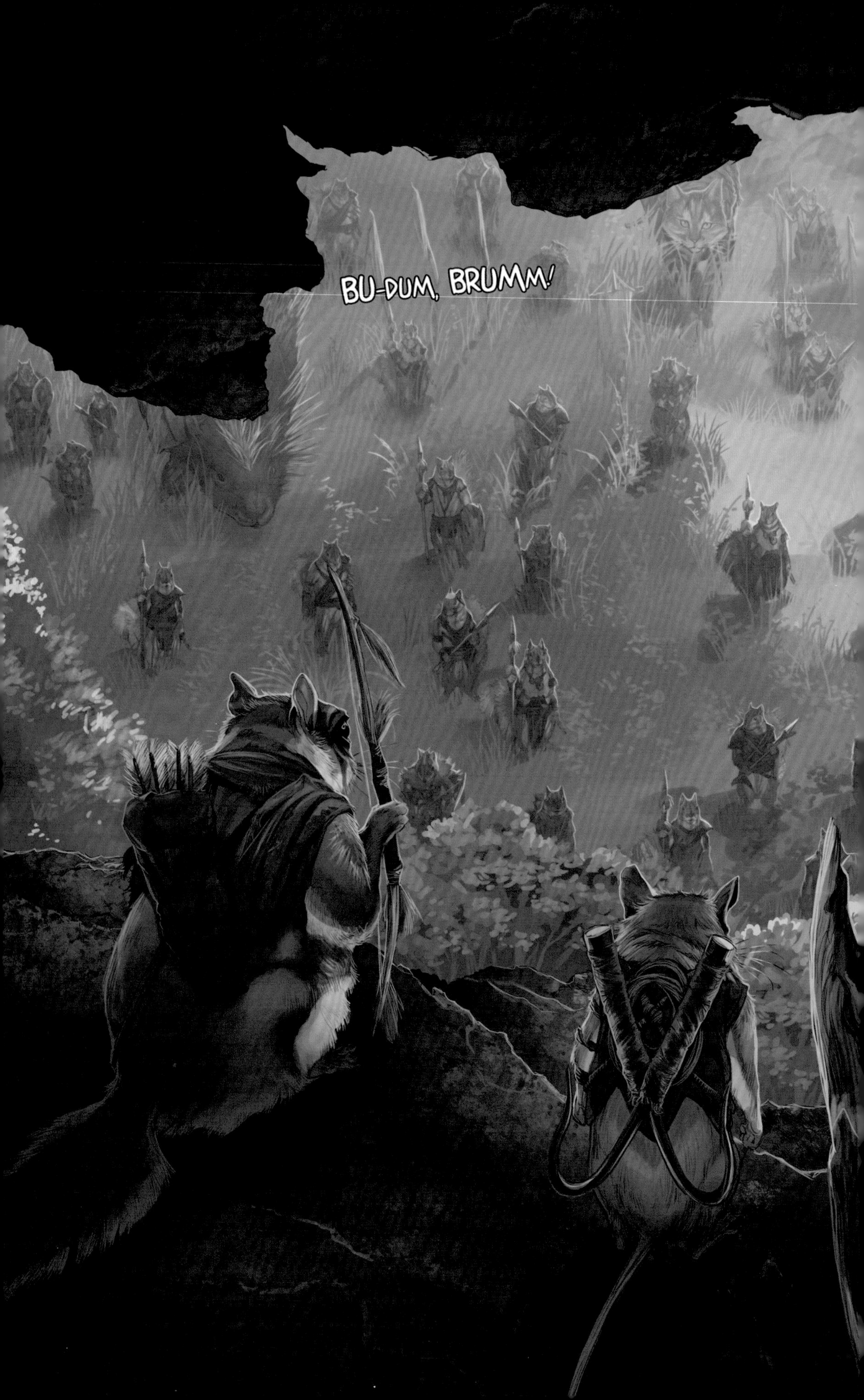
BU-DUM, BRUMM!

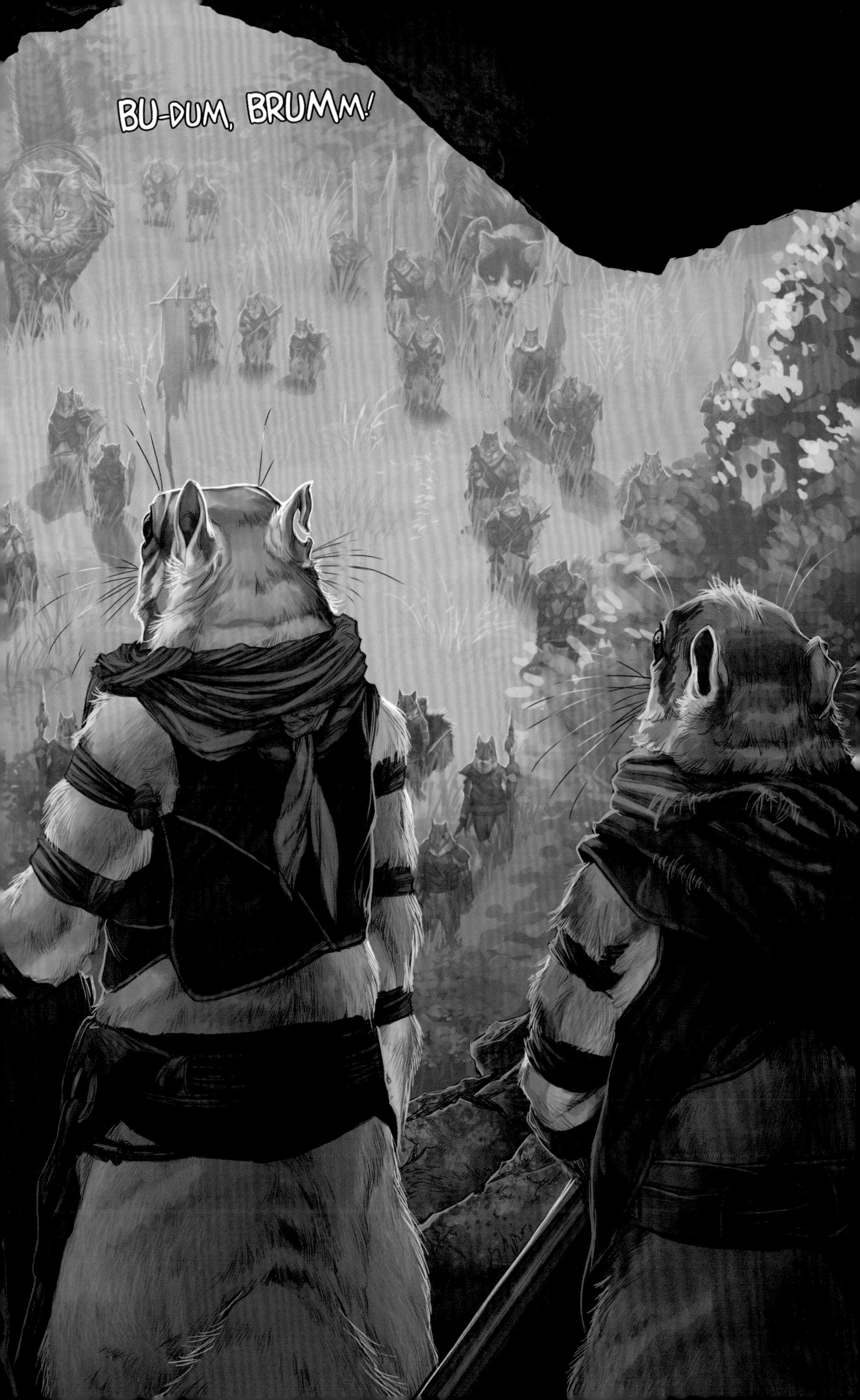
BU-DUM, BRUMM!

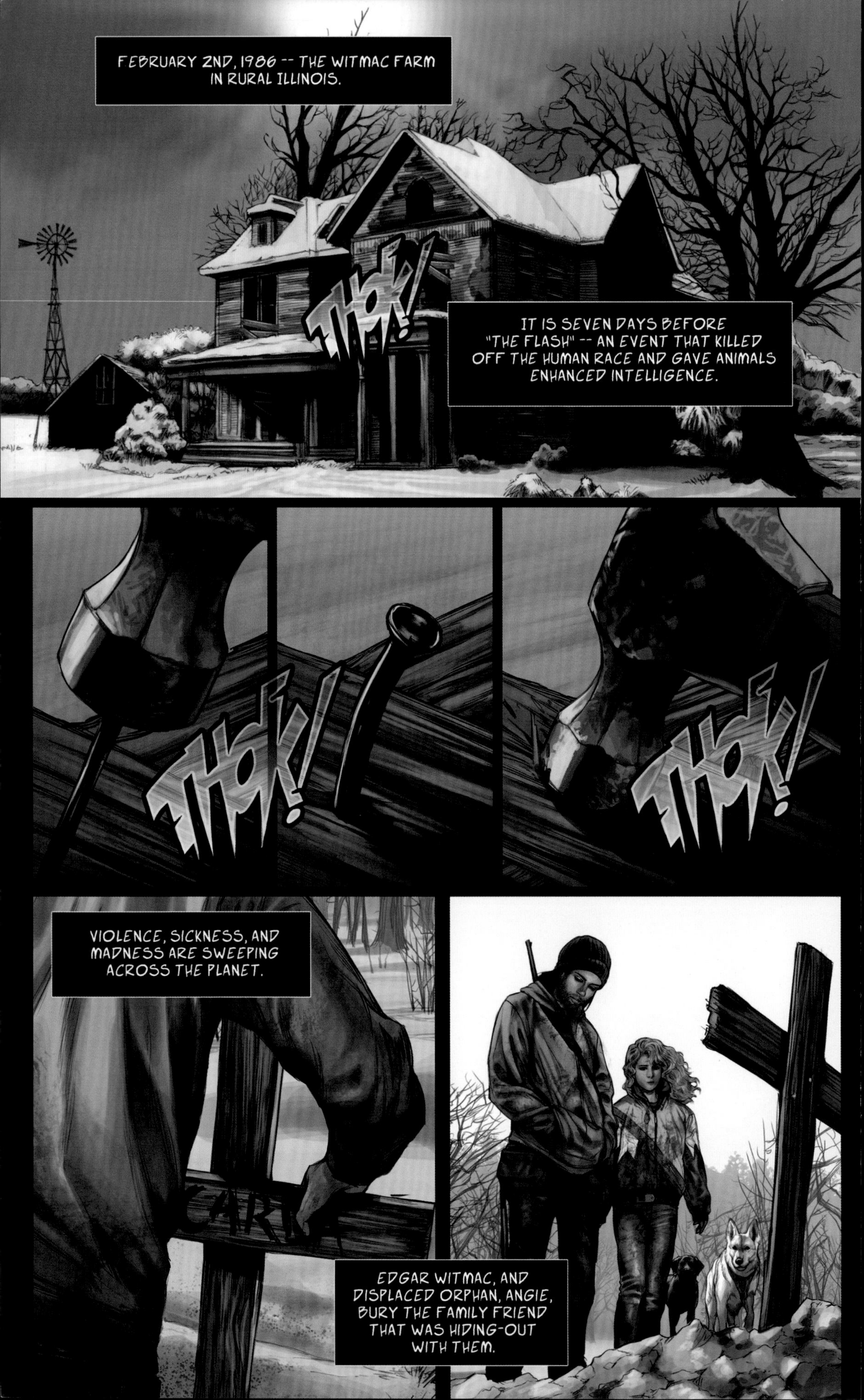
FEBRUARY 2ND, 1986 -- THE WITMAC FARM IN RURAL ILLINOIS.
THOK!
IT IS SEVEN DAYS BEFORE "THE FLASH" -- AN EVENT THAT KILLED OFF THE HUMAN RACE AND GAVE ANIMALS ENHANCED INTELLIGENCE.
THOK!
THOK!
VIOLENCE, SICKNESS, AND MADNESS ARE SWEEPING ACROSS THE PLANET.
EDGAR WITMAC, AND DISPLACED ORPHAN, ANGIE, BURY THE FAMILY FRIEND THAT WAS HIDING-OUT WITH THEM.

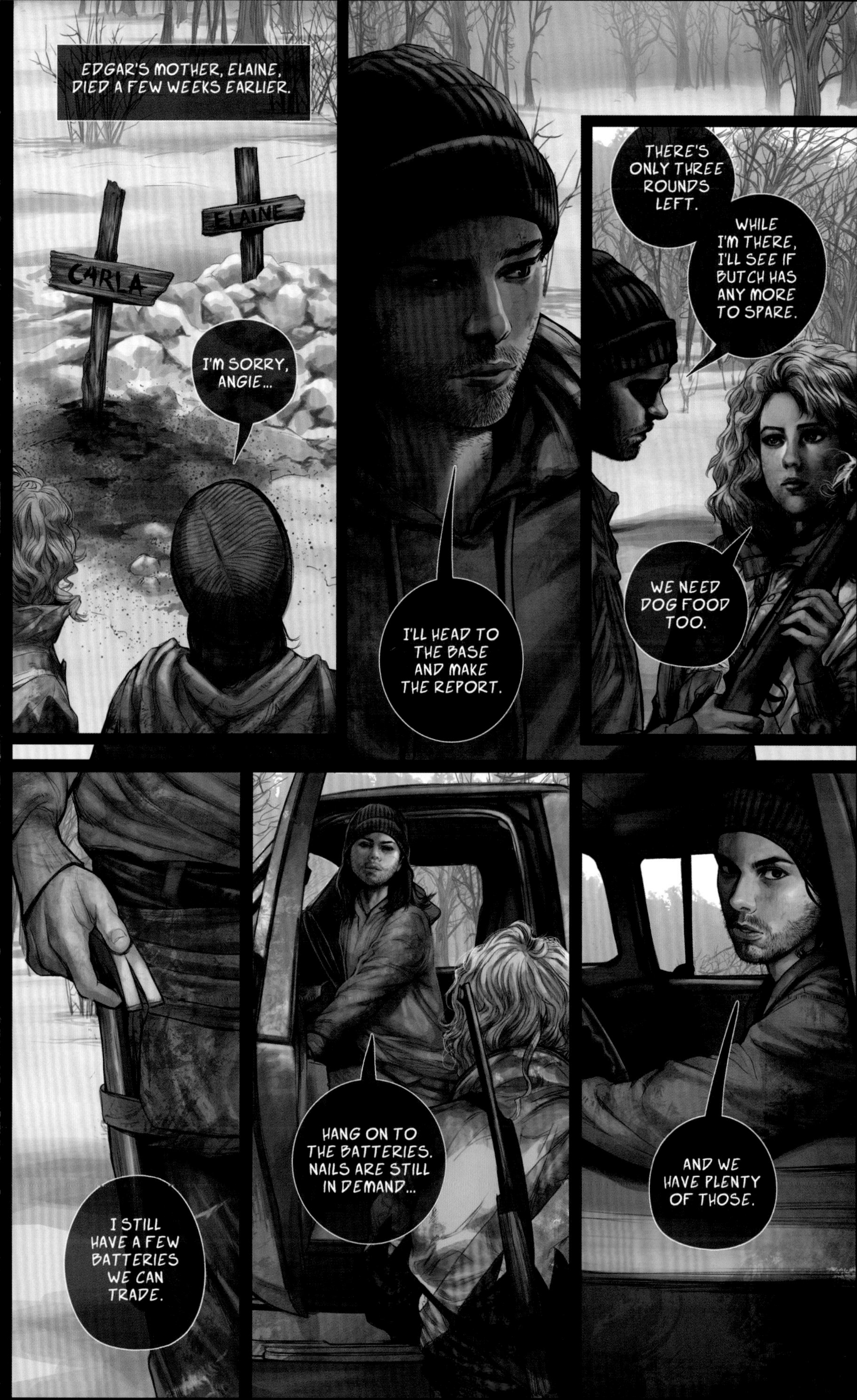
EDGAR'S MOTHER, ELAINE, DIED A FEW WEEKS EARLIER.
ELAINE
CARLA
I'M SORRY, ANGIE...
I'LL HEAD TO THE BASE AND MAKE THE REPORT.
THERE'S ONLY THREE ROUNDS LEFT.
WHILE I'M THERE, I'LL SEE IF BUTCH HAS ANY MORE TO SPARE.
WE NEED DOG FOOD TOO.
I STILL HAVE A FEW BATTERIES WE CAN TRADE.
HANG ON TO THE BATTERIES. NAILS ARE STILL IN DEMAND...
AND WE HAVE PLENTY OF THOSE.

ABOUT ONE MILE FROM THE WITMAC FARM...

...IF IT WEREN'T FOR THE RADICAL CHRISTIANS -- THE ZEALOTS, THE DEATH TOLL WOULD BE HALF OF WHAT IT IS.

NO, NO, NO. SOMETHING'S HAPPENING!

HAVE YOU SEEN THE DYATLOV FOOTAGE?!

THOSE AREN'T PEOPLE! THEY JUST FOUND ANOTHER COLONY UNDERNEATH THE SEARS TOWER WRECKAGE!

THAT'S NOT AN EXCUSE TO START A CIVIL-FUCKING-WAR!

NOOO! THE ONLY WAR IS THE WAR BETWEEN US AND THEM!

RUMBLE-RUMBLE-RUMBLE-

AND AS THE COMET GETS CLOSER WE'LL SEE WHO'S RIGHTEOUS!

RUMBLE- RUMBA -VARAAAIM!

OH, THE COMET... THE RAPTURE? THE APOCALYPSE?!

A MYSTERIOUS PERSON FROM THE PAST IS UNLUCKY ENOUGH TO CROSS EDGAR'S PATH FOR A SECOND TIME.

ILLINOIS LAND OF LINCOLN
CDOSCAR

THERE ARE SOME BIZARRE THINGS HAPPENING, BUT WE NEED TO KEEP OUR HEADS...

THE WAY THE U.N., AND SPECIFICALLY THE UNITED STATES, HAVE BEEN HANDLING THIS IS INSANE!

...C.D. OSCAR...

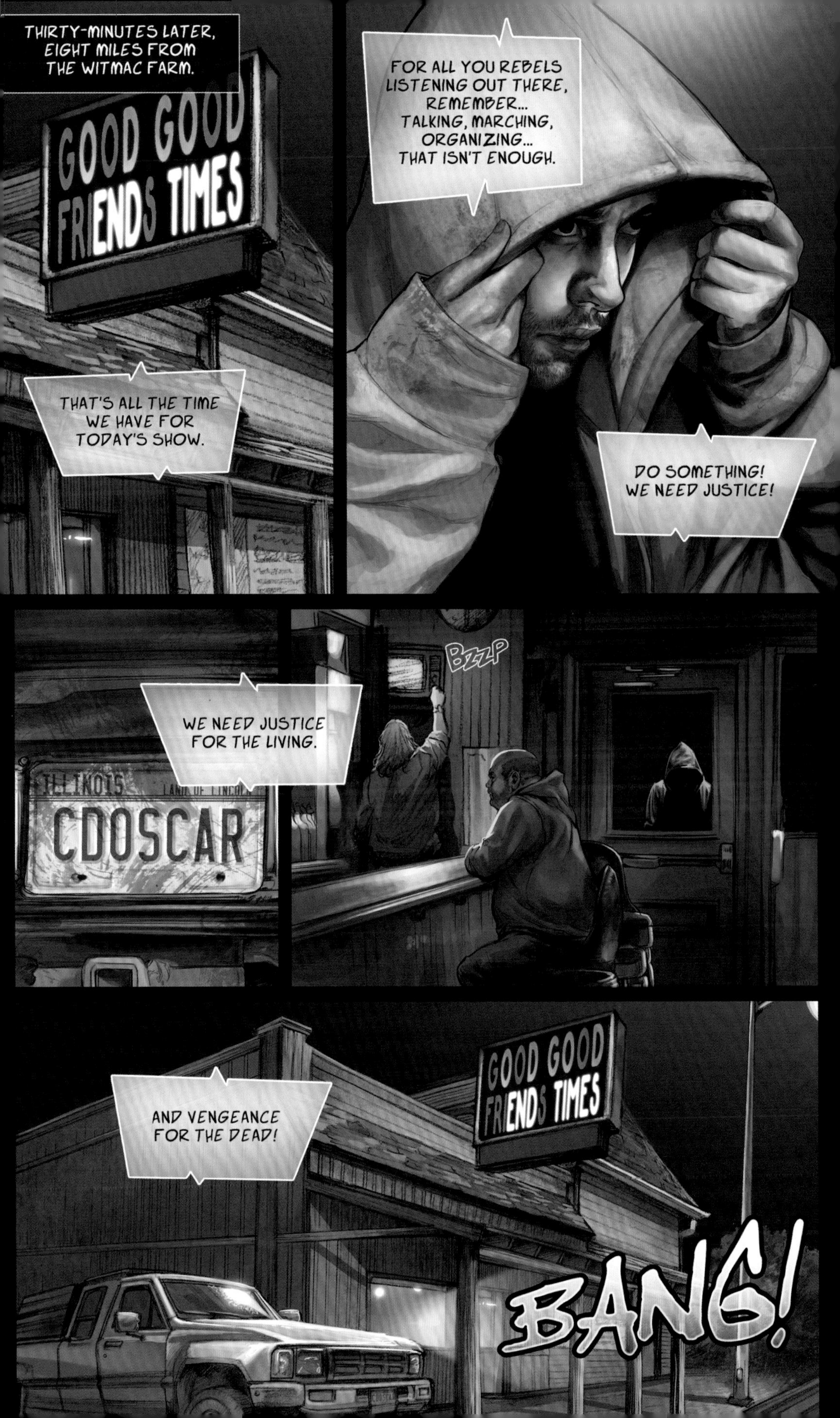
THIRTY-MINUTES LATER, EIGHT MILES FROM THE WITMAC FARM.
GOOD GOOD FRIENDS TIMES
THAT'S ALL THE TIME WE HAVE FOR TODAY'S SHOW.
FOR ALL YOU REBELS LISTENING OUT THERE, REMEMBER... TALKING, MARCHING, ORGANIZING... THAT ISN'T ENOUGH.
DO SOMETHING! WE NEED JUSTICE!
WE NEED JUSTICE FOR THE LIVING.
CDOSCAR
BZZP
AND VENGEANCE FOR THE DEAD!
GOOD GOOD FRIENDS TIMES
BANG!

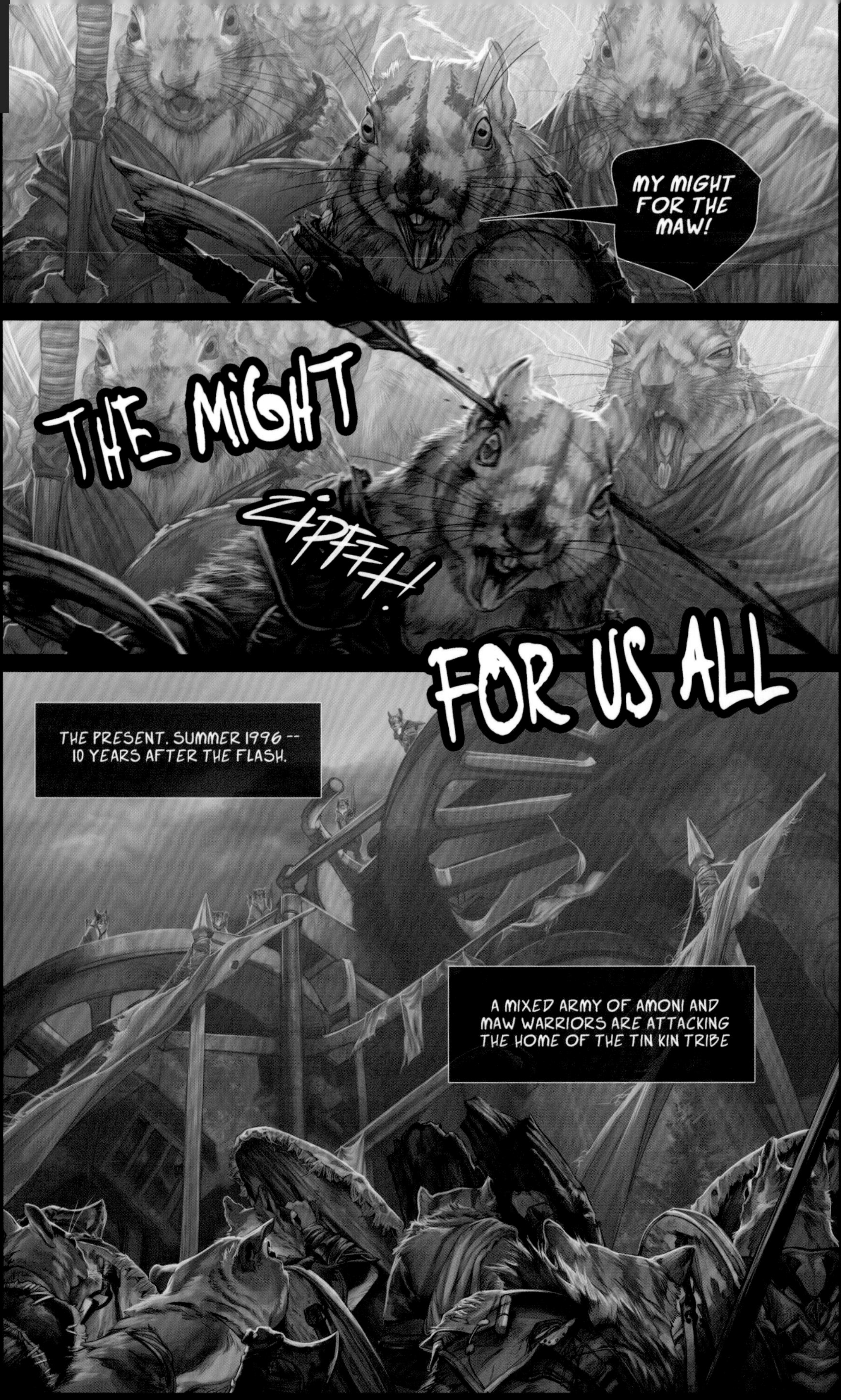
MY MIGHT FOR THE MAW!
THE MIGHT
ZIPFFH!
FOR US ALL
THE PRESENT. SUMMER 1996 -- 10 YEARS AFTER THE FLASH.
A MIXED ARMY OF AMONI AND MAW WARRIORS ARE ATTACKING THE HOME OF THE TIN KIN TRIBE

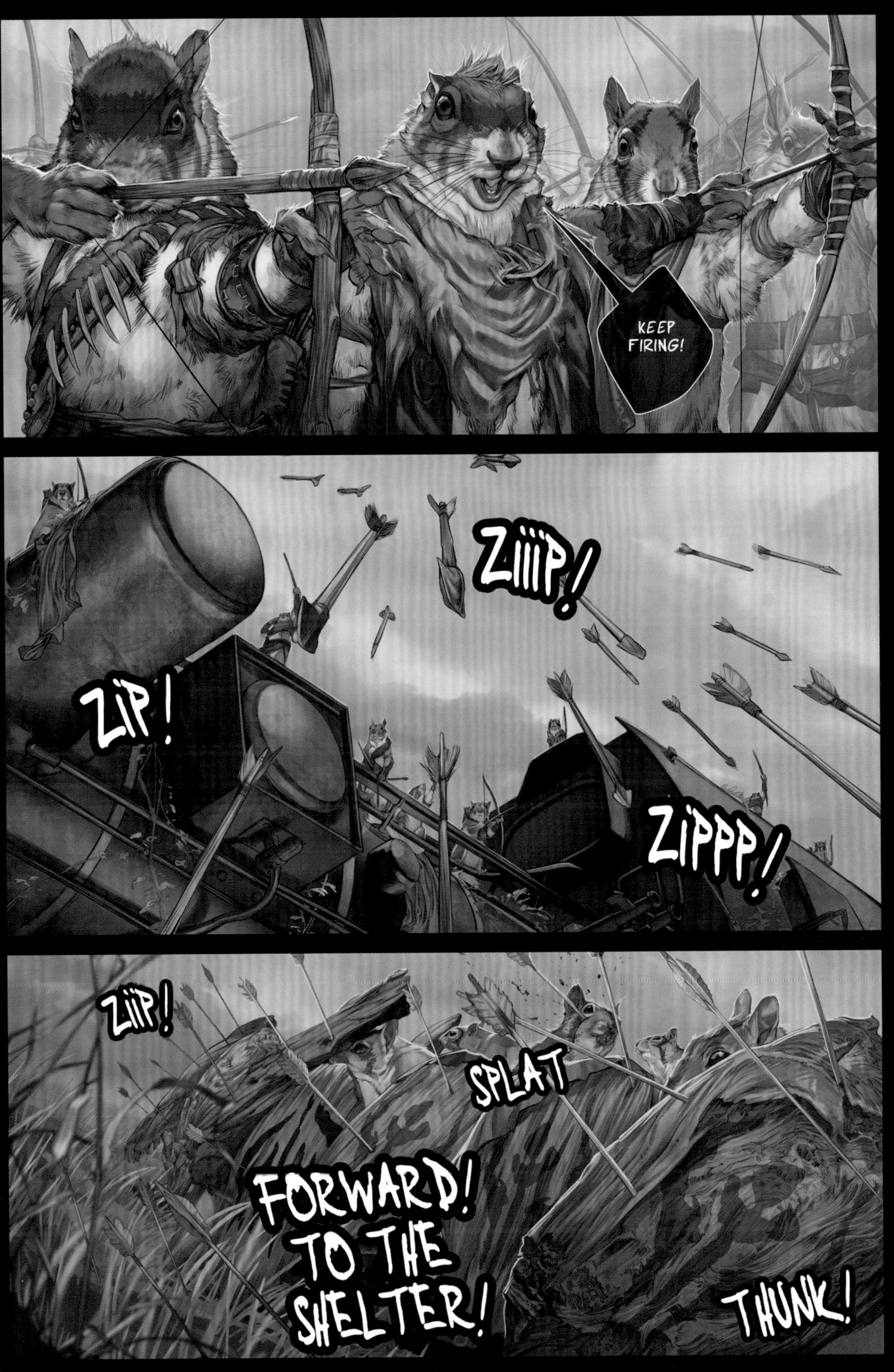
KEEP FIRING!
ZiiiP!
ZiP!
ZiPPP!
ZiiP!
SPLAT
FORWARD! TO THE SHELTER!
THUNK!

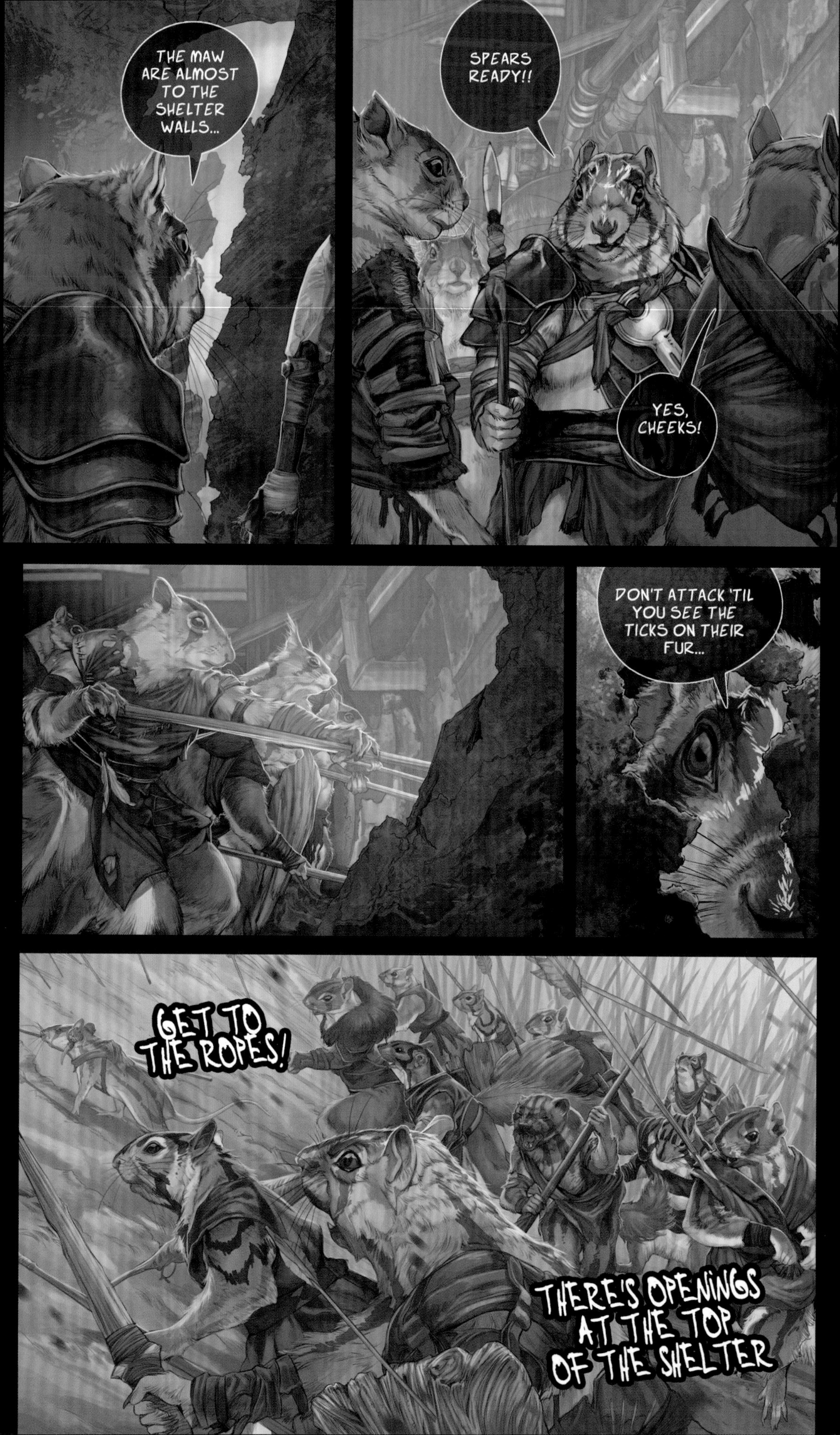
THE MAW ARE ALMOST TO THE SHELTER WALLS...
SPEARS READY!!
YES, CHEEKS!
DON'T ATTACK 'TIL YOU SEE THE TICKS ON THEIR FUR...
GET TO THE ROPES!
THERE'S OPENINGS AT THE TOP OF THE SHELTER

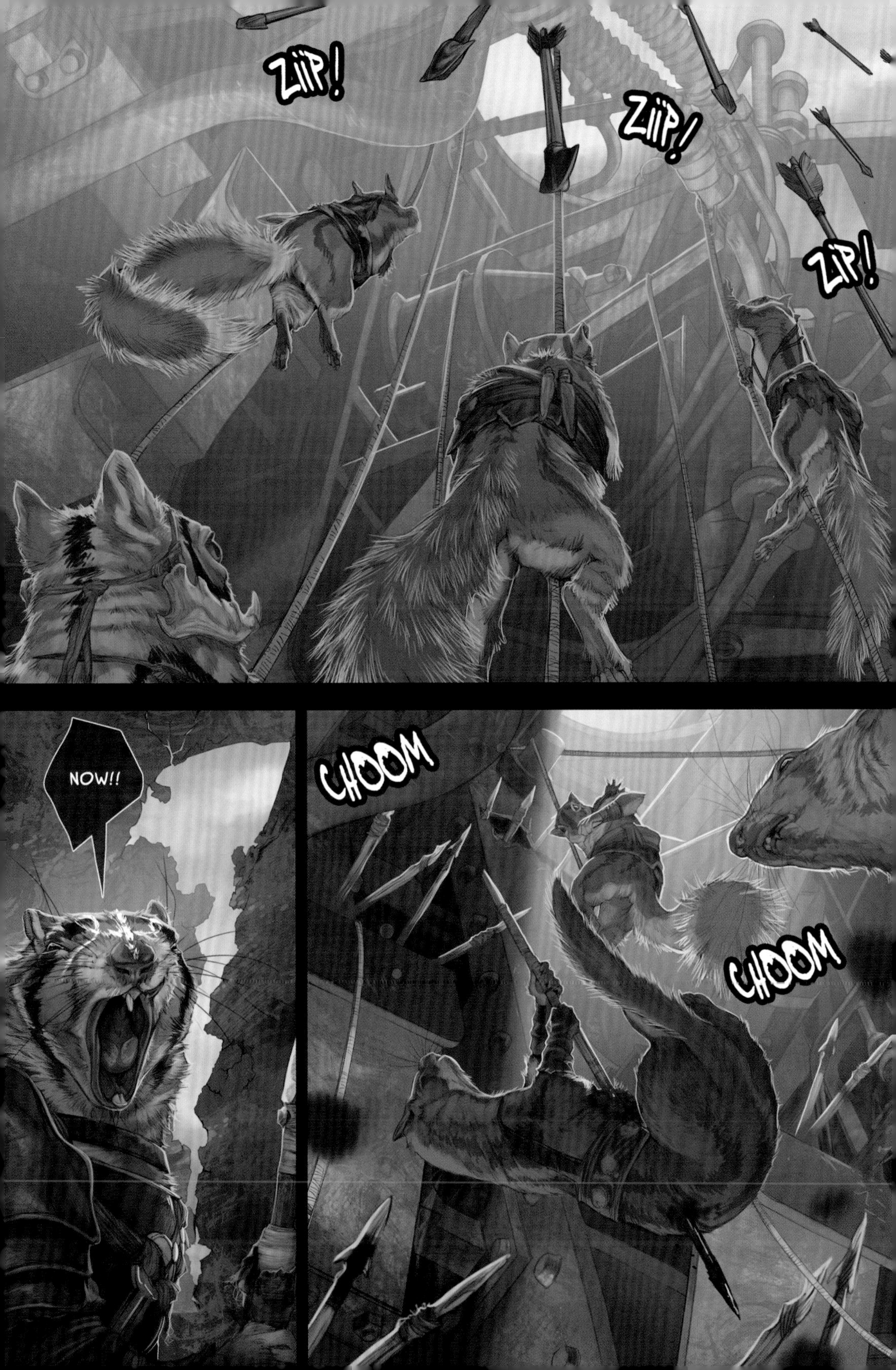
ZIIP!
ZIIP!
ZIP!
NOW!!
CHOOM
CHOOM

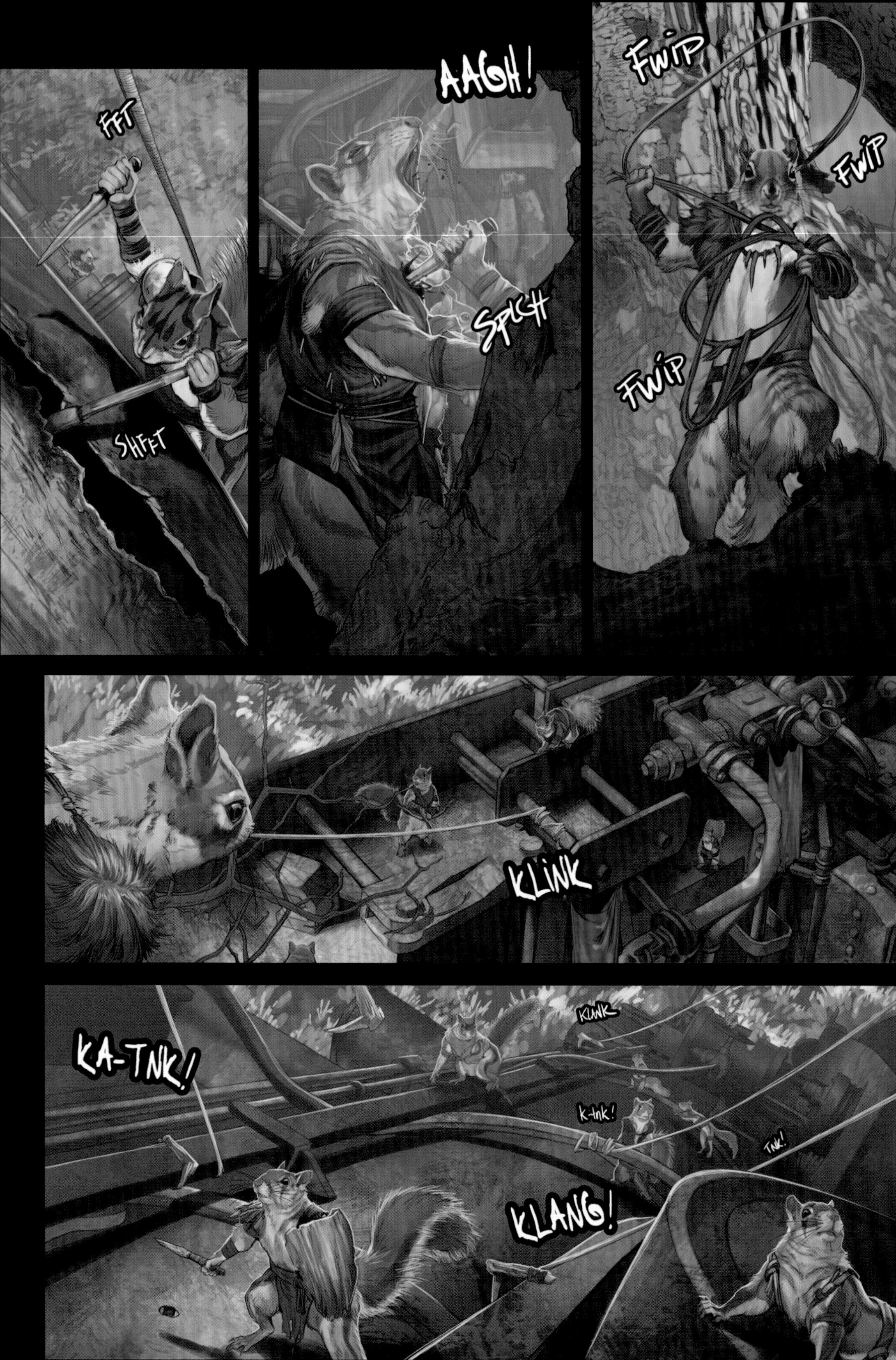
FFT
SHFFT
AAGH!
SPLCH
FWIP
FWIP
FWIP
KLINK
KA-TNK!
KLANK
K-tnk!
TNK!
KLANG!

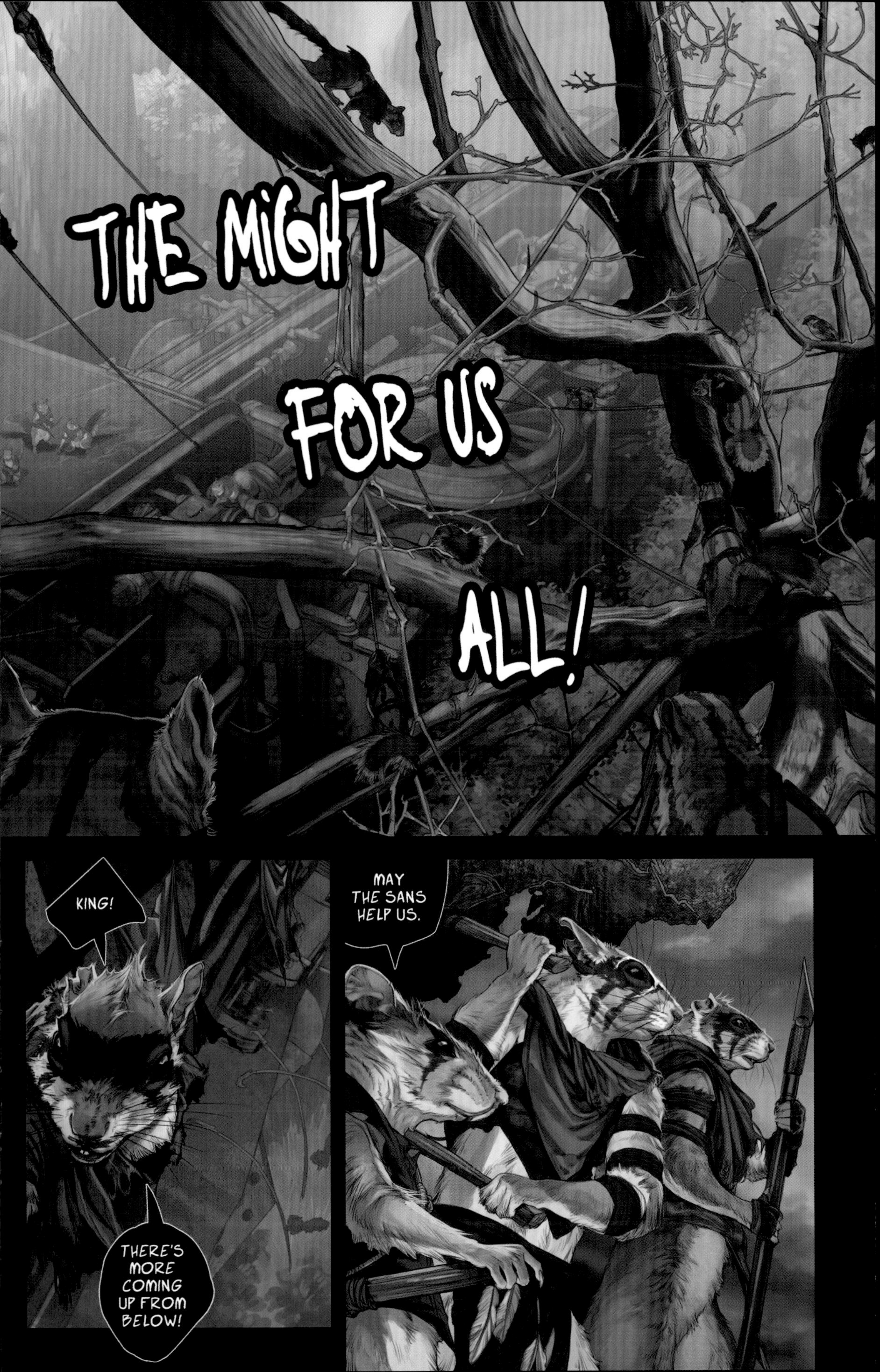
THE MIGHT
FOR US
ALL!
KING!
THERE'S MORE COMING UP FROM BELOW!
MAY THE SANS HELP US.

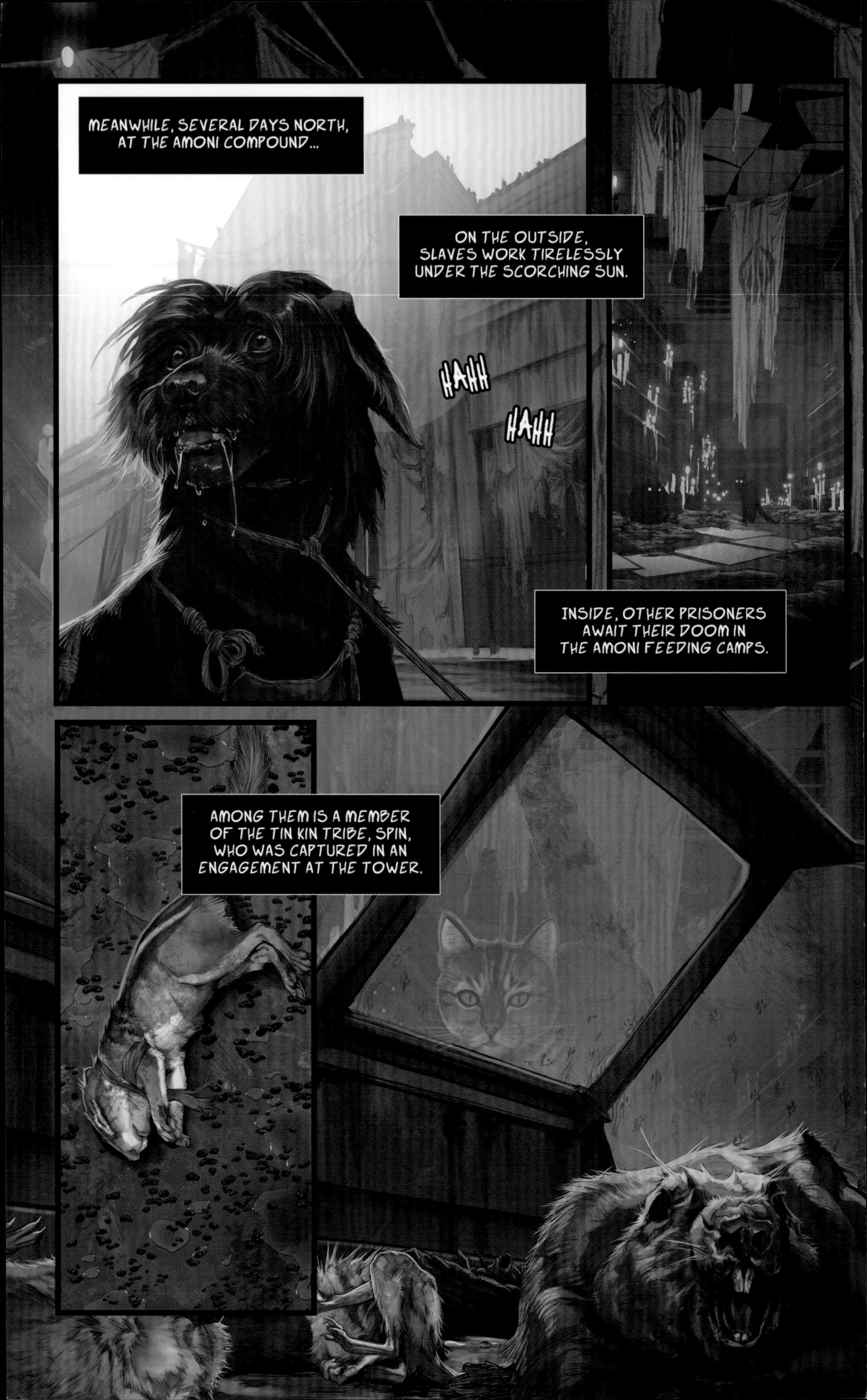

MEANWHILE, SEVERAL DAYS NORTH, AT THE AMONI COMPOUND...
ON THE OUTSIDE, SLAVES WORK TIRELESSLY UNDER THE SCORCHING SUN.
HAHH
HAHH
INSIDE, OTHER PRISONERS AWAIT THEIR DOOM IN THE AMONI FEEDING CAMPS.
AMONG THEM IS A MEMBER OF THE TIN KIN TRIBE, SPIN, WHO WAS CAPTURED IN AN ENGAGEMENT AT THE TOWER.

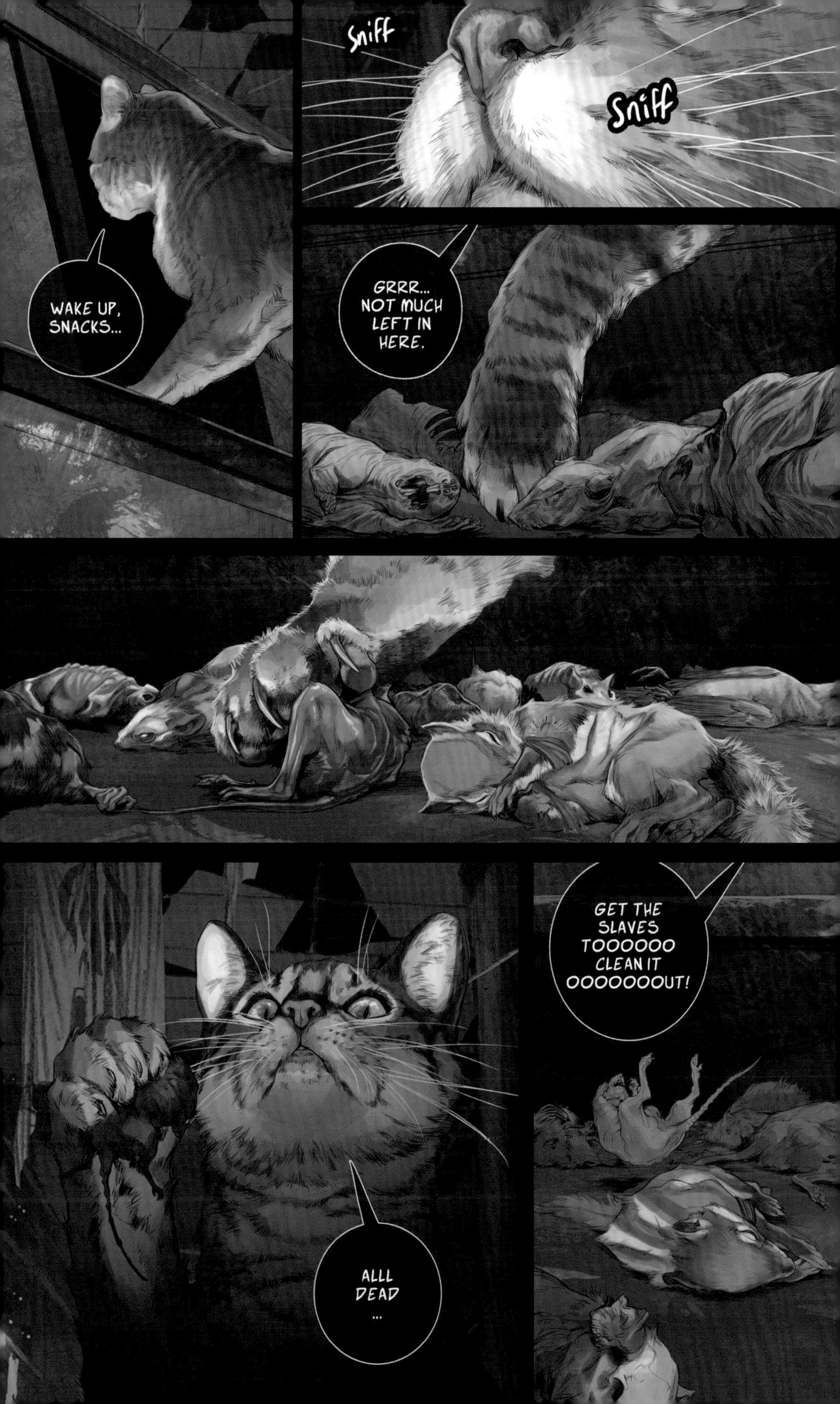
Sniff
Sniff
WAKE UP, SNACKS...
GRRR... NOT MUCH LEFT IN HERE.
ALLL DEAD ...
GET THE SLAVES TOOOOOO CLEAN IT OOOOOOOUT!

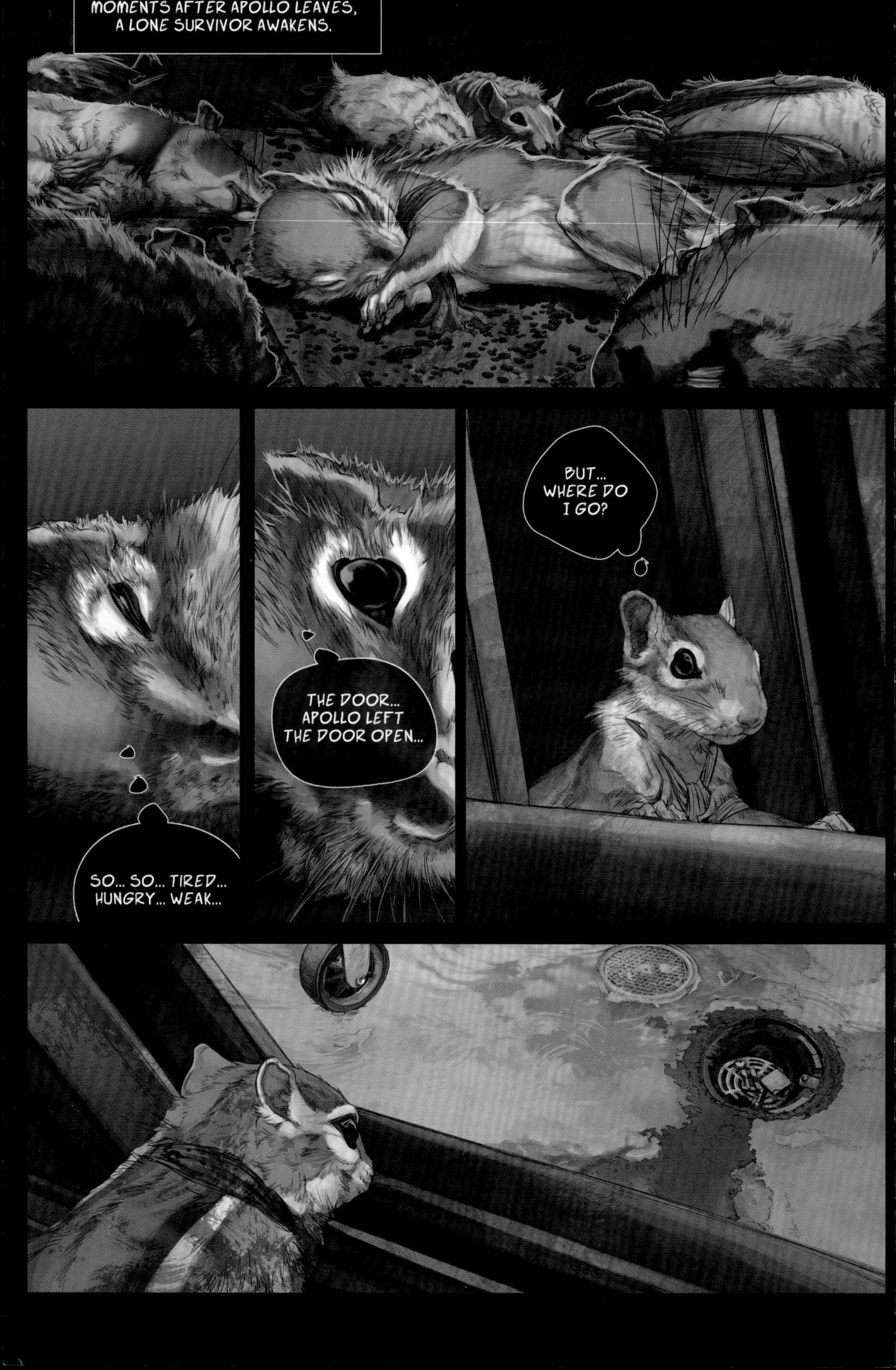
MOMENTS AFTER APOLLO LEAVES, A LONE SURVIVOR AWAKENS.
SO... SO... TIRED... HUNGRY... WEAK...
THE DOOR... APOLLO LEFT THE DOOR OPEN...
BUT... WHERE DO I GO?

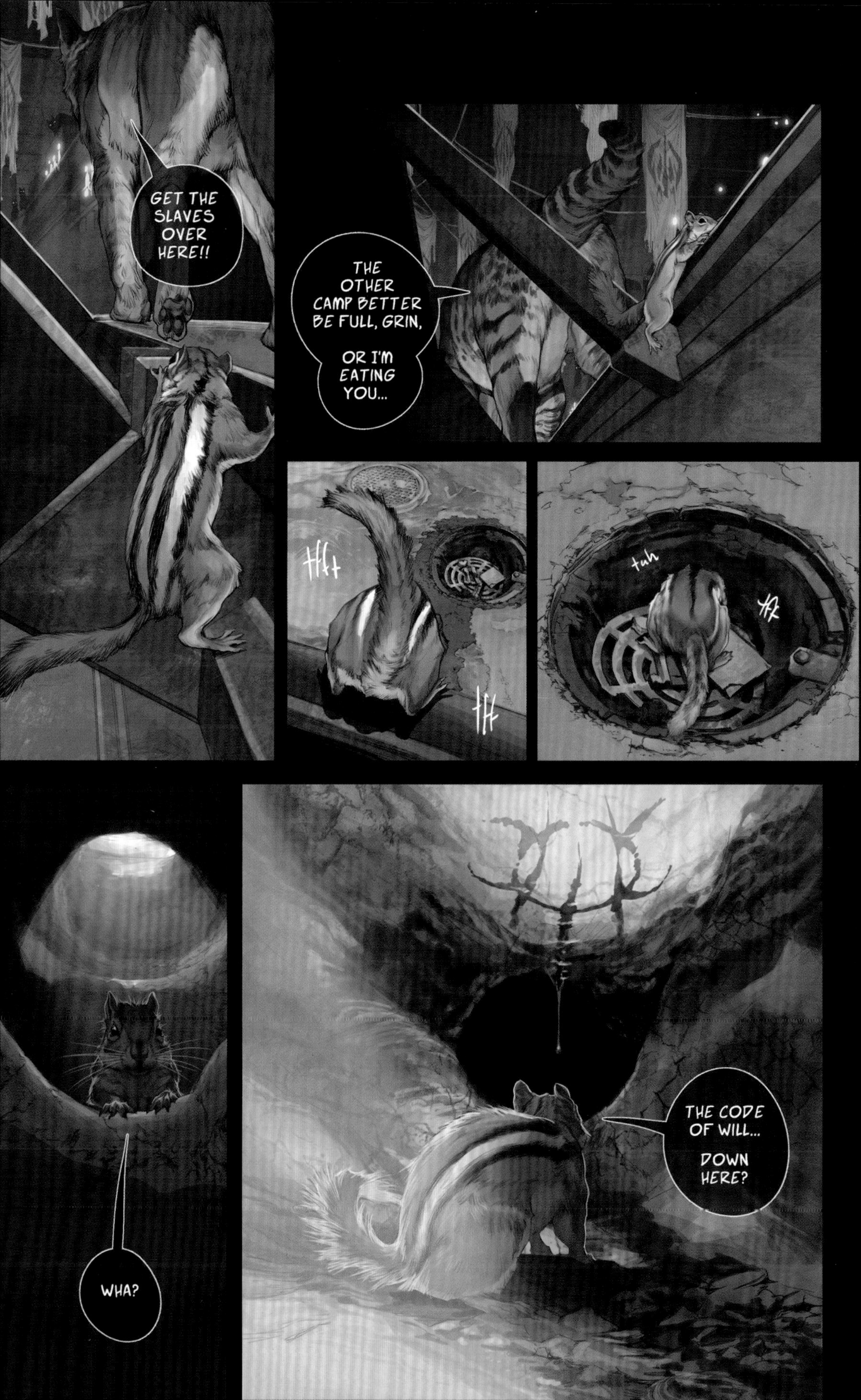

GET THE SLAVES OVER HERE!!
THE OTHER CAMP BETTER BE FULL, GRIN,
OR I'M EATING YOU...
tfft
tft
tuh
WHA?
THE CODE OF WILL...
DOWN HERE?

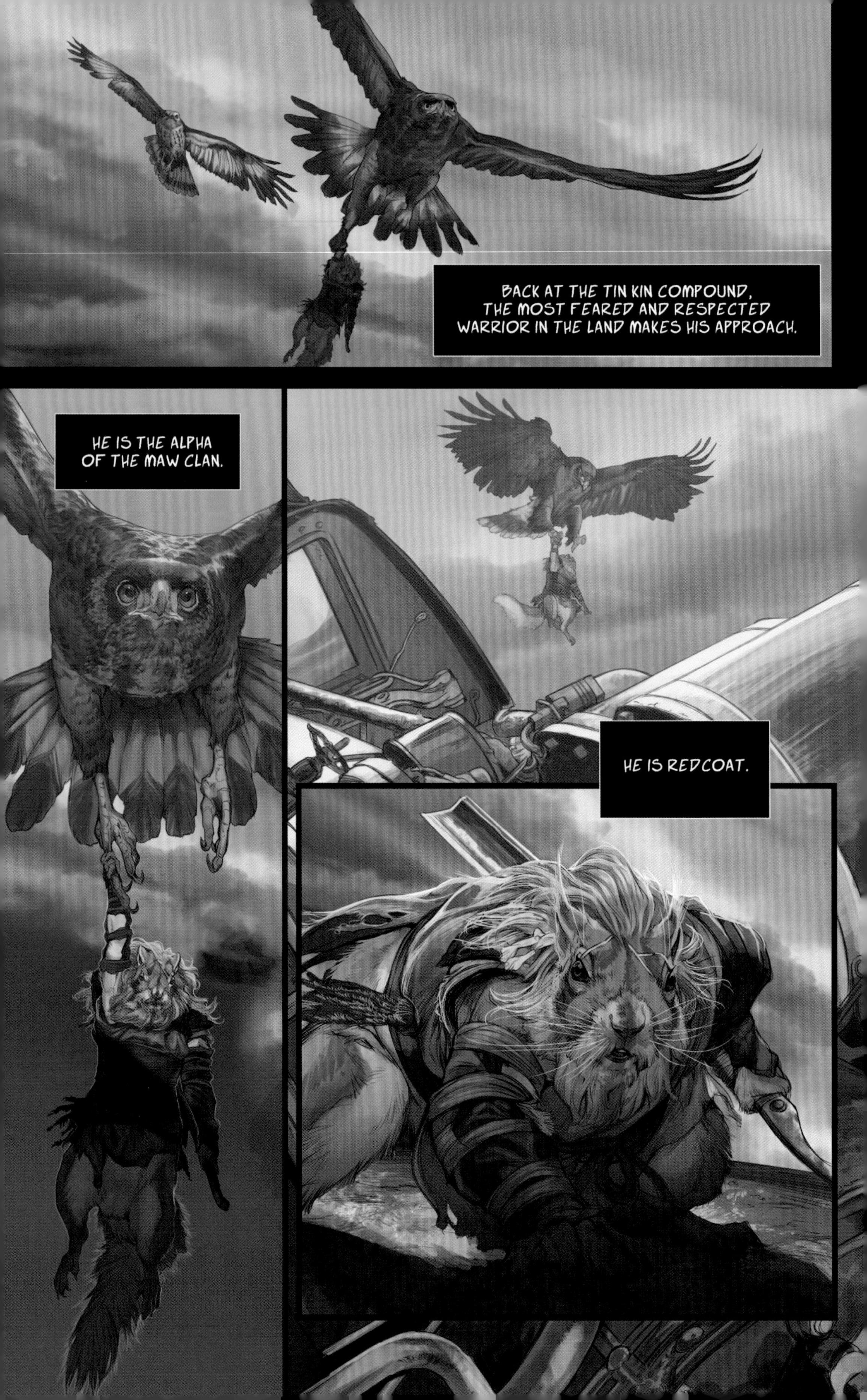
BACK AT THE TIN KIN COMPOUND, THE MOST FEARED AND RESPECTED WARRIOR IN THE LAND MAKES HIS APPROACH.
HE IS THE ALPHA OF THE MAW CLAN.
HE IS REDCOAT.

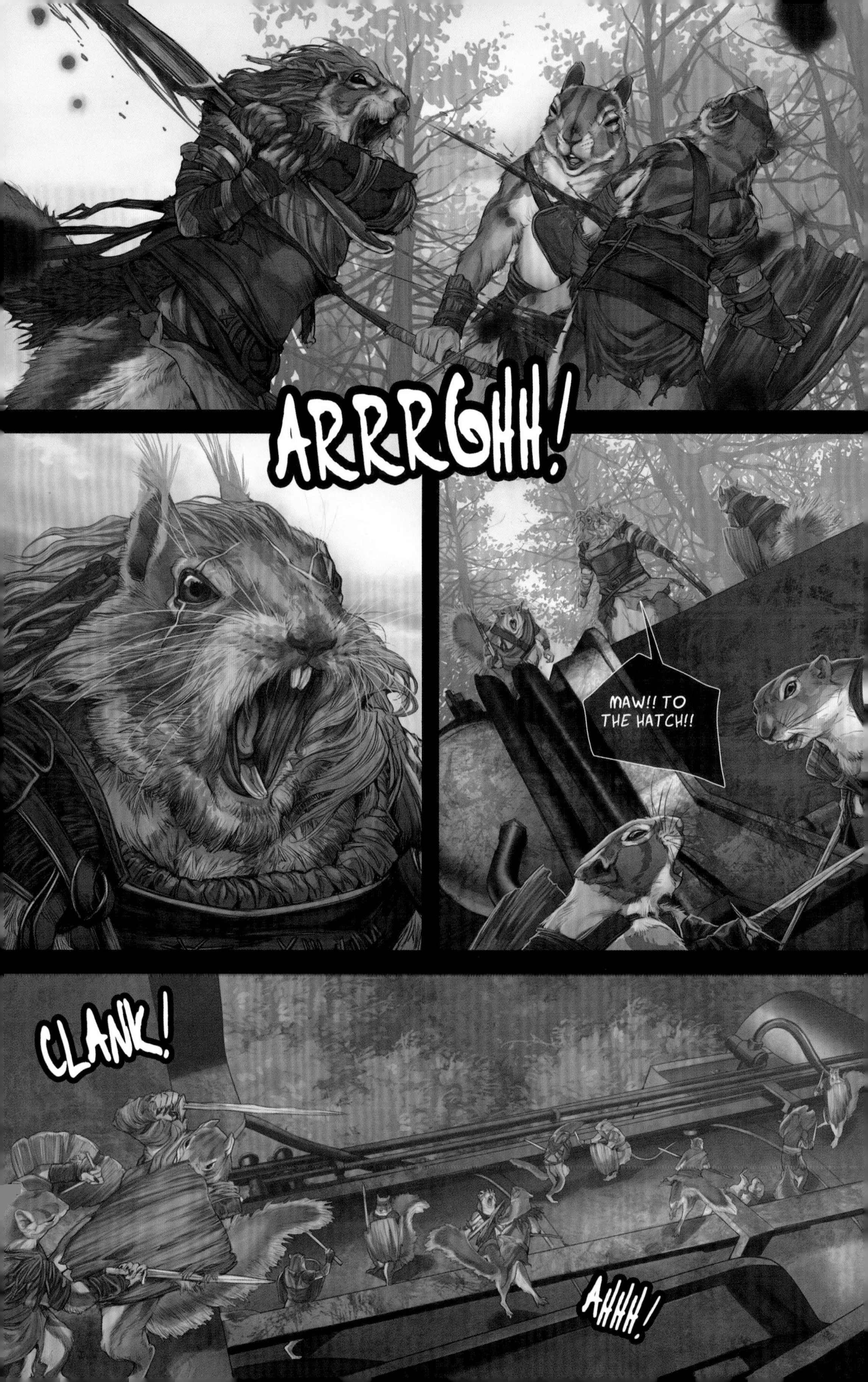
ARRRGHH!
MAW!! TO
THE HATCH!!
CLANK!
AHHH!

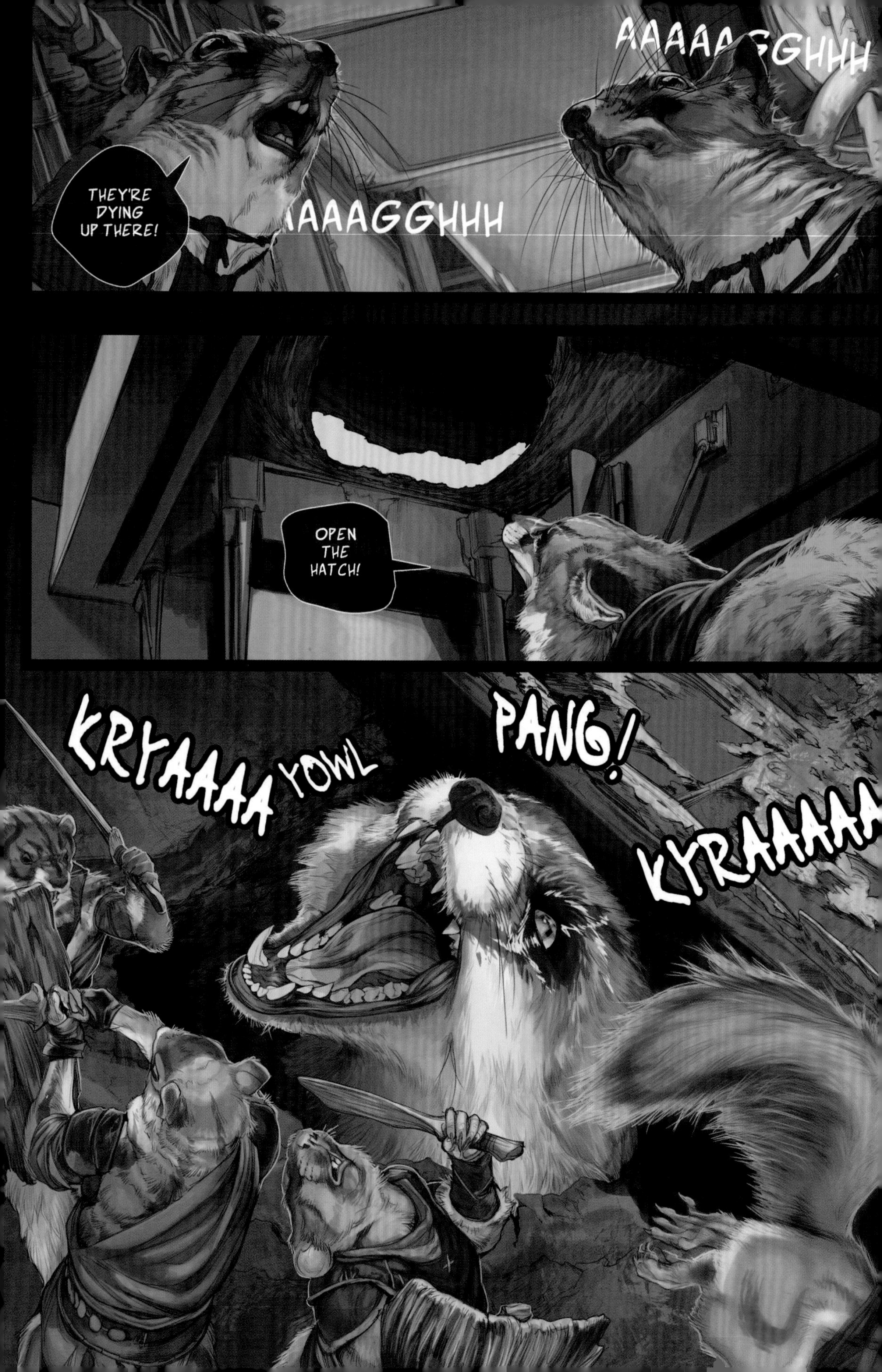
AAAAAGGHHH
THEY'RE DYING UP THERE!
AAAAGGHHH
OPEN THE HATCH!
KRYAAAA
YOWL
PANG!
KYRAAAAA

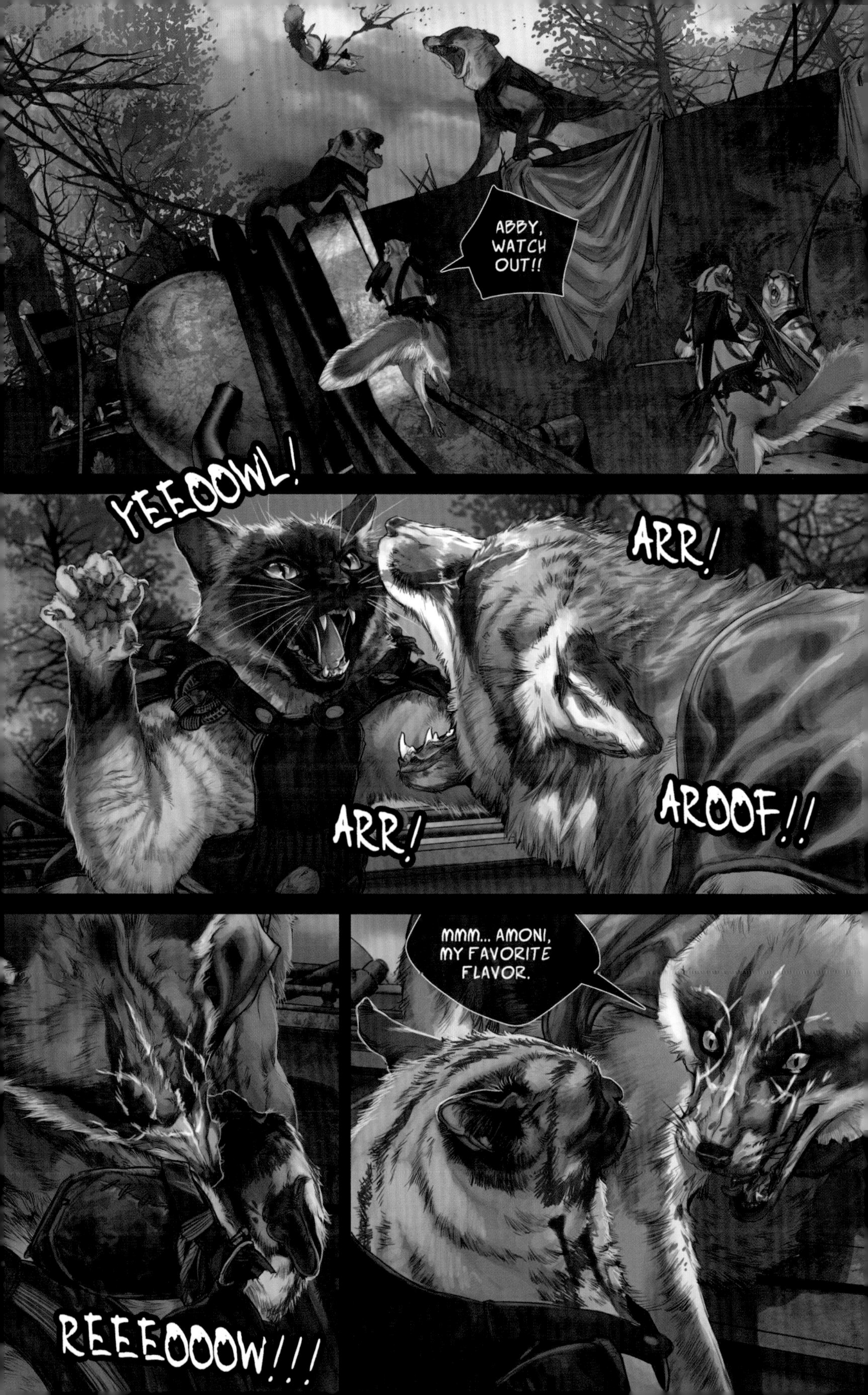
ABBY, WATCH OUT!!
YEEOOWL!
ARR!
ARR!
AROOF!!
REEEOOOW!!!
MMM... AMONI, MY FAVORITE FLAVOR.

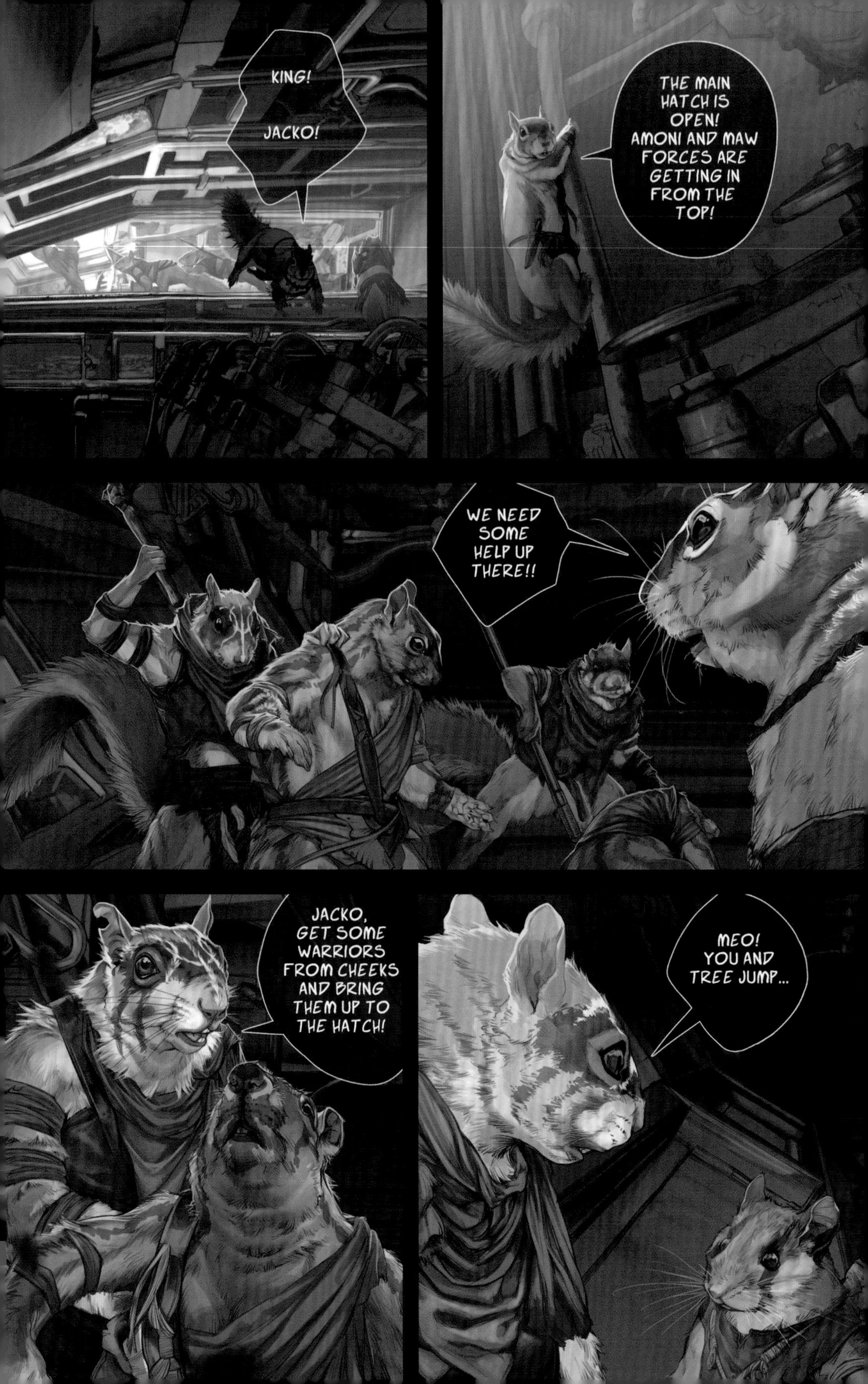
KING!
JACKO!
THE MAIN HATCH IS OPEN! AMONI AND MAW FORCES ARE GETTING IN FROM THE TOP!
WE NEED SOME HELP UP THERE!!
JACKO, GET SOME WARRIORS FROM CHEEKS AND BRING THEM UP TO THE HATCH!
MEO! YOU AND TREE JUMP...

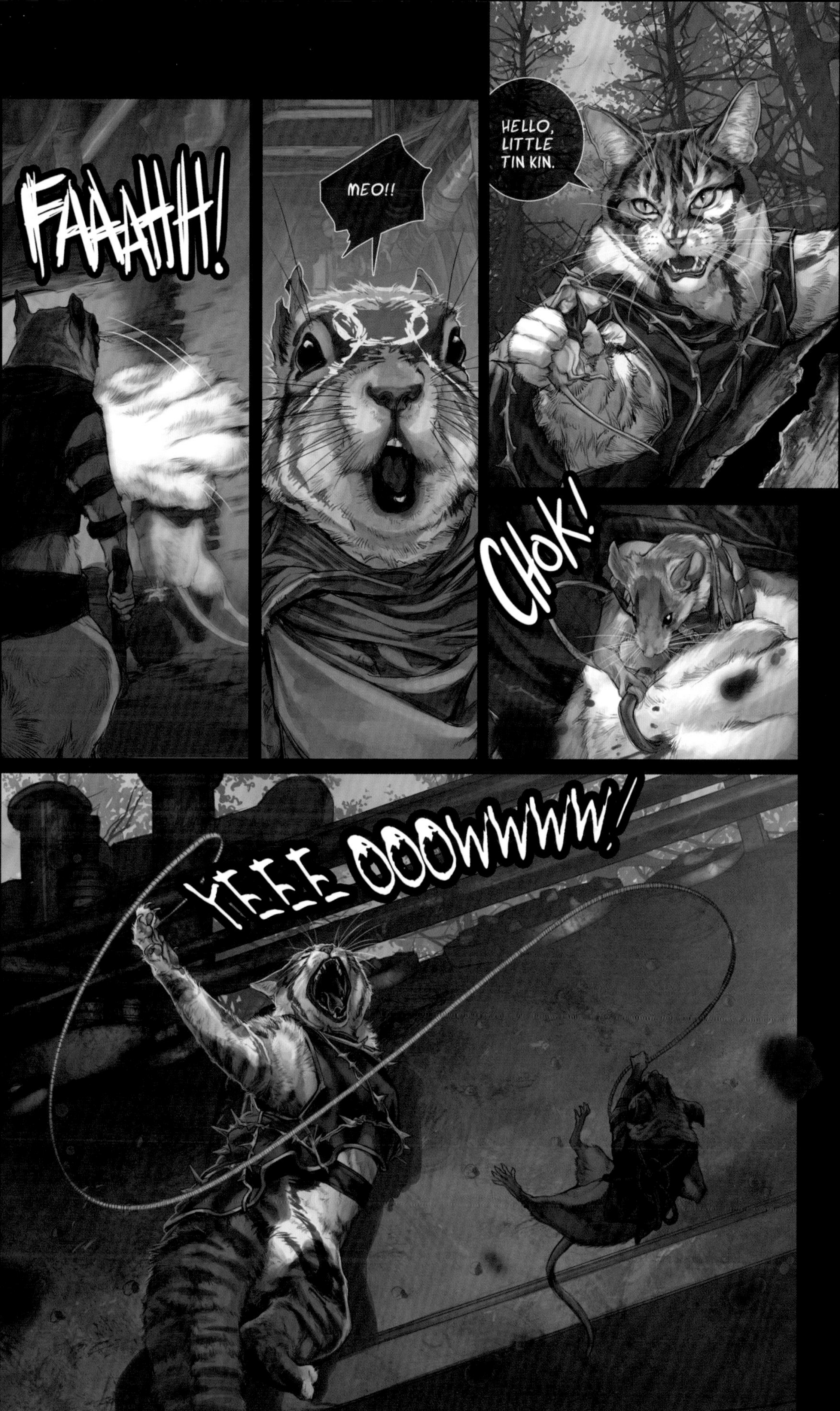
FAAHH!
MEO!!
HELLO, LITTLE TIN KIN.
CHOK!
YEEE OOOWWWW!

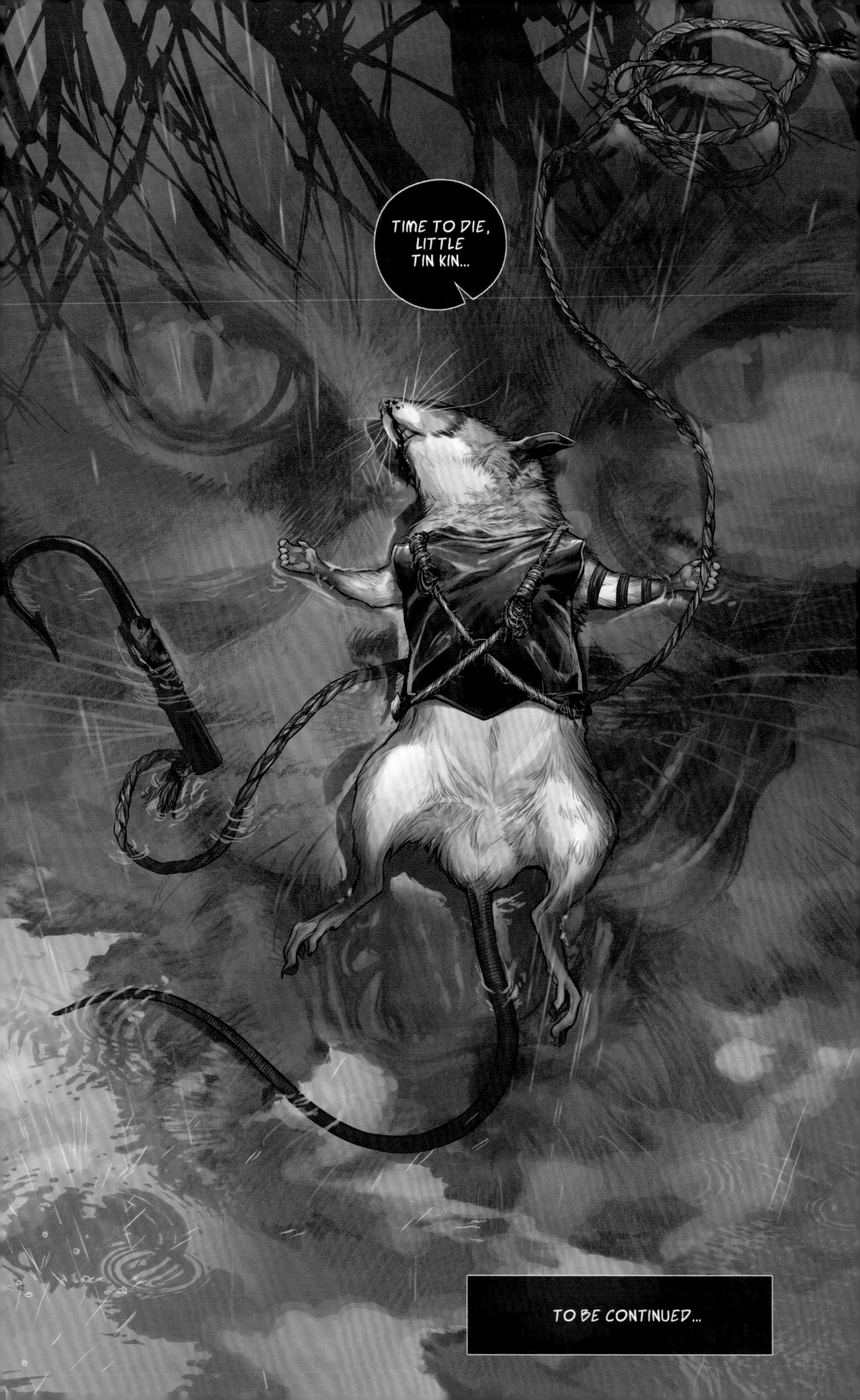
TIME TO DIE, LITTLE TIN KIN...
TO BE CONTINUED...

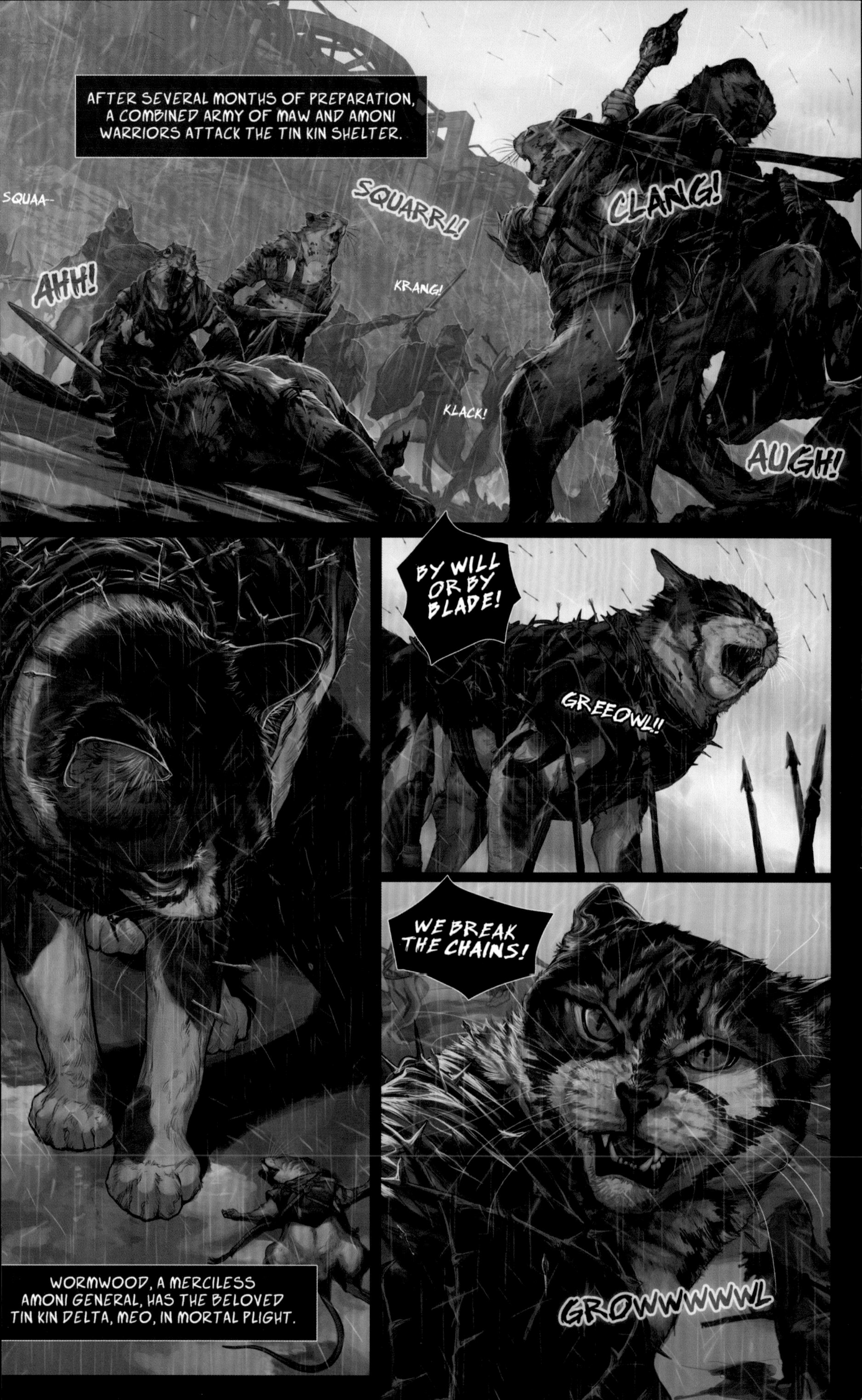
AFTER SEVERAL MONTHS OF PREPARATION, A COMBINED ARMY OF MAW AND AMONI WARRIORS ATTACK THE TIN KIN SHELTER.
SQUAA-
SQUARRL!
CLANG!
AHH!
KRANG!
KLACK!
AUGH!
BY WILL OR BY BLADE!
GREEOWL!!
WE BREAK THE CHAINS!
WORMWOOD, A MERCILESS AMONI GENERAL, HAS THE BELOVED TIN KIN DELTA, MEO, IN MORTAL PLIGHT.
GROWWWWWL

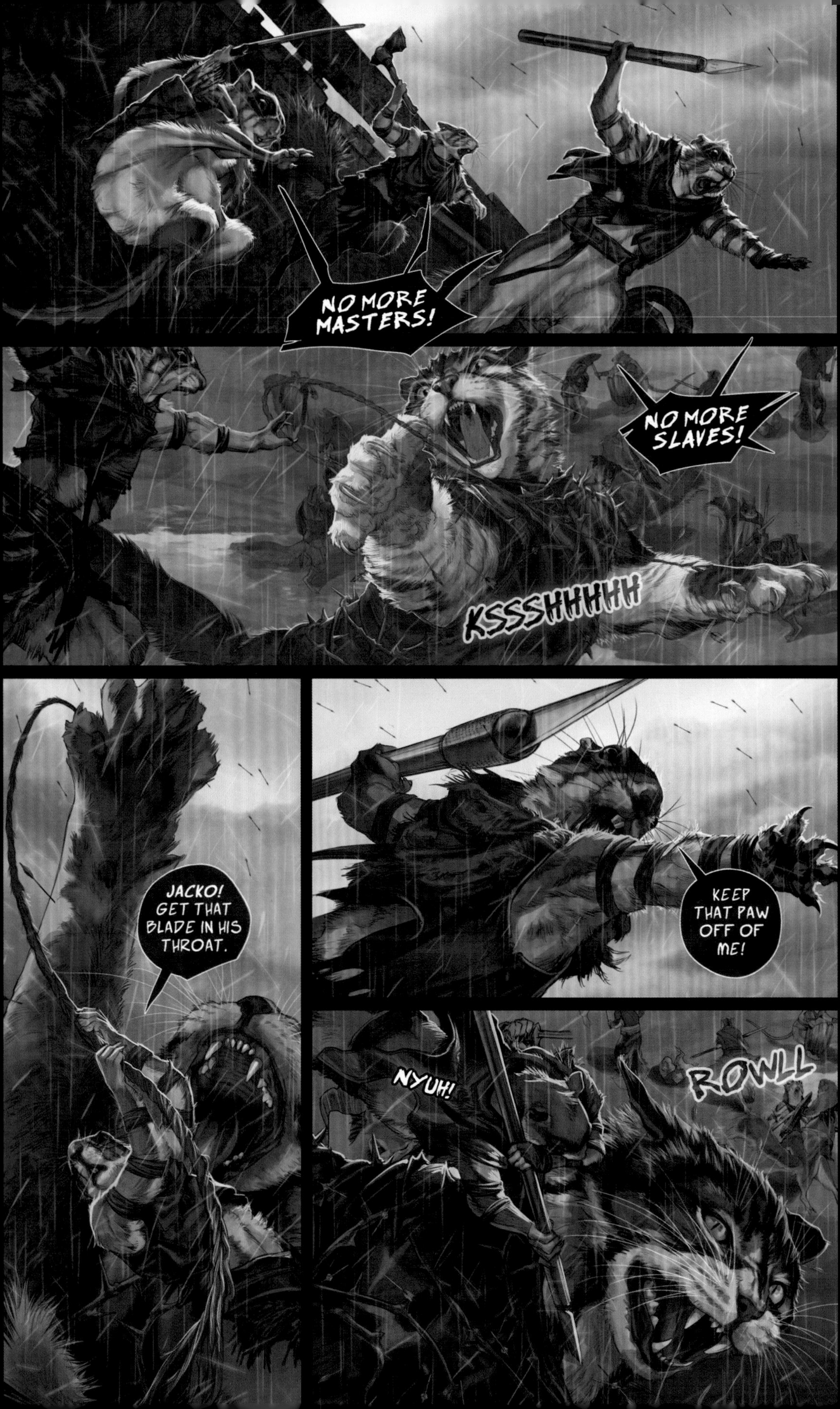
NO MORE MASTERS!
NO MORE SLAVES!
KSSSHHHHH
JACKO! GET THAT BLADE IN HIS THROAT.
KEEP THAT PAW OFF OF ME!
NYUH!
ROWLL

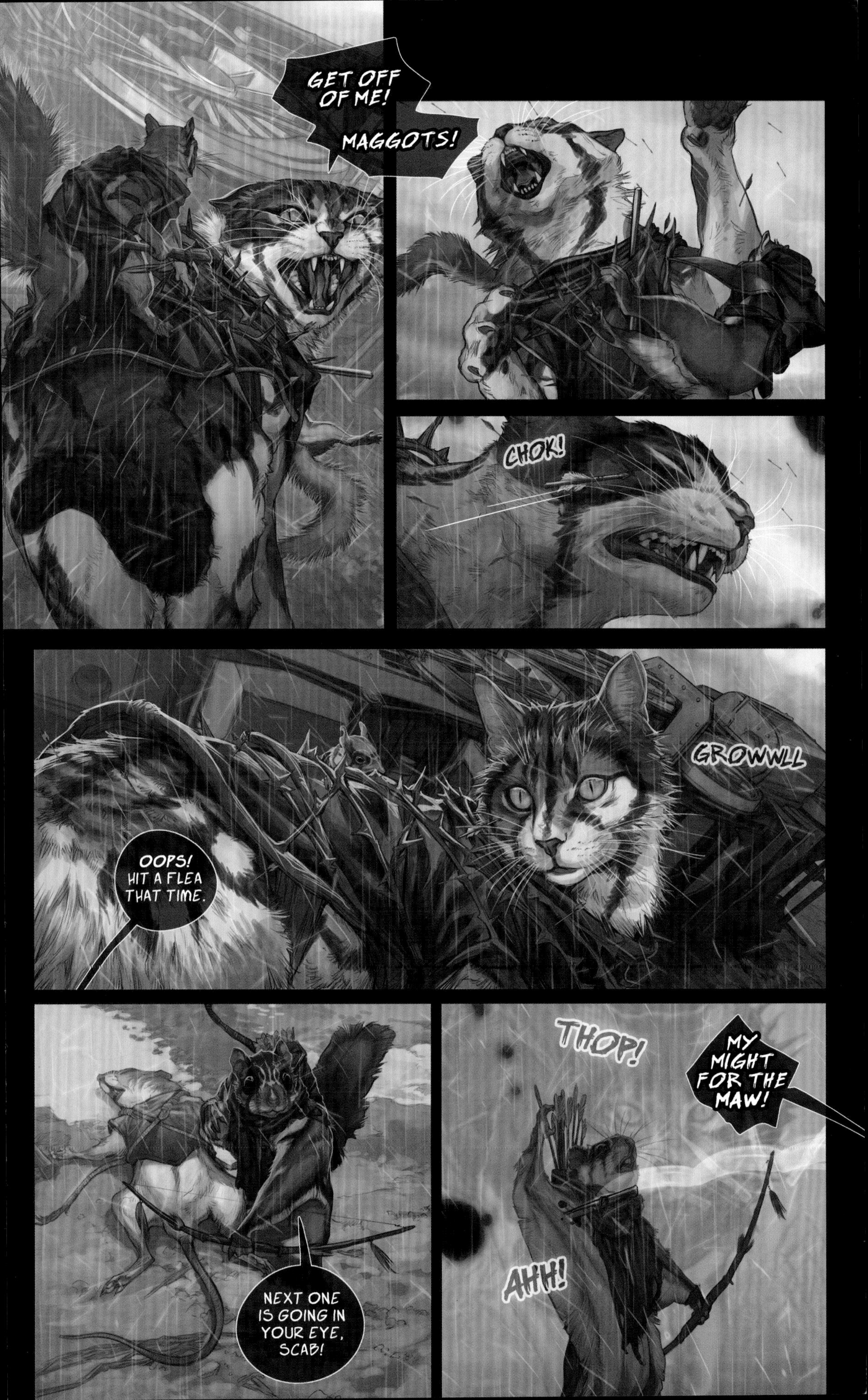
GET OFF OF ME!
MAGGOTS!
CHOK!
GROWWLL
OOPS! HIT A FLEA THAT TIME.
NEXT ONE IS GOING IN YOUR EYE, SCAB!
THOP!
MY MIGHT FOR THE MAW!
AHH!

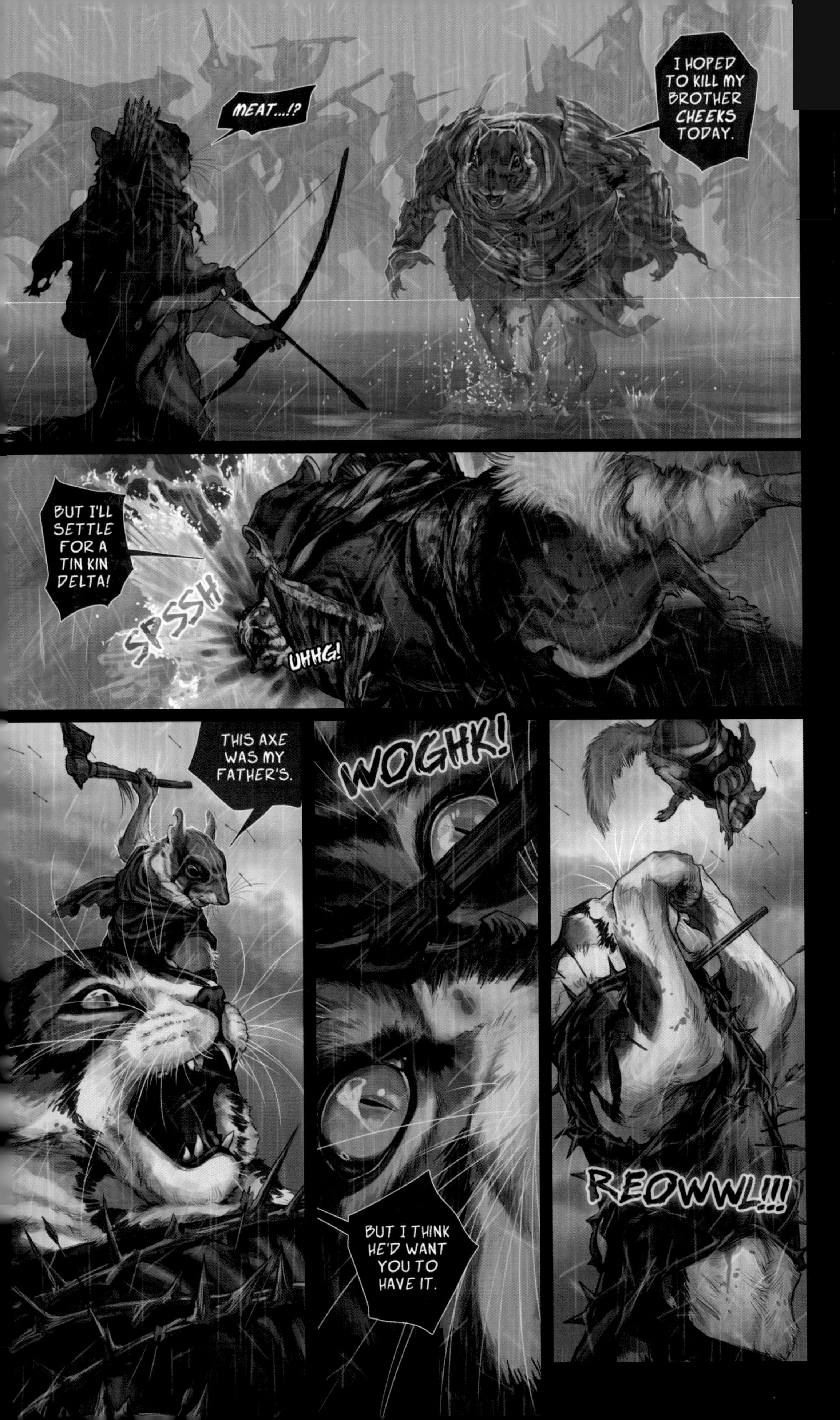

MEAT...!?
I HOPED TO KILL MY BROTHER CHEEKS TODAY.
BUT I'LL SETTLE FOR A TIN KIN DELTA!
SPSSH
UHHG!
THIS AXE WAS MY FATHER'S.
WOGHK!
BUT I THINK HE'D WANT YOU TO HAVE IT.
REOWWL!!!

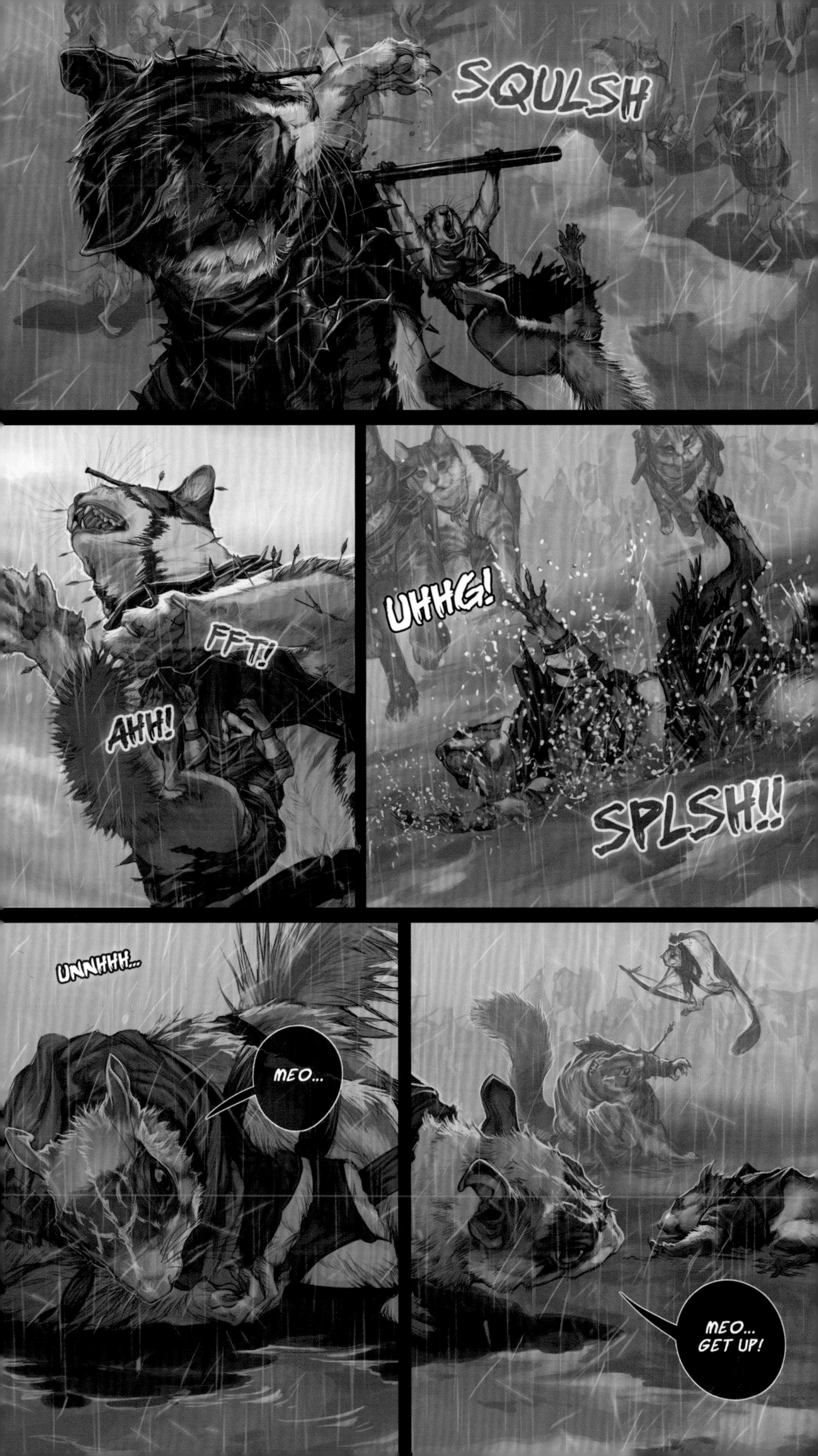
SQULSH
FFT!
AHH!
UHHG!
SPLSH!!
UNHHH...
MEO...
MEO... GET UP!

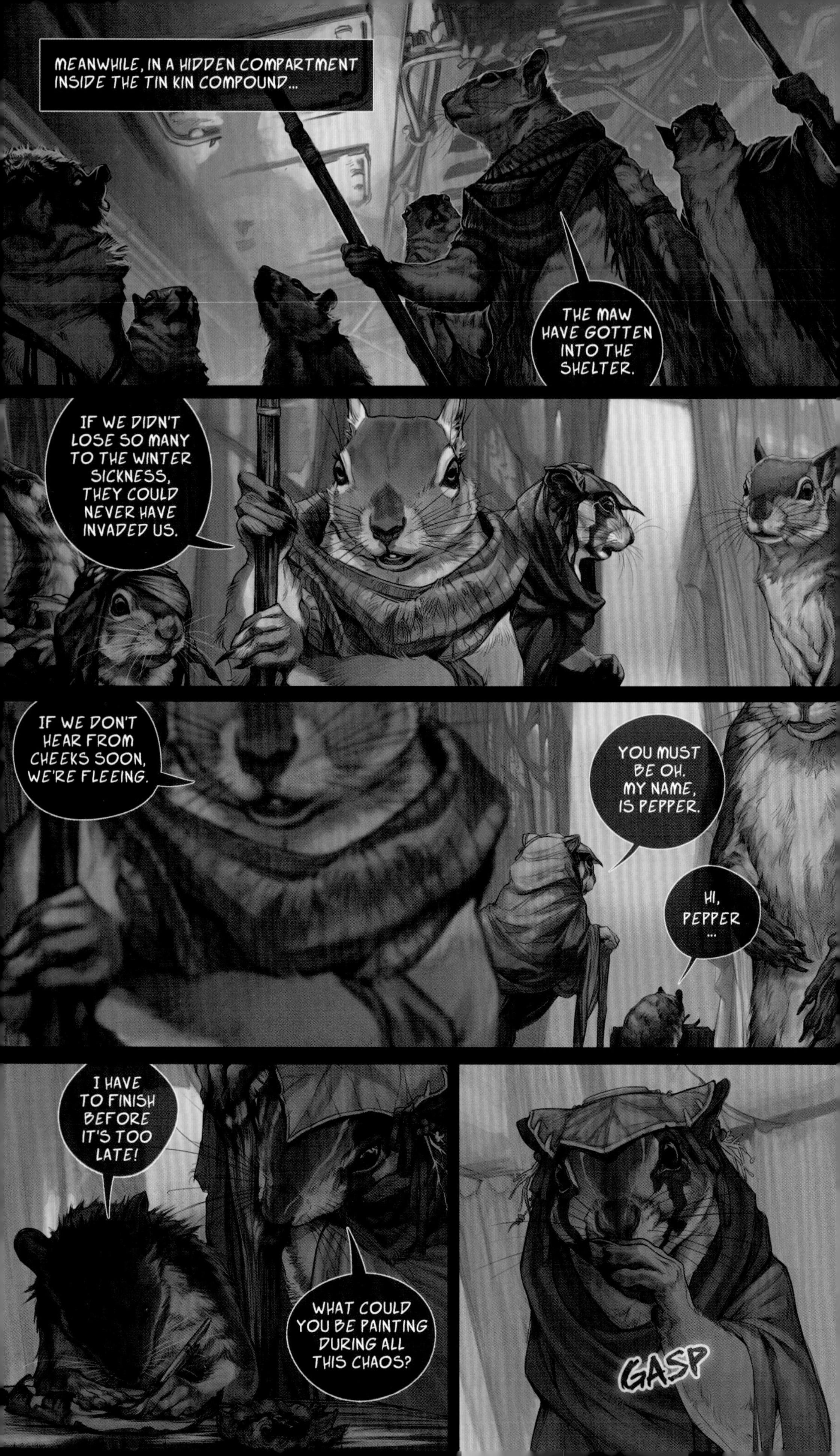
MEANWHILE, IN A HIDDEN COMPARTMENT INSIDE THE TIN KIN COMPOUND...
THE MAW HAVE GOTTEN INTO THE SHELTER.
IF WE DIDN'T LOSE SO MANY TO THE WINTER SICKNESS, THEY COULD NEVER HAVE INVADED US.
IF WE DON'T HEAR FROM CHEEKS SOON, WE'RE FLEEING.
YOU MUST BE OH. MY NAME, IS PEPPER.
HI, PEPPER ...
I HAVE TO FINISH BEFORE IT'S TOO LATE!
WHAT COULD YOU BE PAINTING DURING ALL THIS CHAOS?
GASP

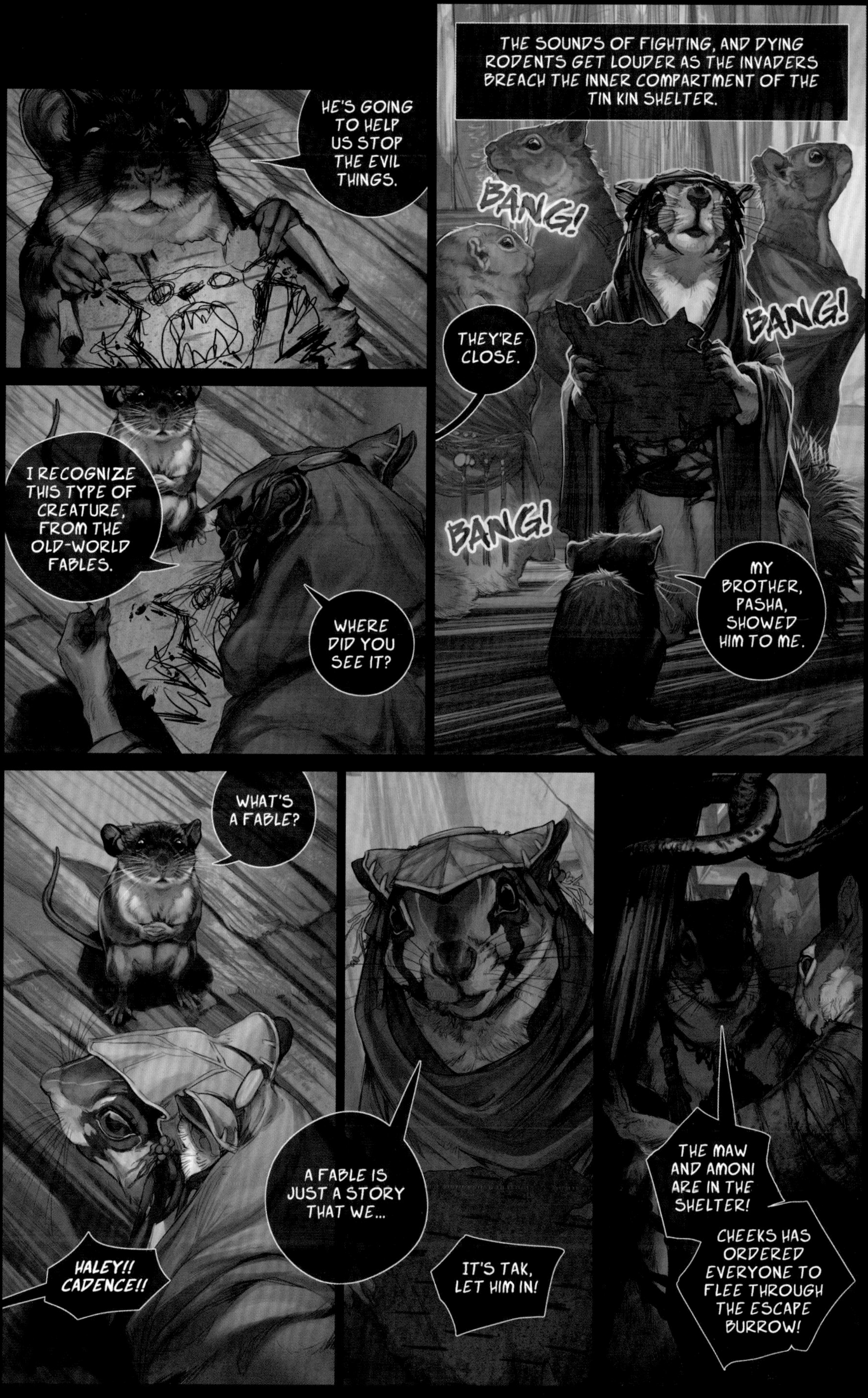

HE'S GOING TO HELP US STOP THE EVIL THINGS.
I RECOGNIZE THIS TYPE OF CREATURE, FROM THE OLD-WORLD FABLES.
WHERE DID YOU SEE IT?
THE SOUNDS OF FIGHTING, AND DYING RODENTS GET LOUDER AS THE INVADERS BREACH THE INNER COMPARTMENT OF THE TIN KIN SHELTER.
BANG!
BANG!
BANG!
THEY'RE CLOSE.
MY BROTHER, PASHA, SHOWED HIM TO ME.
WHAT'S A FABLE?
HALEY!! CADENCE!!
A FABLE IS JUST A STORY THAT WE...
IT'S TAK, LET HIM IN!
THE MAW AND AMONI ARE IN THE SHELTER!
CHEEKS HAS ORDERED EVERYONE TO FLEE THROUGH THE ESCAPE BURROW!

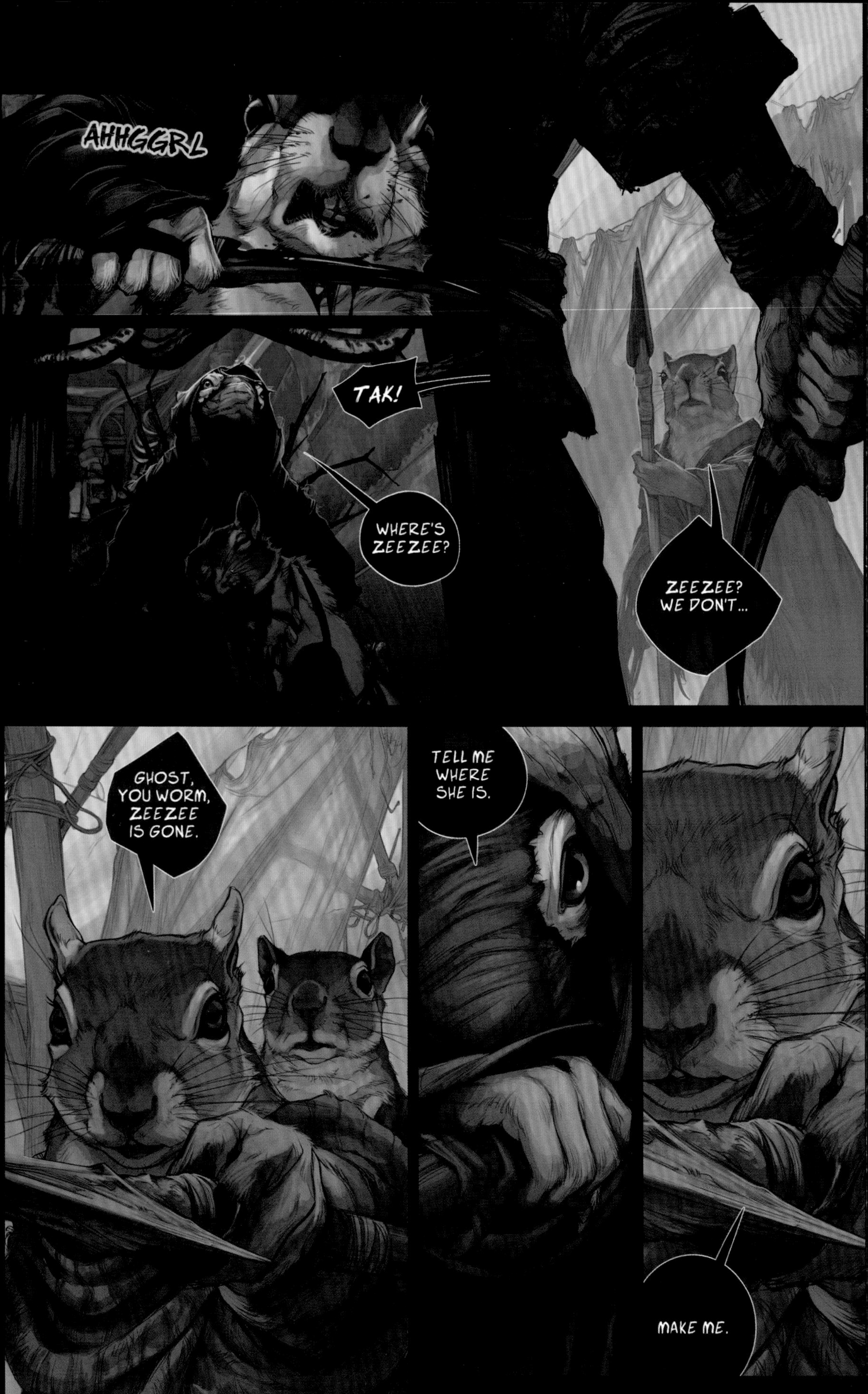
AHHGGRL
TAK!
WHERE'S ZEEZEE?
ZEEZEE? WE DON'T...
GHOST, YOU WORM, ZEEZEE IS GONE.
TELL ME WHERE SHE IS.
MAKE ME.

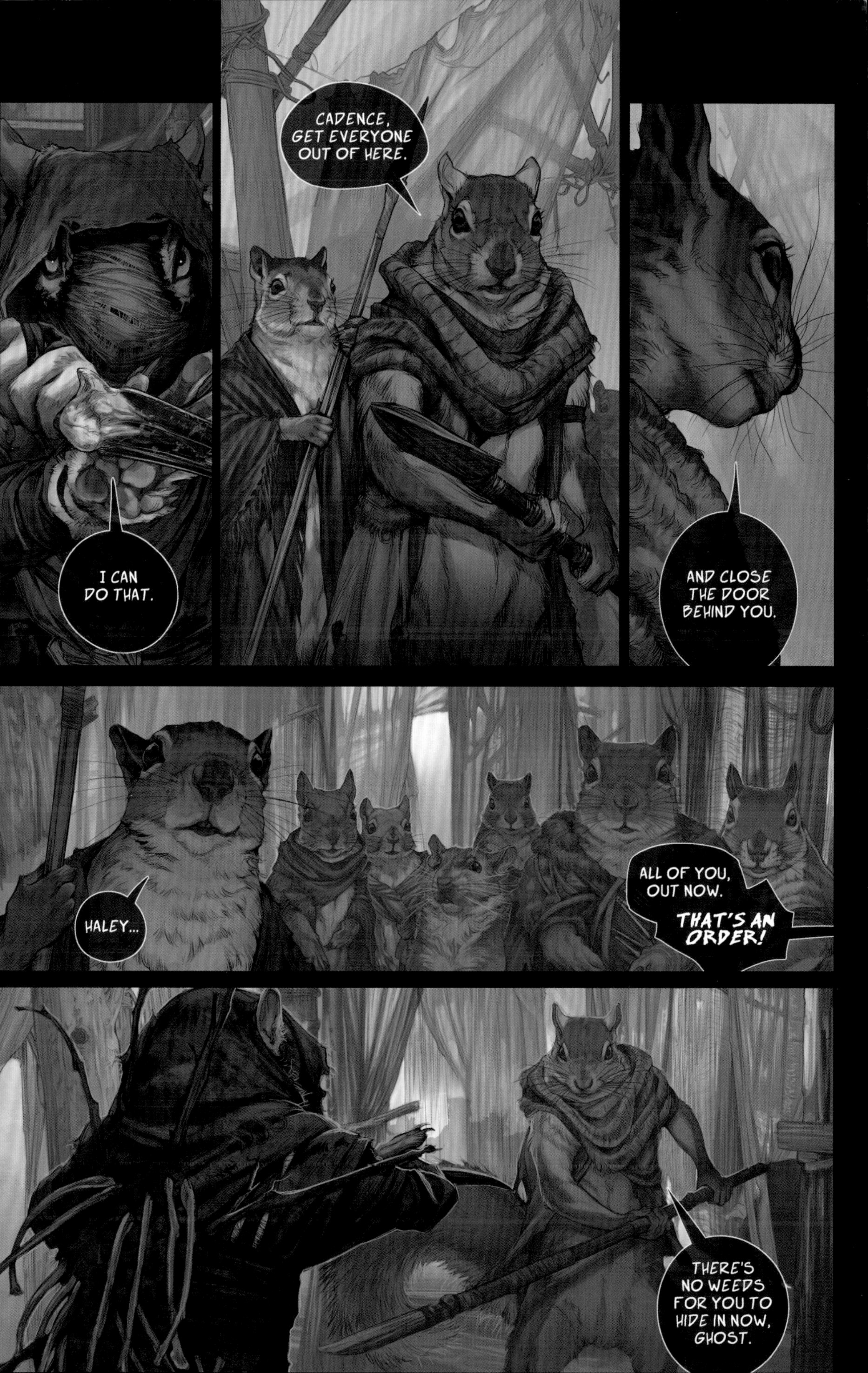
CADENCE, GET EVERYONE OUT OF HERE.
I CAN DO THAT.
AND CLOSE THE DOOR BEHIND YOU.
HALEY...
ALL OF YOU, OUT NOW.
THAT'S AN ORDER!
THERE'S NO WEEDS FOR YOU TO HIDE IN NOW, GHOST.

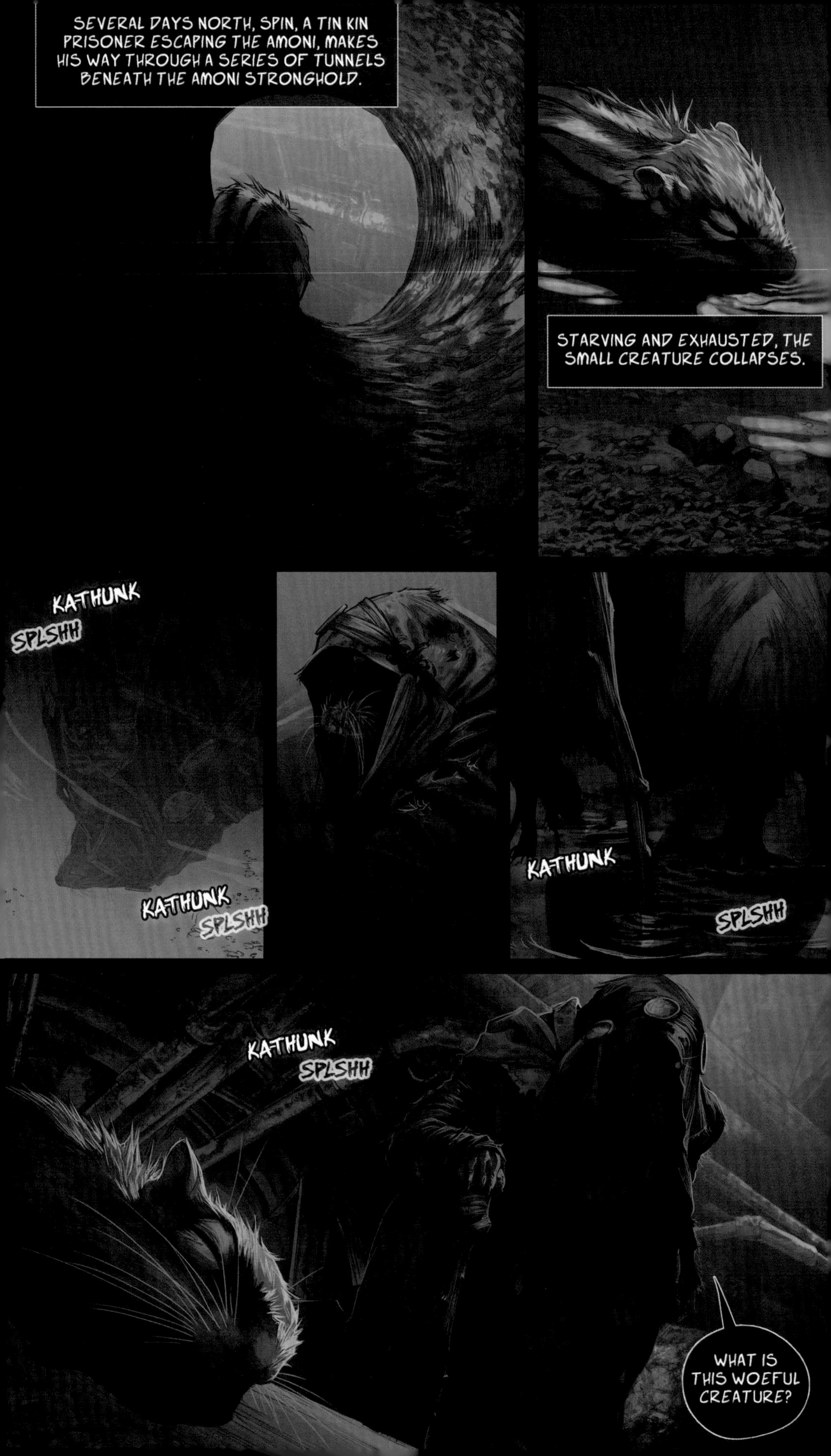
SEVERAL DAYS NORTH, SPIN, A TIN KIN PRISONER ESCAPING THE AMONI, MAKES HIS WAY THROUGH A SERIES OF TUNNELS BENEATH THE AMONI STRONGHOLD.
STARVING AND EXHAUSTED, THE SMALL CREATURE COLLAPSES.
KATHUNK
SPLSHH
KATHUNK
SPLSHH
KATHUNK
SPLSHH
KATHUNK
SPLSHH
WHAT IS THIS WOEFUL CREATURE?

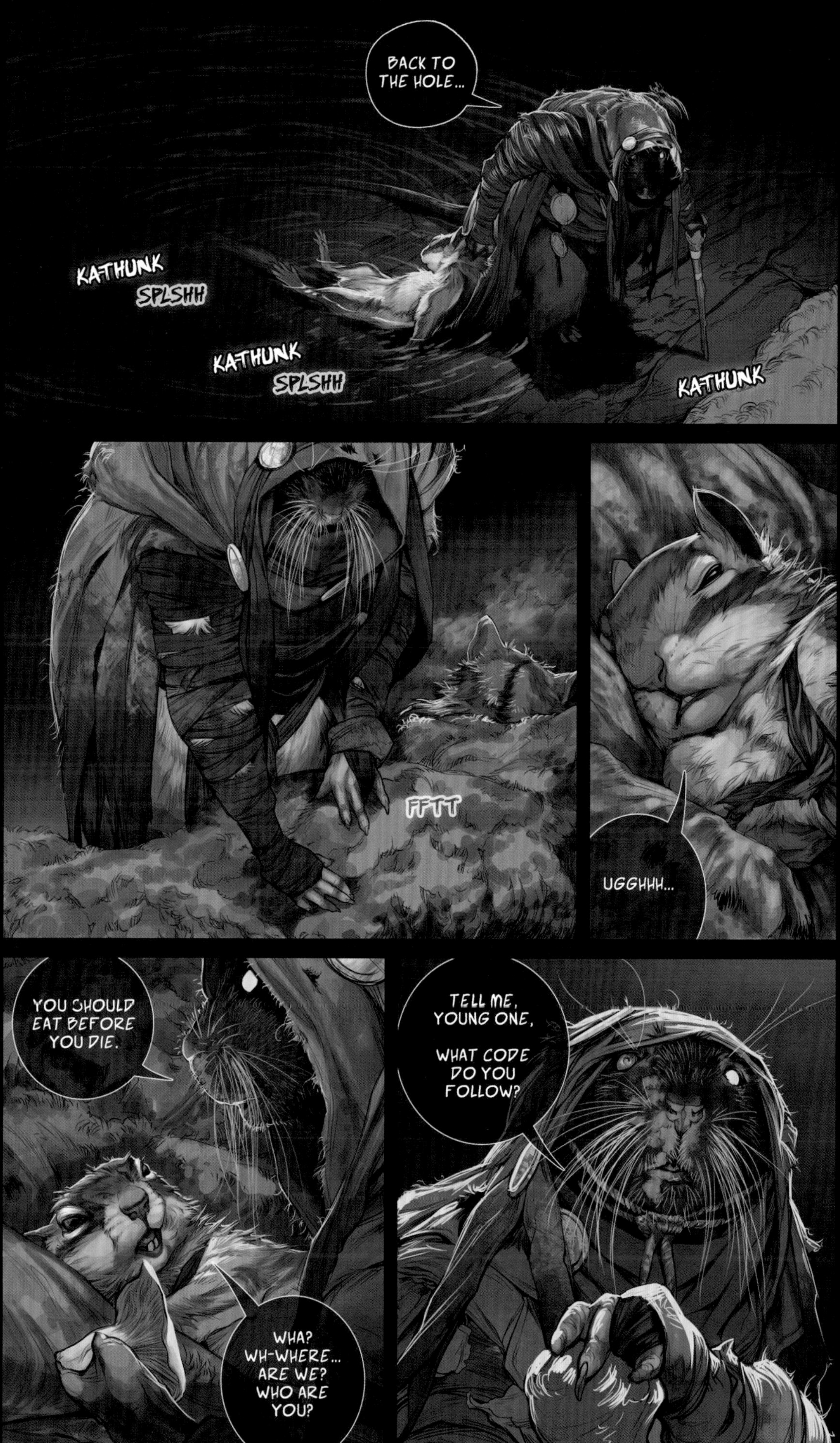
BACK TO THE HOLE...
KATHUNK
SPLSHH
KATHUNK
SPLSHH
KATHUNK
FFTT
UGGHHH...
YOU SHOULD EAT BEFORE YOU DIE.
WHA? WH-WHERE... ARE WE? WHO ARE YOU?
TELL ME, YOUNG ONE,
WHAT CODE DO YOU FOLLOW?

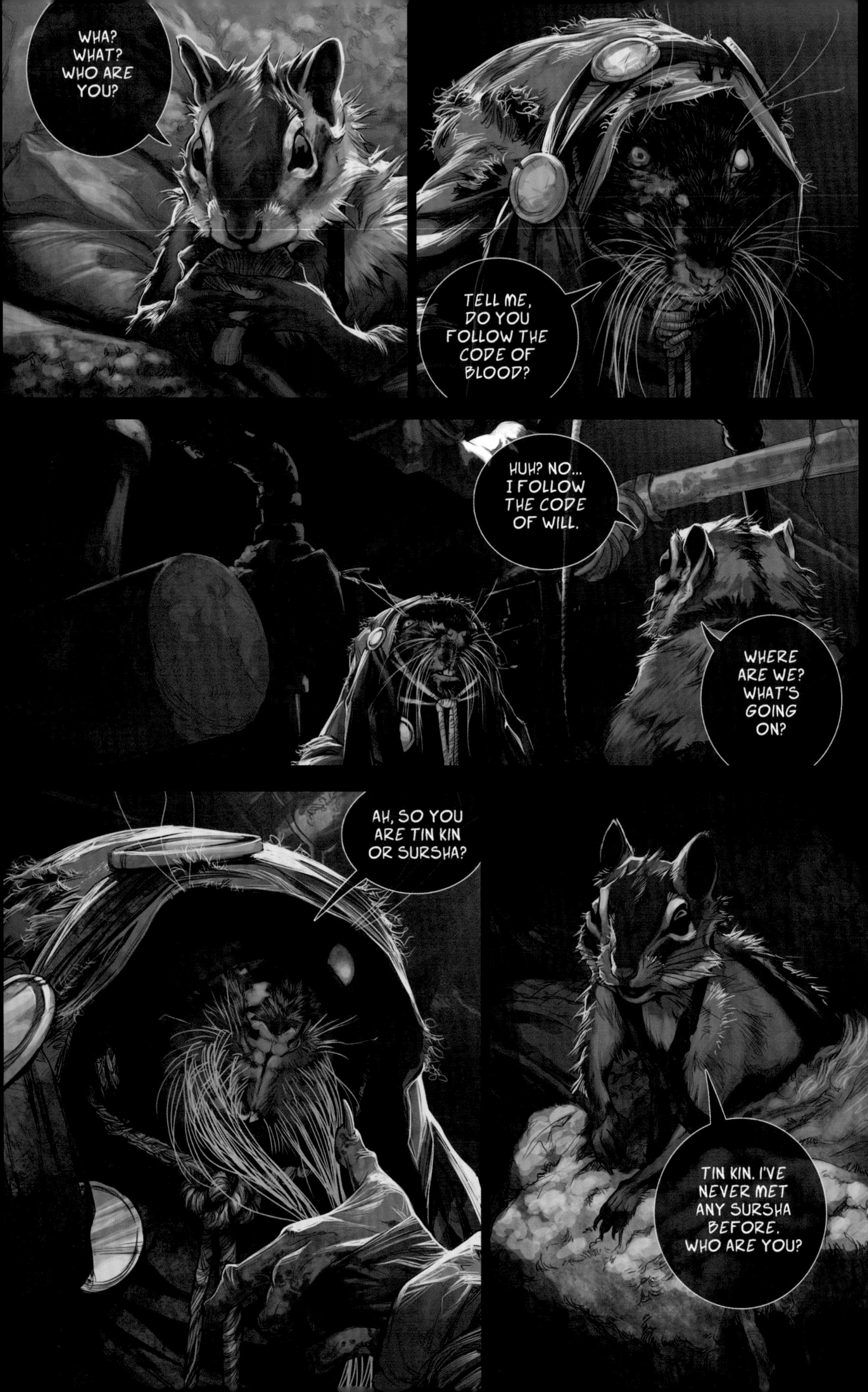
WHA? WHAT? WHO ARE YOU?
TELL ME, DO YOU FOLLOW THE CODE OF BLOOD?
HUH? NO... I FOLLOW THE CODE OF WILL.
WHERE ARE WE? WHAT'S GOING ON?
AH, SO YOU ARE TIN KIN OR SURSHA?
TIN KIN. I'VE NEVER MET ANY SURSHA BEFORE. WHO ARE YOU?

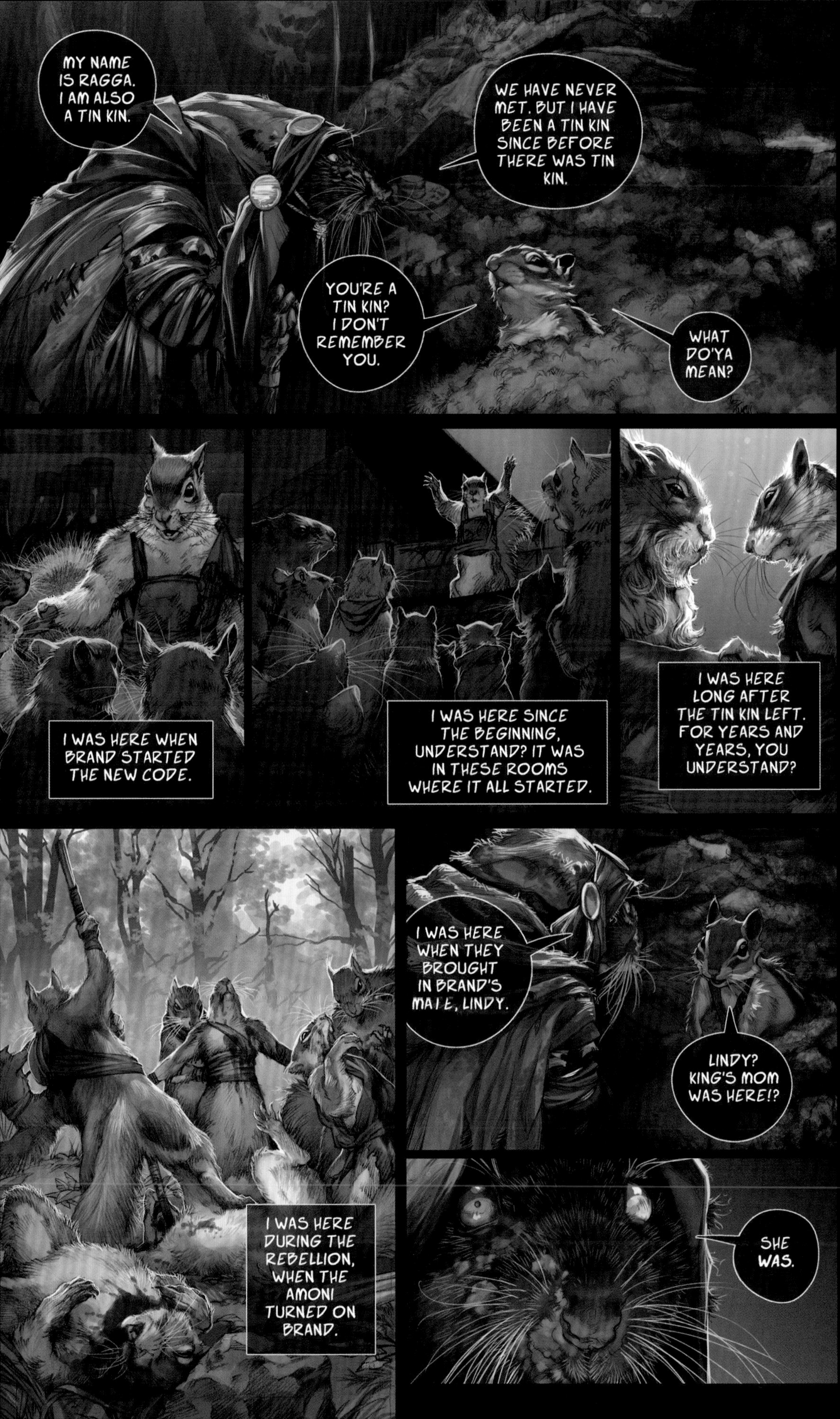
MY NAME IS RAGGA. I AM ALSO A TIN KIN.
WE HAVE NEVER MET. BUT I HAVE BEEN A TIN KIN SINCE BEFORE THERE WAS TIN KIN.
YOU'RE A TIN KIN? I DON'T REMEMBER YOU.
WHAT DO'YA MEAN?
I WAS HERE WHEN BRAND STARTED THE NEW CODE.
I WAS HERE SINCE THE BEGINNING, UNDERSTAND? IT WAS IN THESE ROOMS WHERE IT ALL STARTED.
I WAS HERE LONG AFTER THE TIN KIN LEFT. FOR YEARS AND YEARS, YOU UNDERSTAND?
I WAS HERE DURING THE REBELLION, WHEN THE AMONI TURNED ON BRAND.
I WAS HERE WHEN THEY BROUGHT IN BRAND'S MATE, LINDY.
LINDY? KING'S MOM WAS HERE!?
SHE WAS.

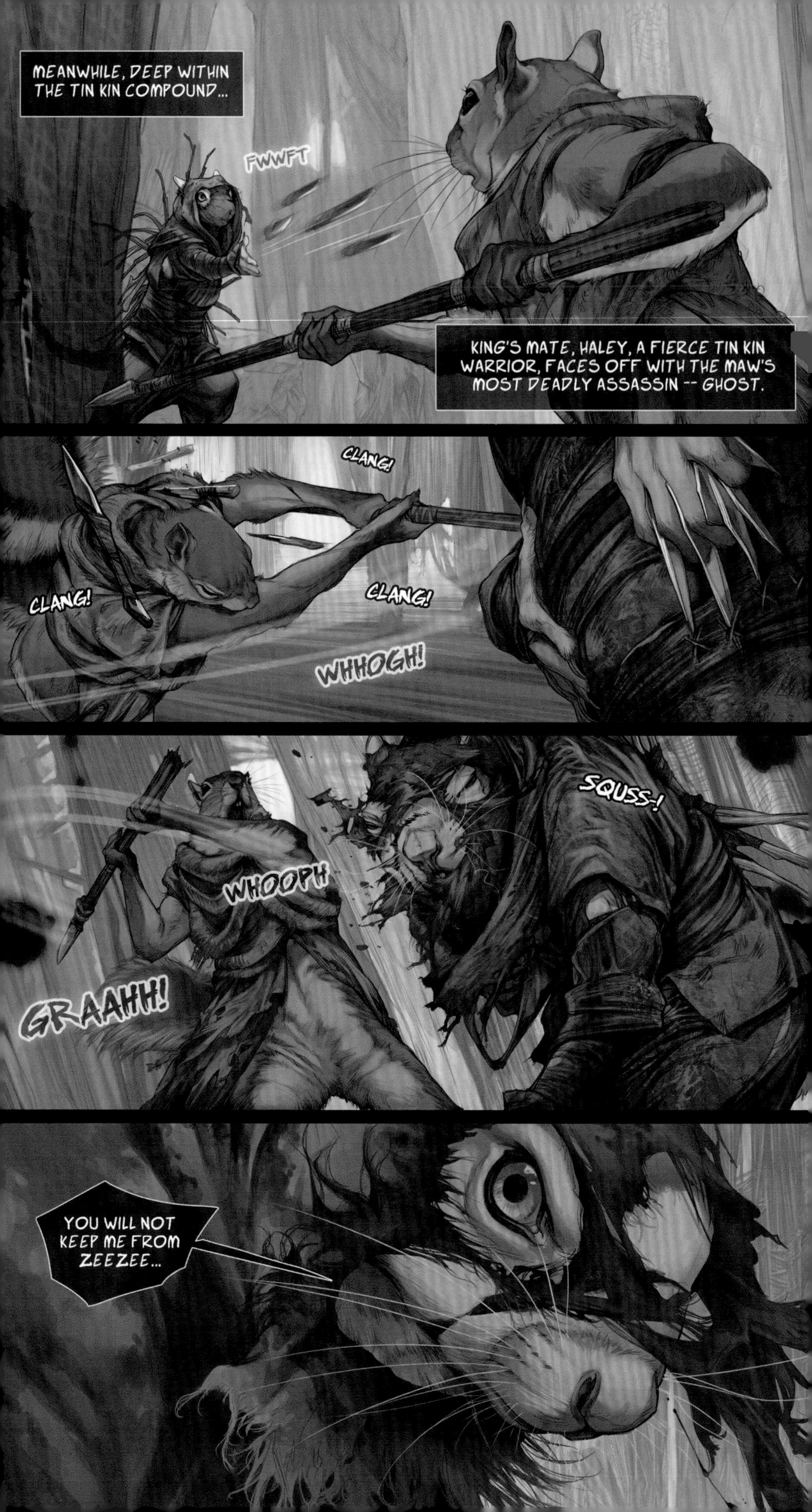
MEANWHILE, DEEP WITHIN THE TIN KIN COMPOUND...
FWWFT
KING'S MATE, HALEY, A FIERCE TIN KIN WARRIOR, FACES OFF WITH THE MAW'S MOST DEADLY ASSASSIN -- GHOST.
CLANG!
CLANG!
CLANG!
WHHOGH!
SQUSS-!
WHOOPH
GRAAHH!
YOU WILL NOT KEEP ME FROM ZEEZEE...

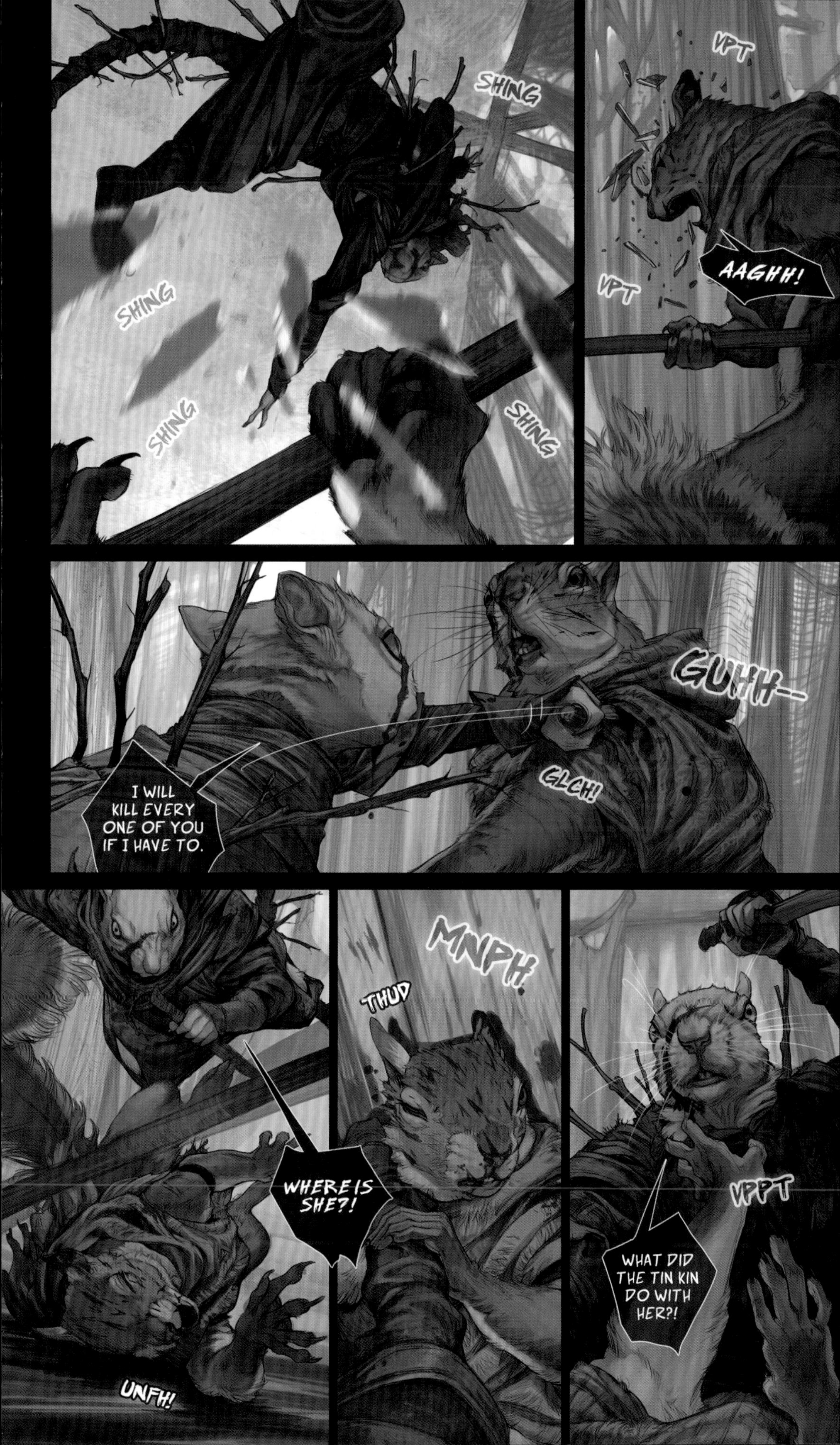
SHING
SHING
SHING
SHING
VPT
VPT
AAGHH!
GUHH--
GLCH!
I WILL KILL EVERY ONE OF YOU IF I HAVE TO.
WHERE IS SHE?!
UNFH!
MNPH.
THUD
VPPT
WHAT DID THE TIN KIN DO WITH HER?!

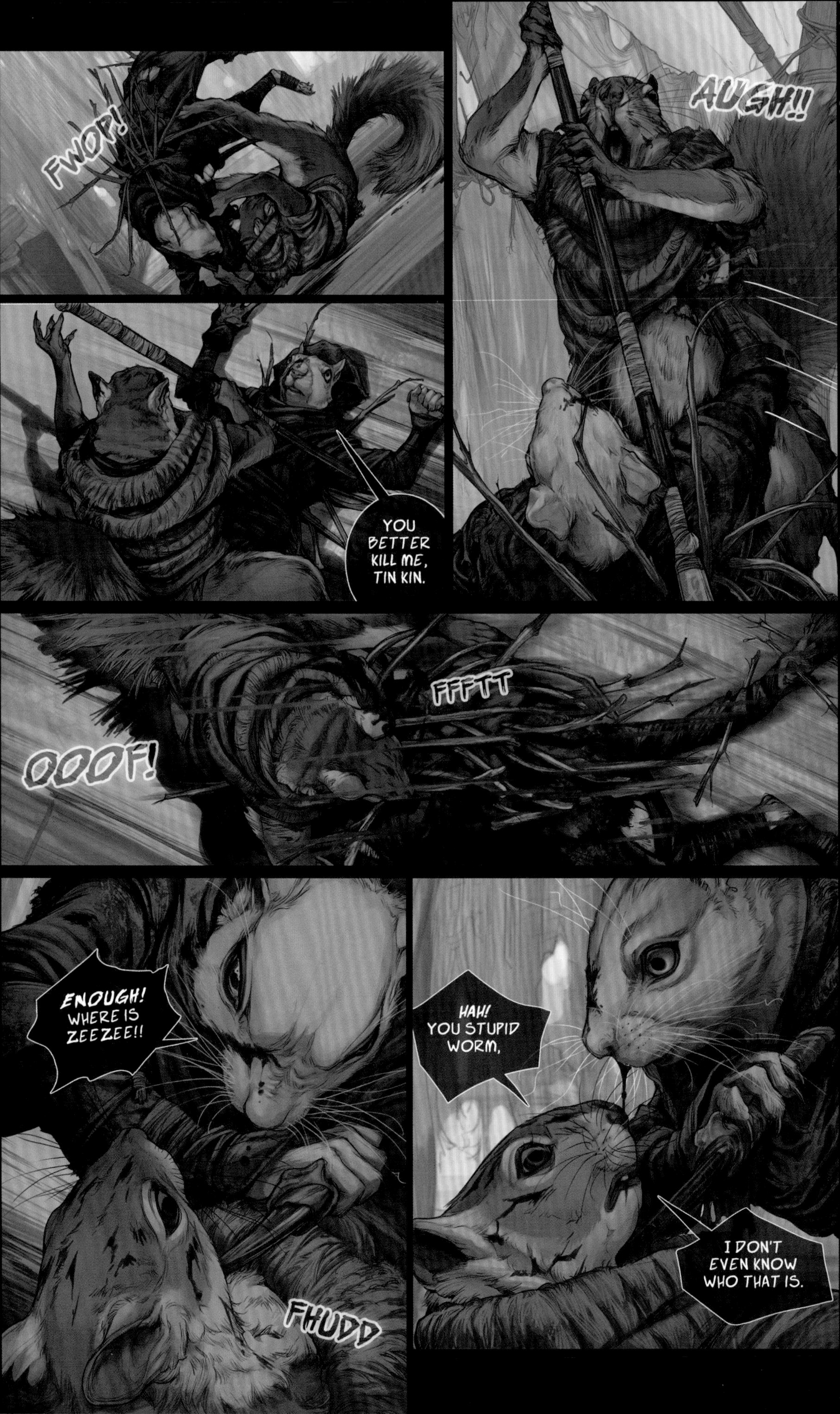
FWOP!
AUGH!!
YOU BETTER KILL ME, TIN KIN.
FFFTT
OOOF!
ENOUGH! WHERE IS ZEEZEE!!
FHUDD
HAH! YOU STUPID WORM,
I DON'T EVEN KNOW WHO THAT IS.

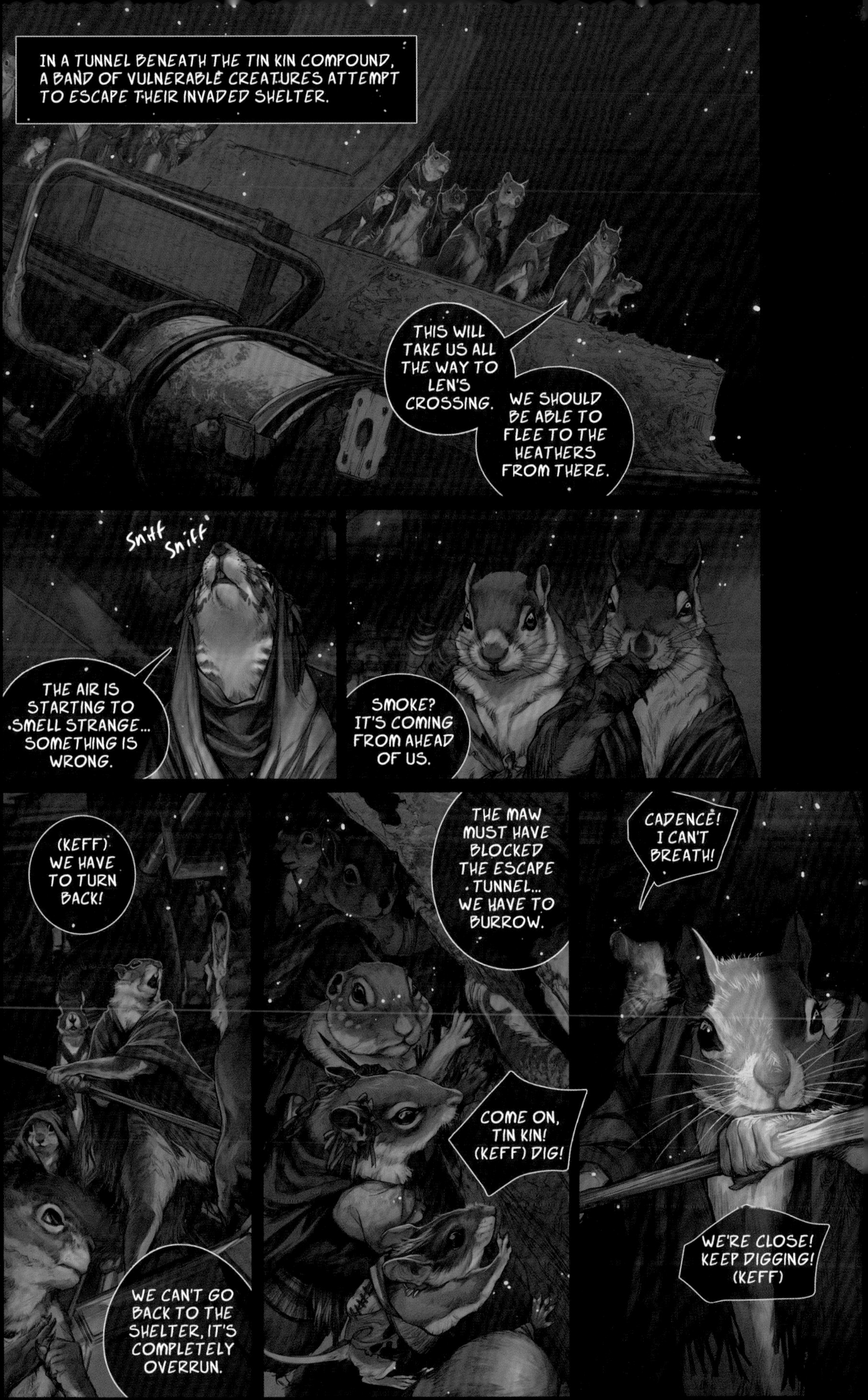
IN A TUNNEL BENEATH THE TIN KIN COMPOUND, A BAND OF VULNERABLE CREATURES ATTEMPT TO ESCAPE THEIR INVADED SHELTER.
THIS WILL TAKE US ALL THE WAY TO LEN'S CROSSING.
WE SHOULD BE ABLE TO FLEE TO THE HEATHERS FROM THERE.
Sniff Sniff
THE AIR IS STARTING TO SMELL STRANGE... SOMETHING IS WRONG.
SMOKE? IT'S COMING FROM AHEAD OF US.
(KEFF) WE HAVE TO TURN BACK!
WE CAN'T GO BACK TO THE SHELTER, IT'S COMPLETELY OVERRUN.
THE MAW MUST HAVE BLOCKED THE ESCAPE TUNNEL... WE HAVE TO BURROW.
COME ON, TIN KIN! (KEFF) DIG!
CADENCE! I CAN'T BREATH!
WE'RE CLOSE! KEEP DIGGING! (KEFF)

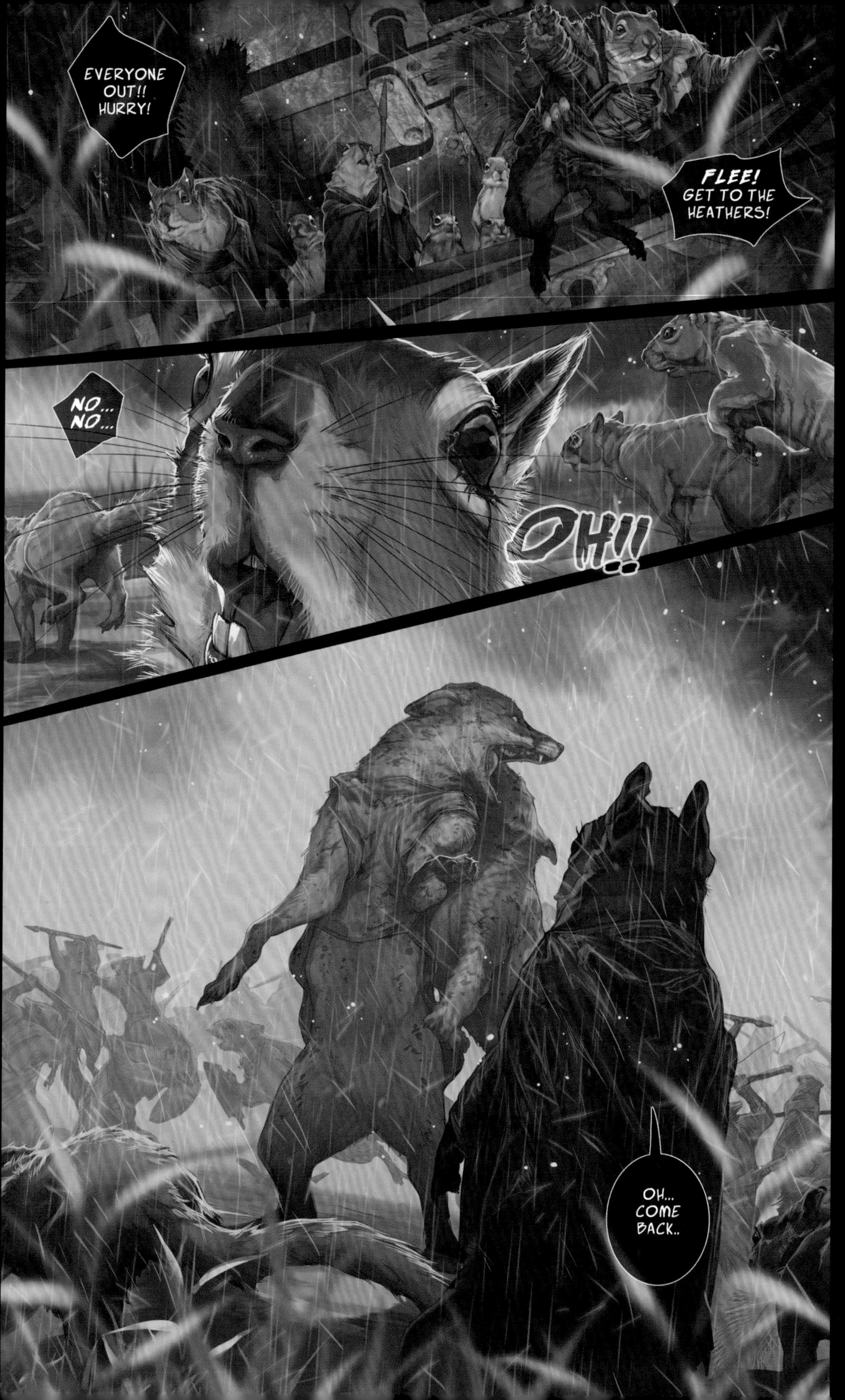
EVERYONE OUT!! HURRY!
FLEE! GET TO THE HEATHERS!
NO... NO...
OH!!
OH... COME BACK..

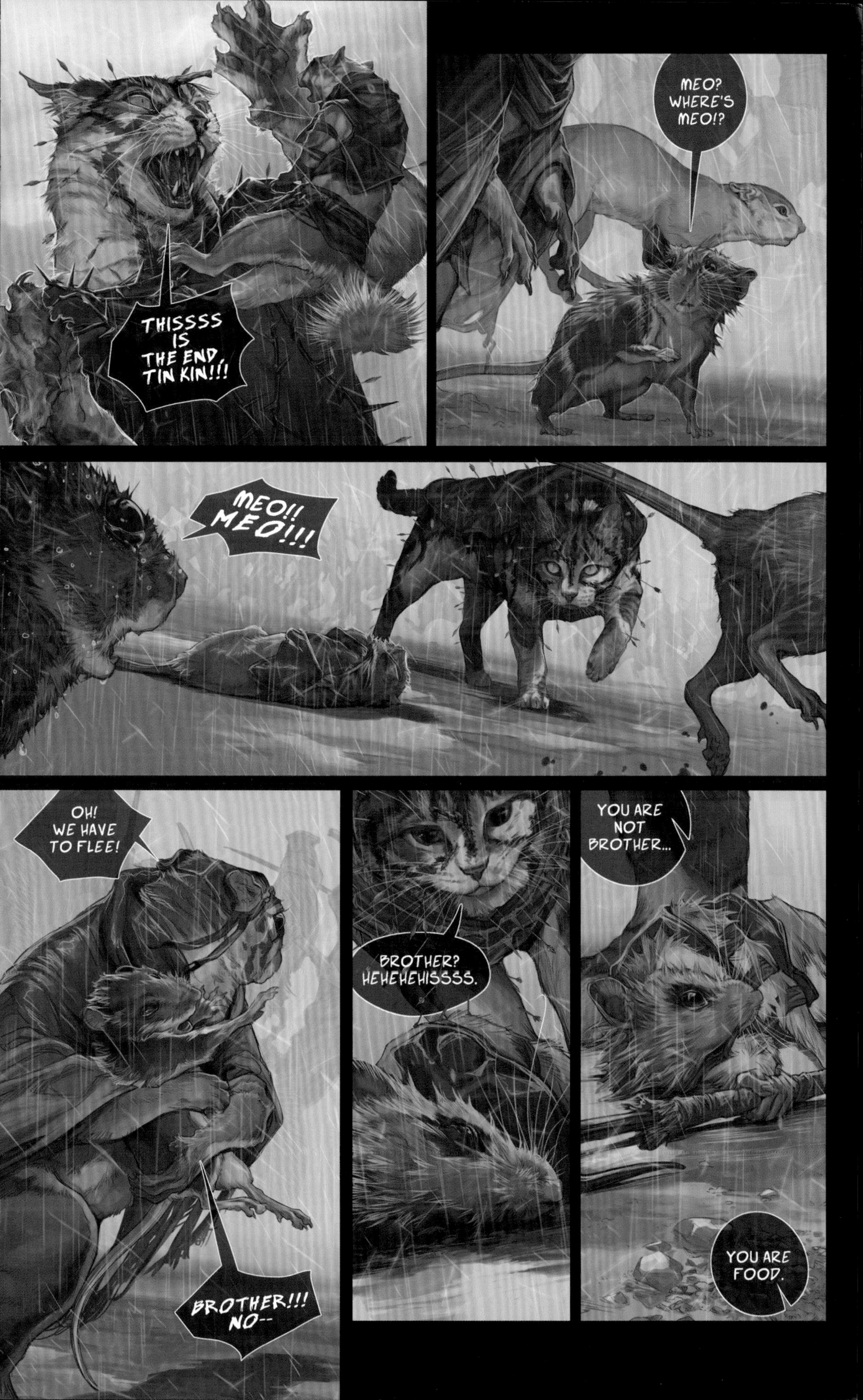
THISSSS IS THE END TIN KIN!!!
MEO? WHERE'S MEO!?
MEO!! MEO!!!
OH! WE HAVE TO FLEE!
BROTHER!!! NO--
BROTHER? HEHEHEHISSSS.
YOU ARE NOT BROTHER...
YOU ARE FOOD.

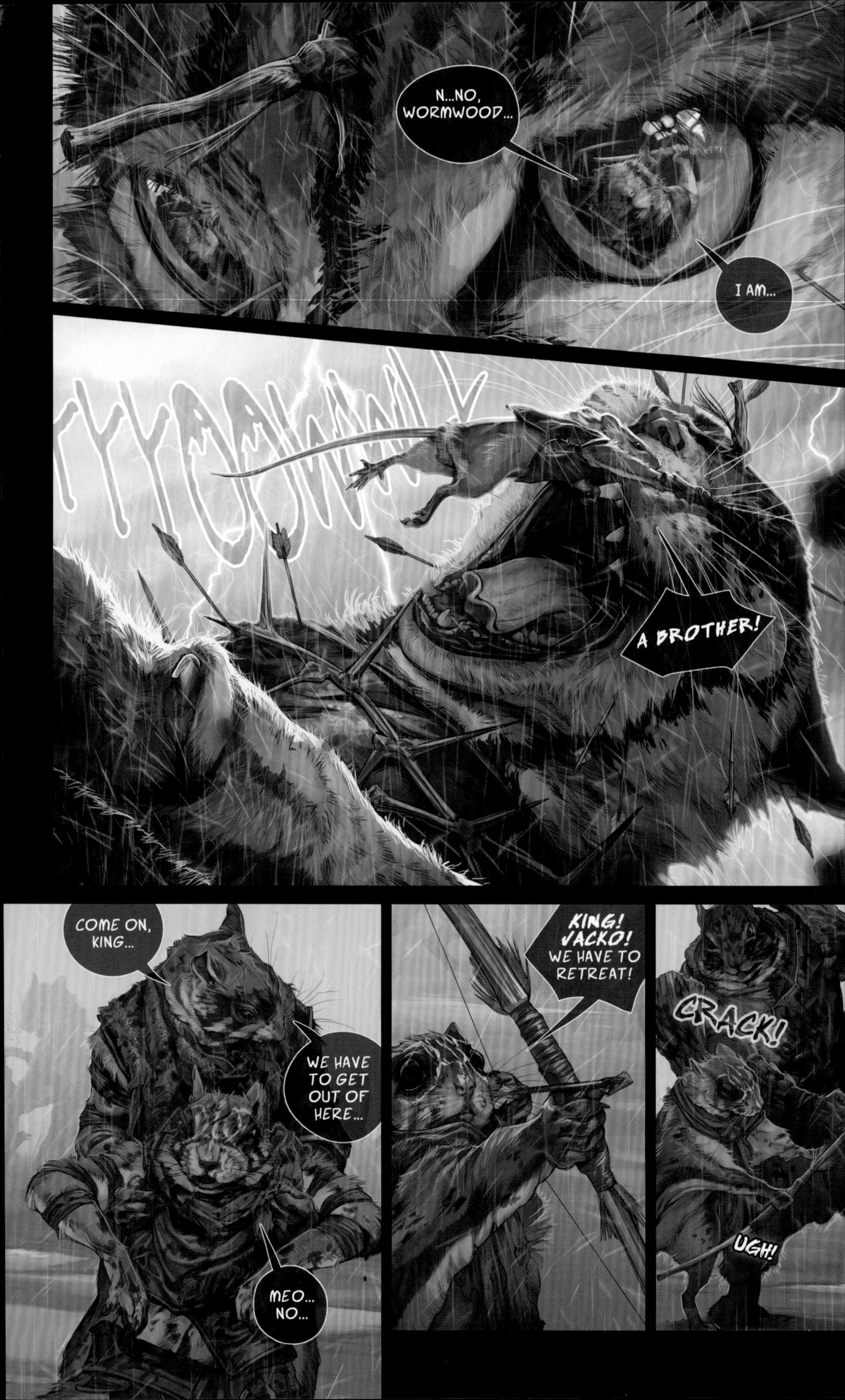

N...NO, WORMWOOD...
I AM...
A BROTHER!
COME ON, KING...
WE HAVE TO GET OUT OF HERE...
MEO... NO...
KING! JACKO! WE HAVE TO RETREAT!
CRACK!
UGH!

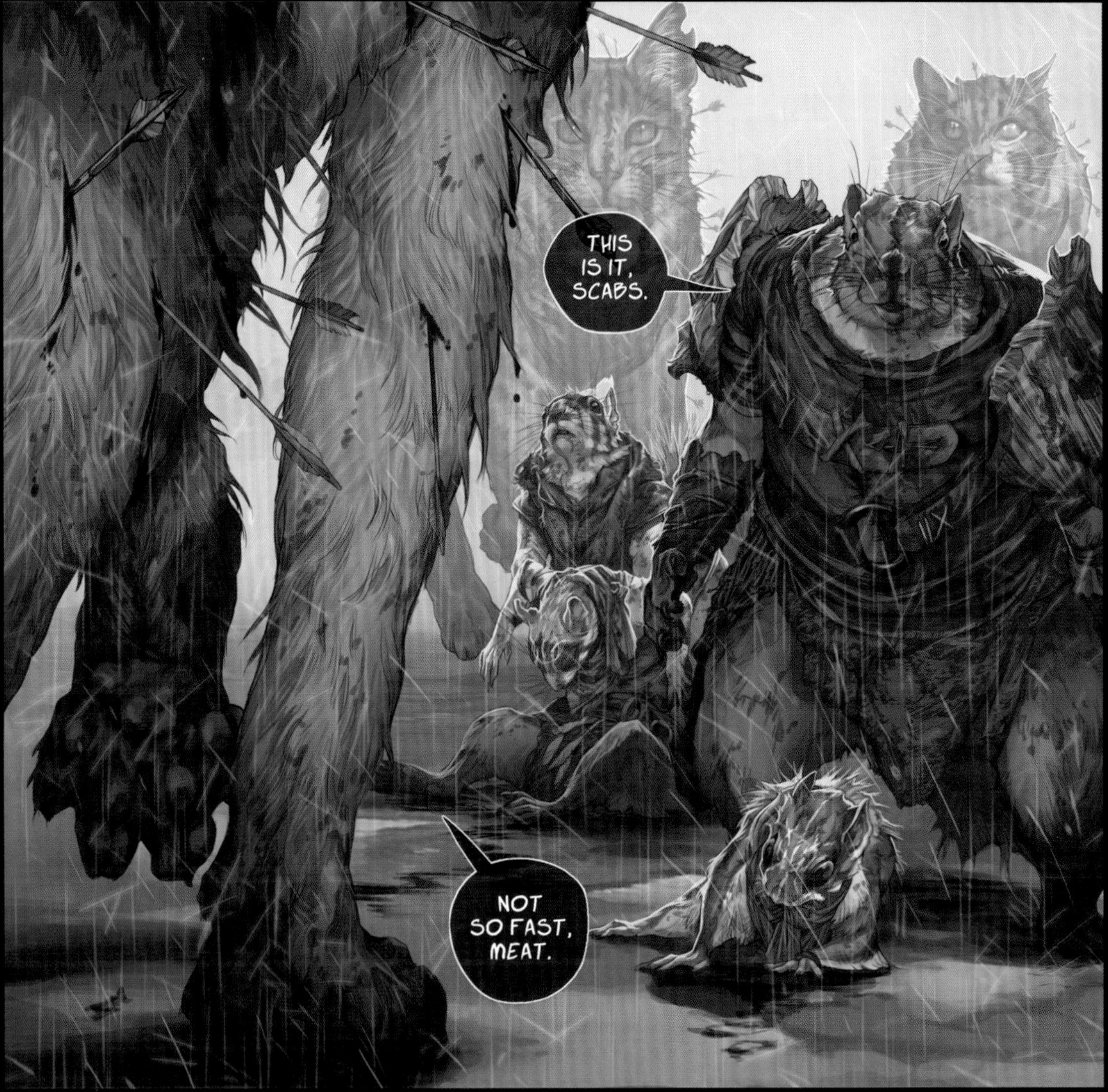
THIS IS IT, SCABS.
NOT SO FAST, MEAT.

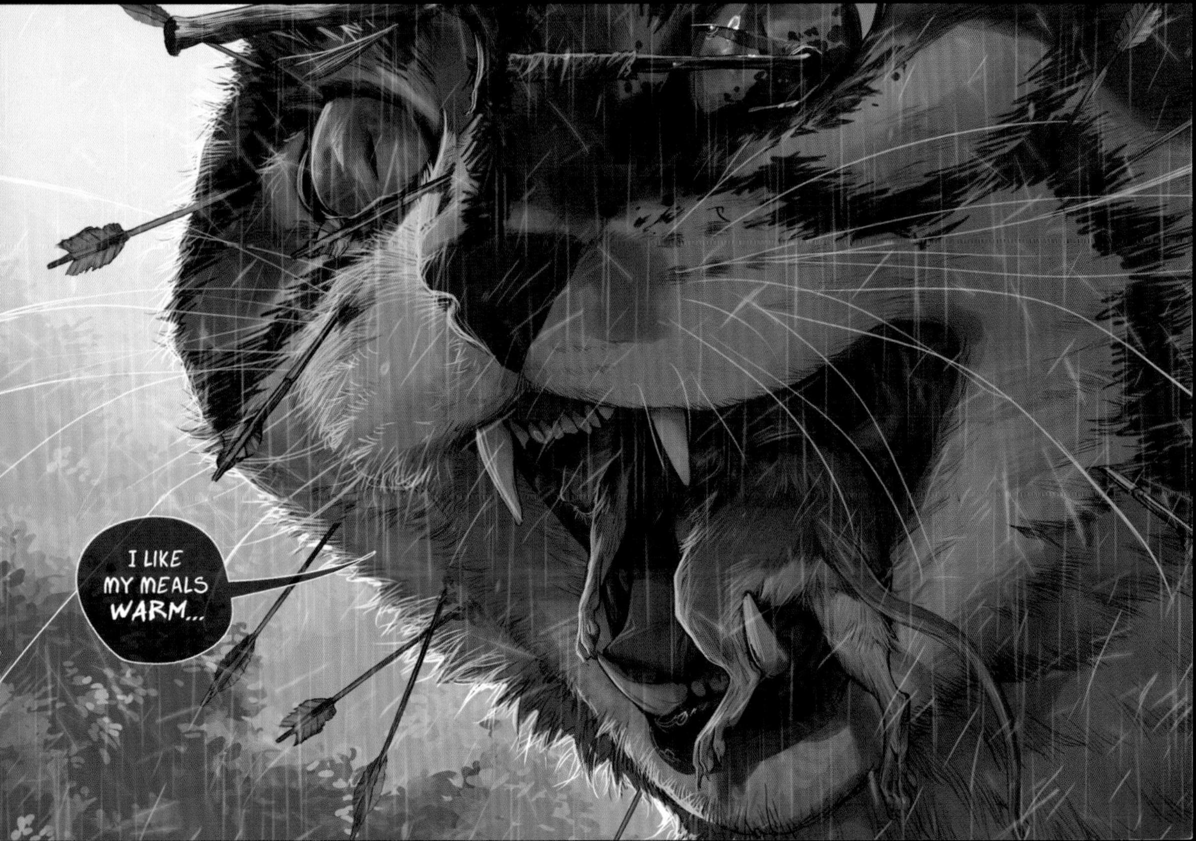
I LIKE MY MEALS WARM...

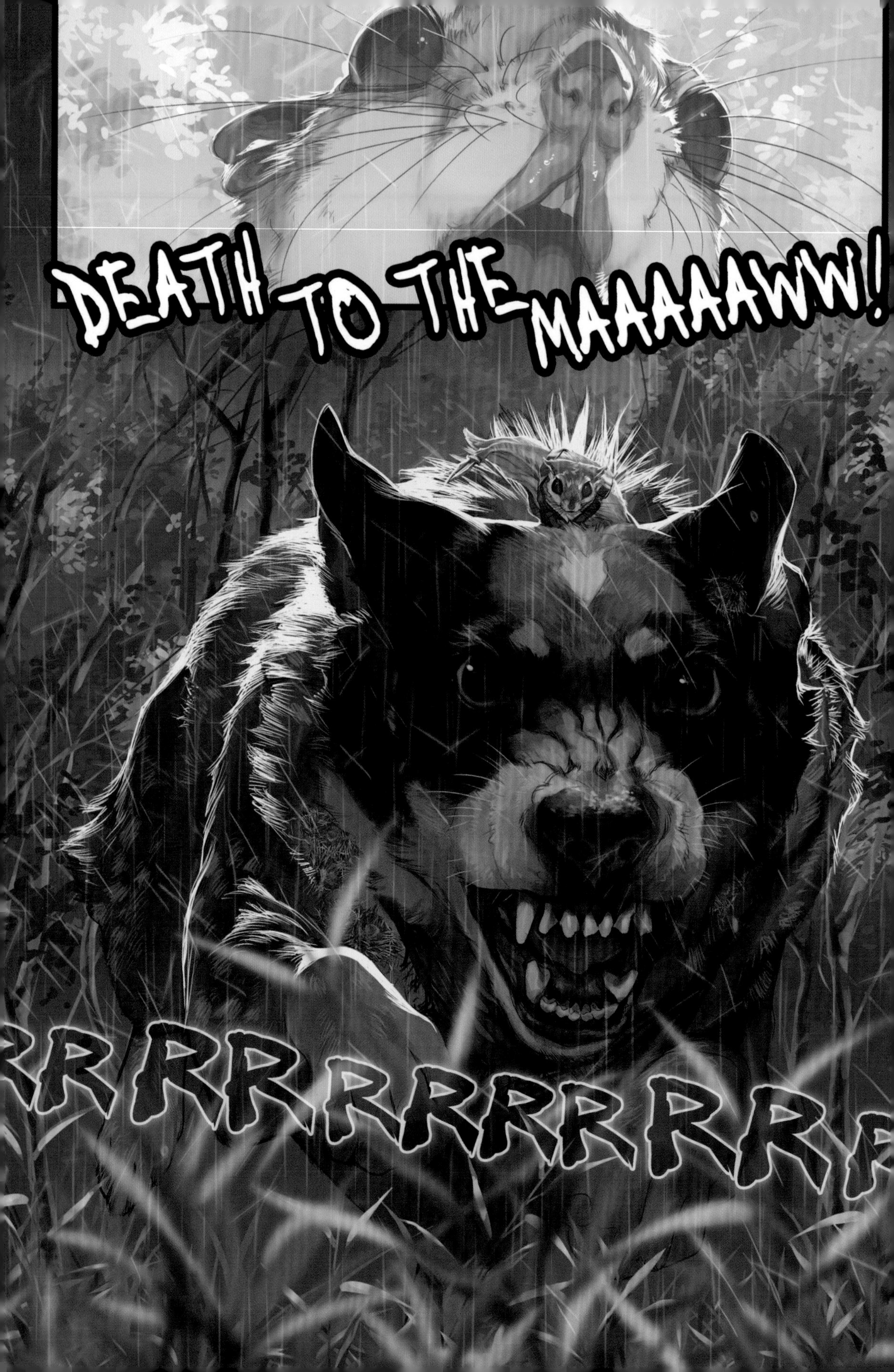

DEATH TO THE MAAAAAWW!
RRRRRRRRRRRRR

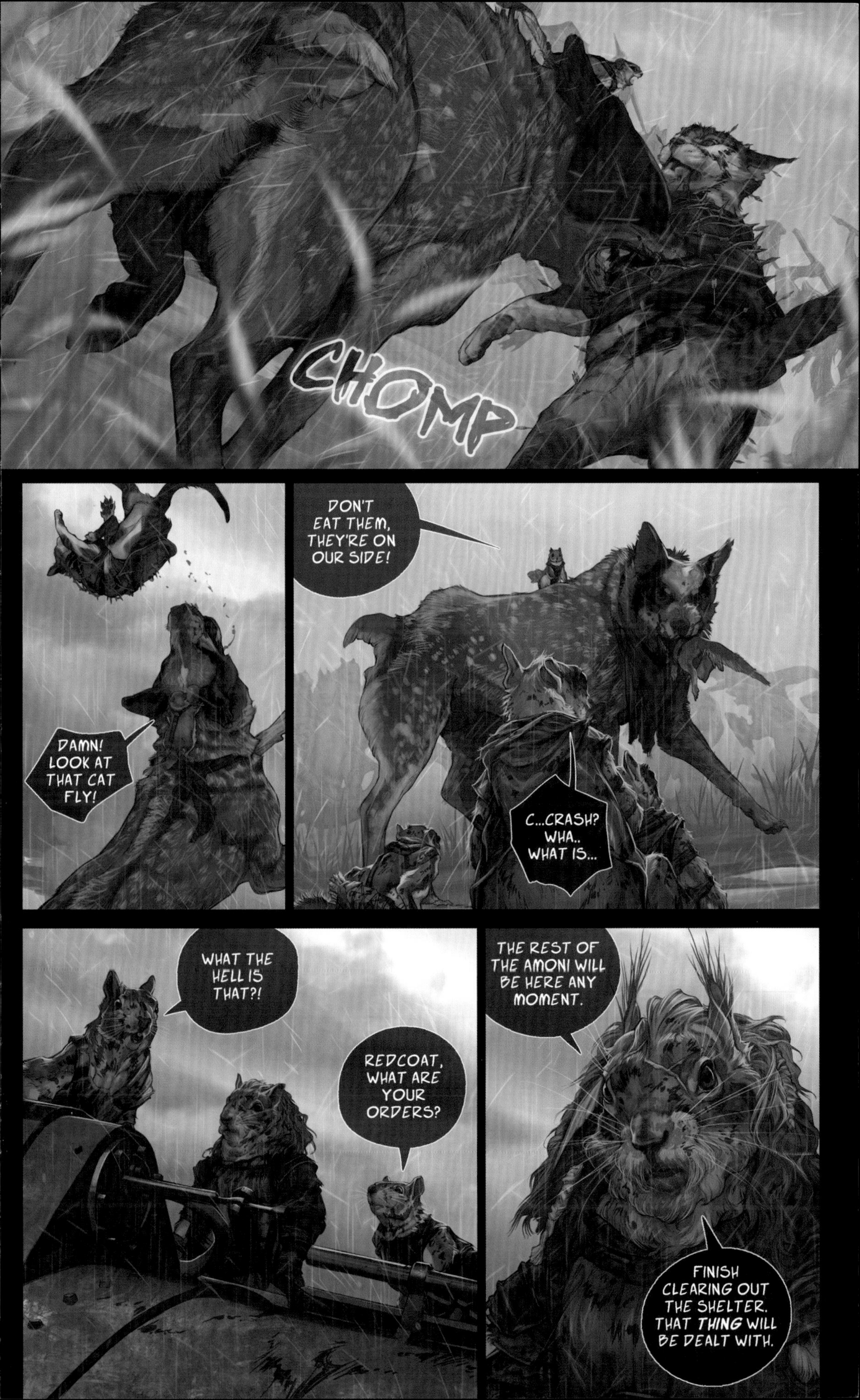
CHOMP
DAMN! LOOK AT THAT CAT FLY!
DON'T EAT THEM, THEY'RE ON OUR SIDE!
C...CRASH? WHA.. WHAT IS...
WHAT THE HELL IS THAT?!
REDCOAT, WHAT ARE YOUR ORDERS?
THE REST OF THE AMONI WILL BE HERE ANY MOMENT.
FINISH CLEARING OUT THE SHELTER. THAT *THING* WILL BE DEALT WITH.

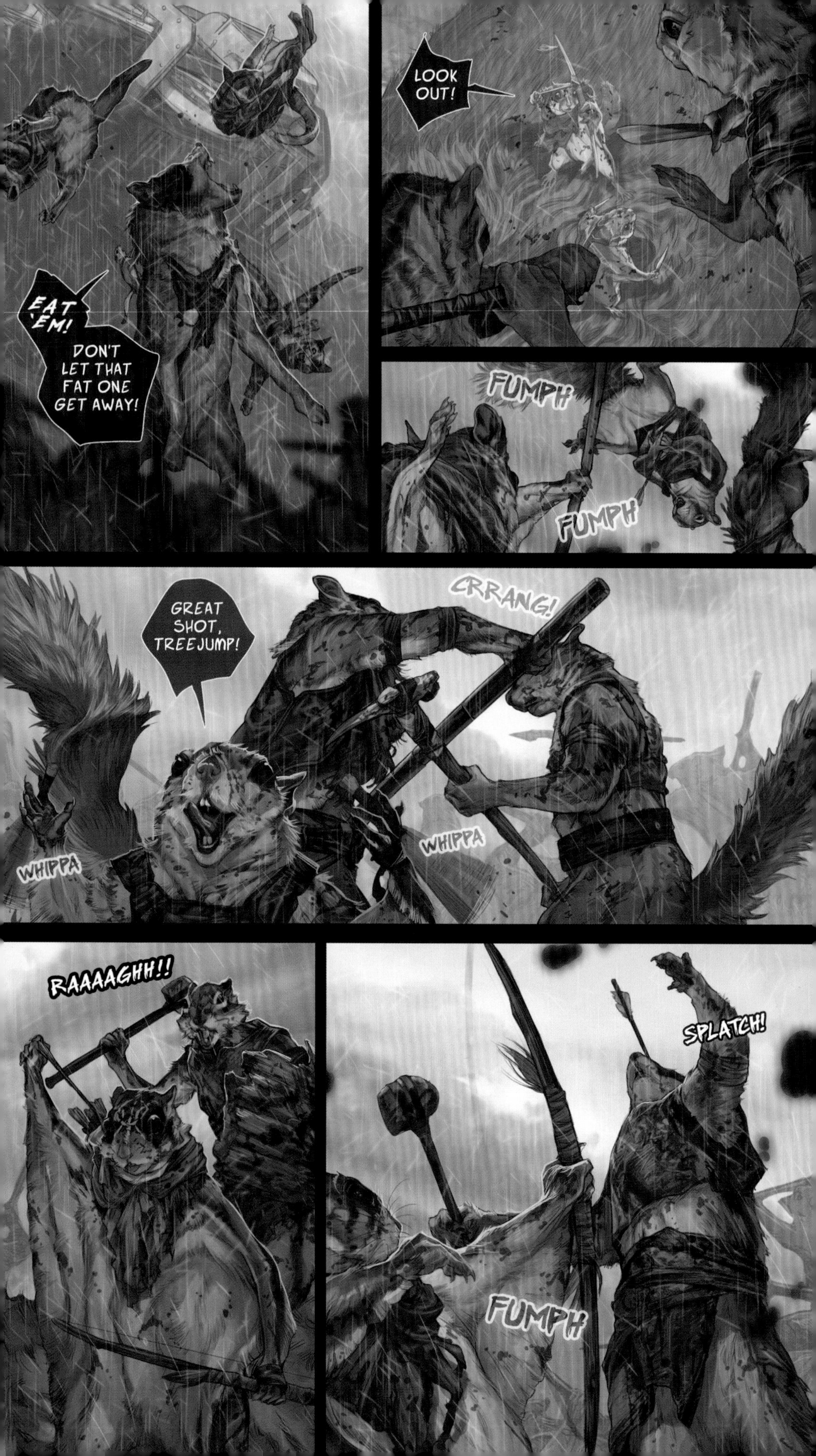
EAT 'EM!
DON'T LET THAT FAT ONE GET AWAY!
LOOK OUT!
FUMPH
FUMPH
GREAT SHOT, TREEJUMP!
CRRANG!
WHIPPA
WHIPPA
RAAAAGHH!!
SPLATCH!
FUMPH

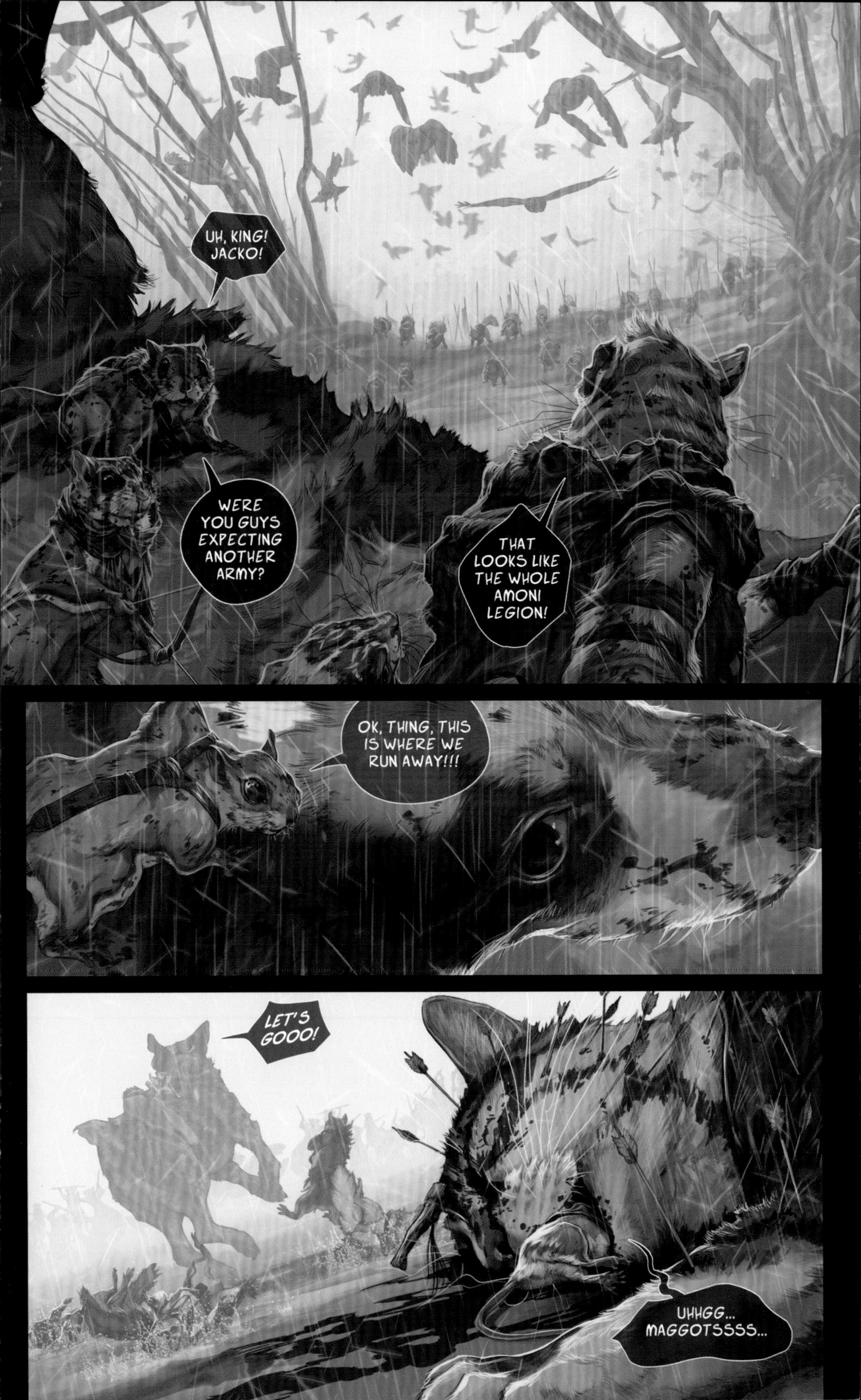
UH, KING! JACKO!
WERE YOU GUYS EXPECTING ANOTHER ARMY?
THAT LOOKS LIKE THE WHOLE AMONI LEGION!
OK, THING, THIS IS WHERE WE RUN AWAY!!!
LET'S GOOO!
UHHGG... MAGGOTSSSS...

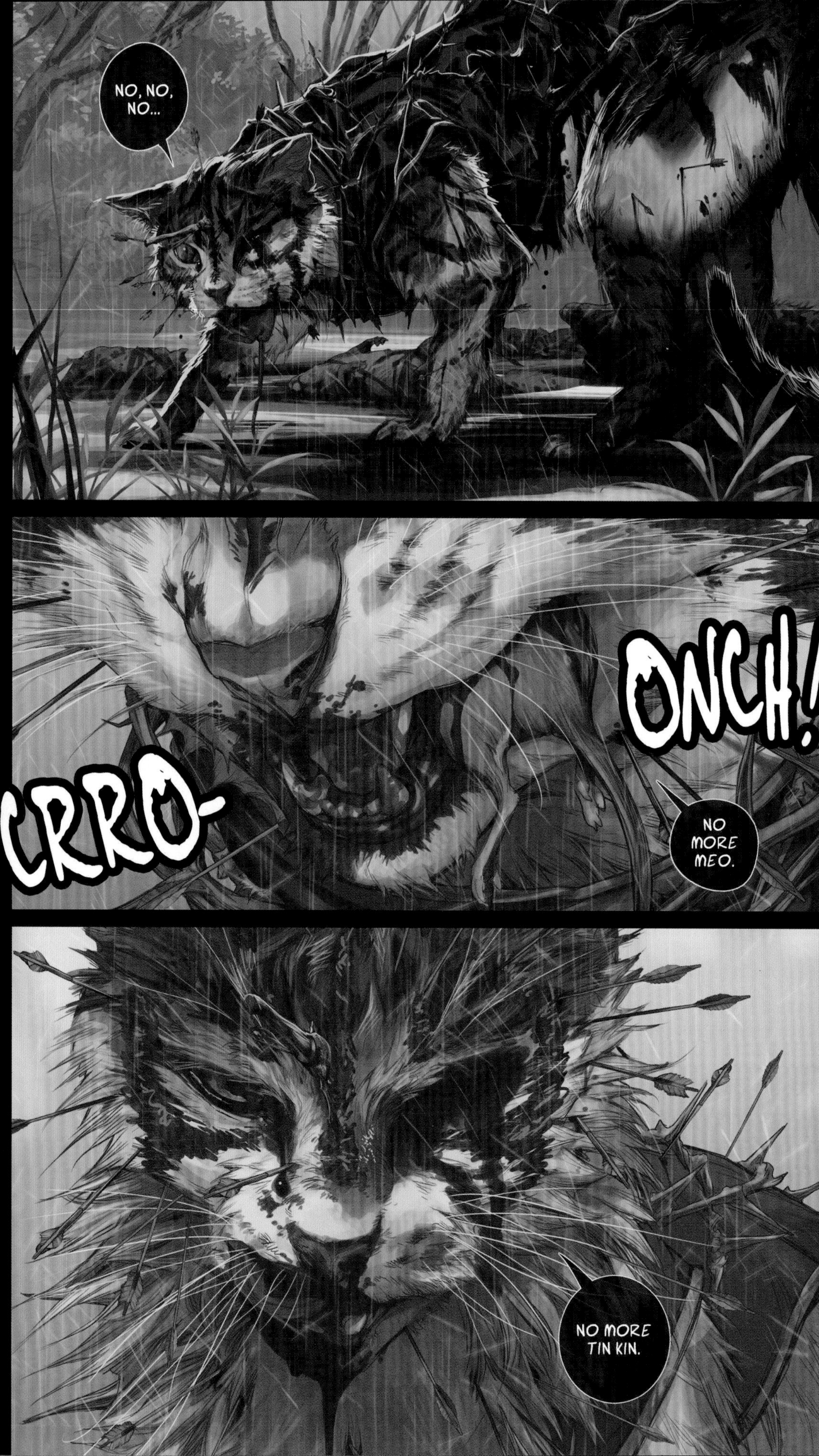
NO, NO, NO...
CRRO-
ONCH!
NO MORE MEO.
NO MORE TIN KIN.

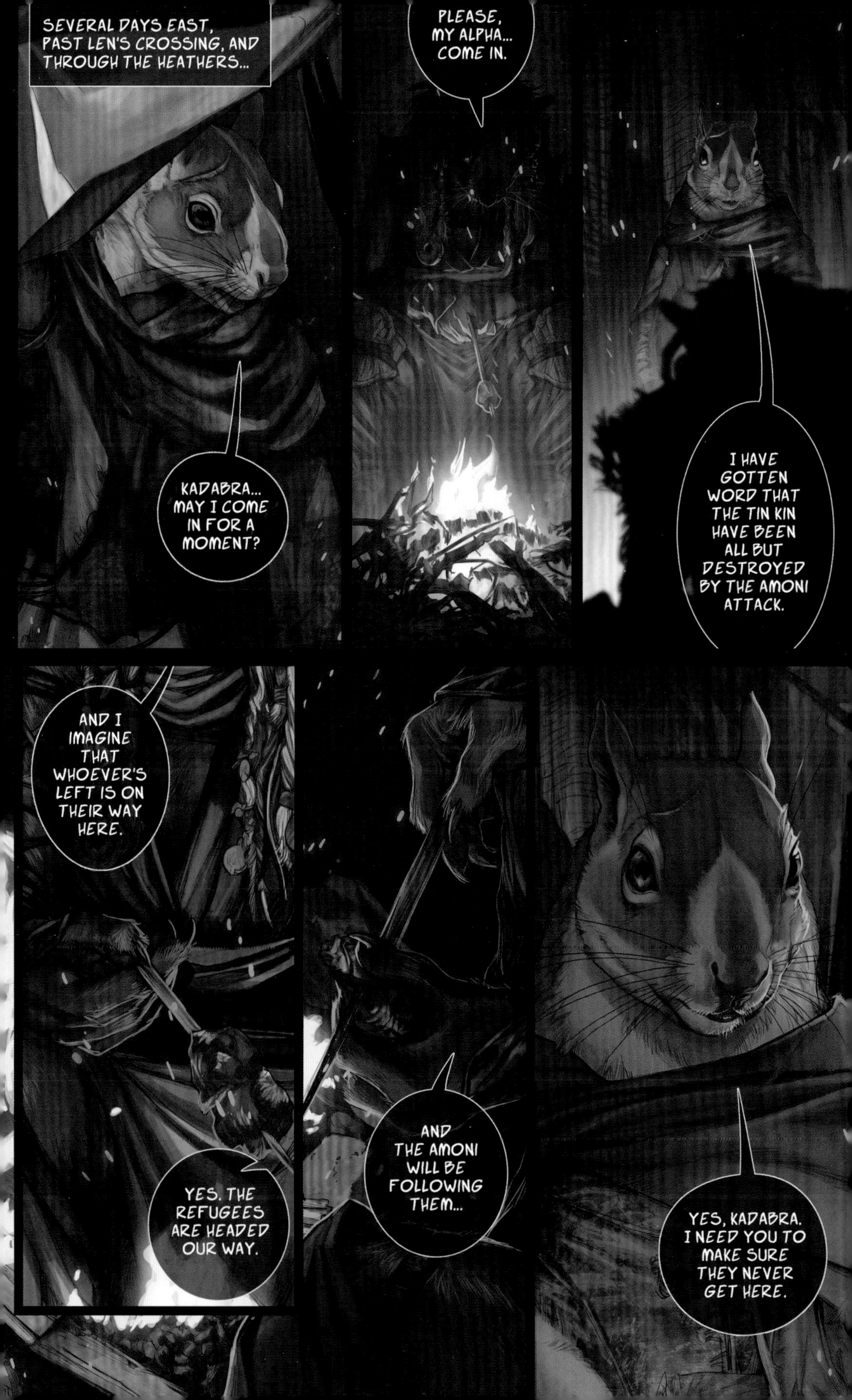
SEVERAL DAYS EAST, PAST LEN'S CROSSING, AND THROUGH THE HEATHERS...
KADABRA... MAY I COME IN FOR A MOMENT?
PLEASE, MY ALPHA... COME IN.
I HAVE GOTTEN WORD THAT THE TIN KIN HAVE BEEN ALL BUT DESTROYED BY THE AMONI ATTACK.
AND I IMAGINE THAT WHOEVER'S LEFT IS ON THEIR WAY HERE.
YES. THE REFUGEES ARE HEADED OUR WAY.
AND THE AMONI WILL BE FOLLOWING THEM...
YES, KADABRA. I NEED YOU TO MAKE SURE THEY NEVER GET HERE.

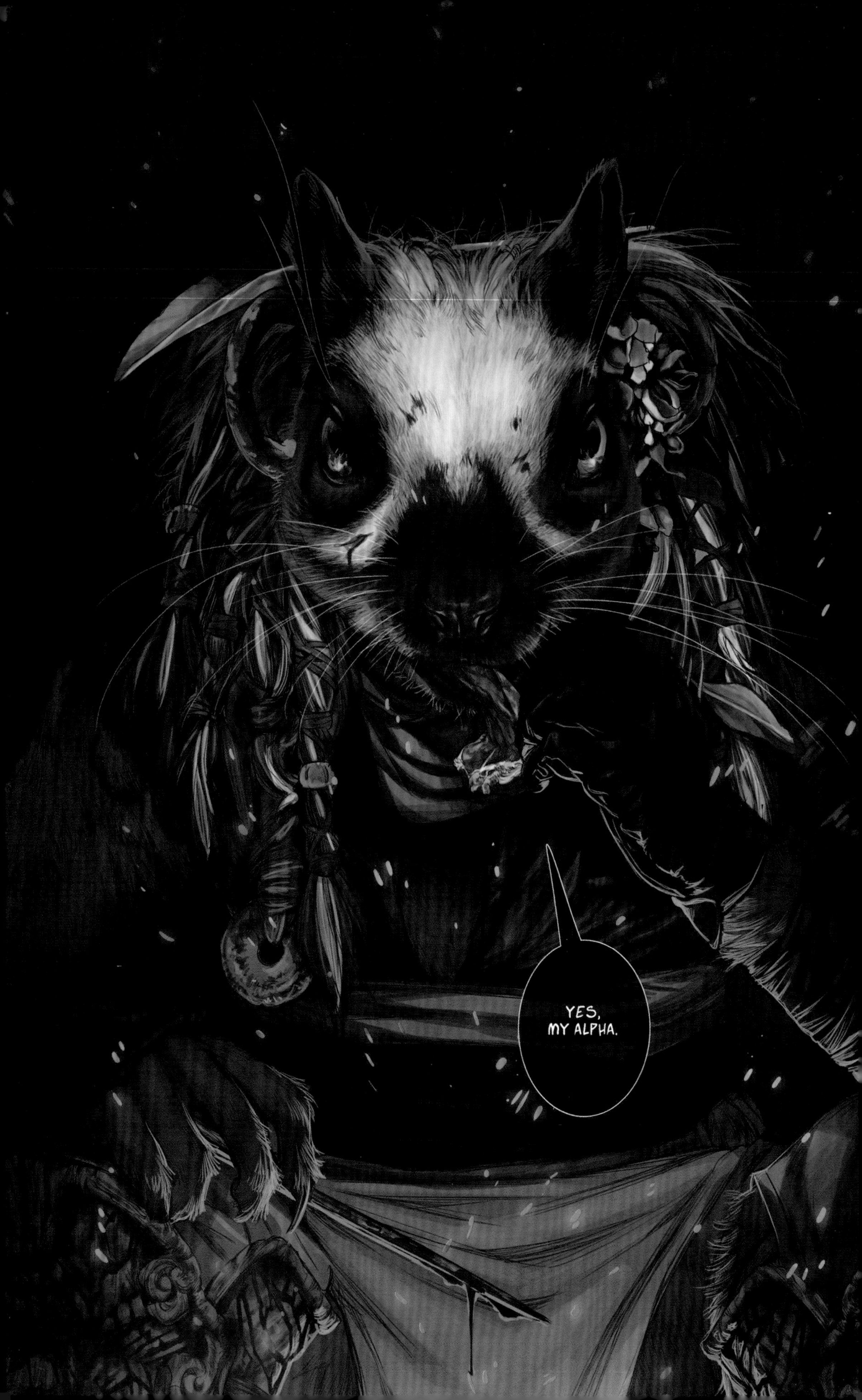
YES, MY ALPHA.

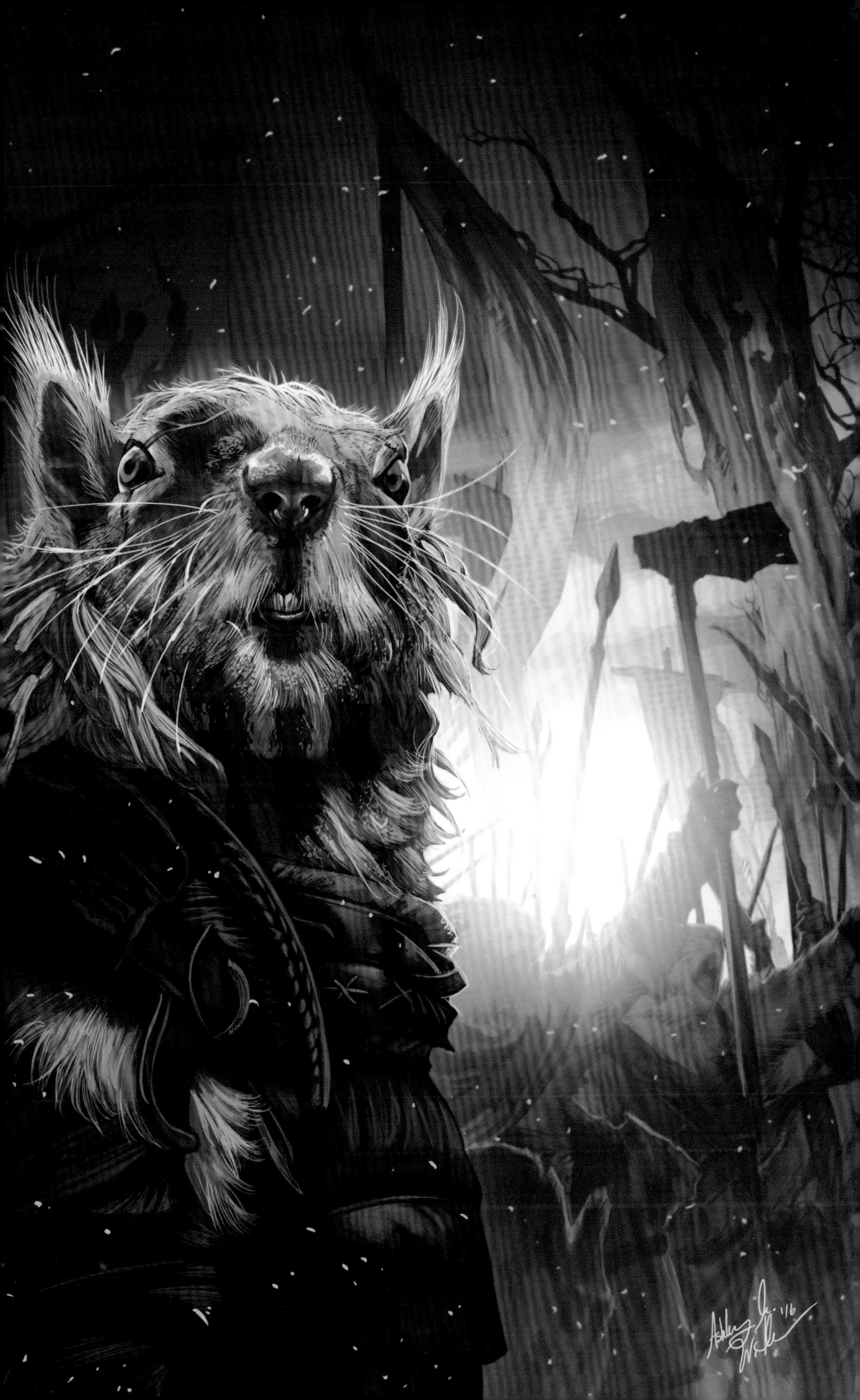

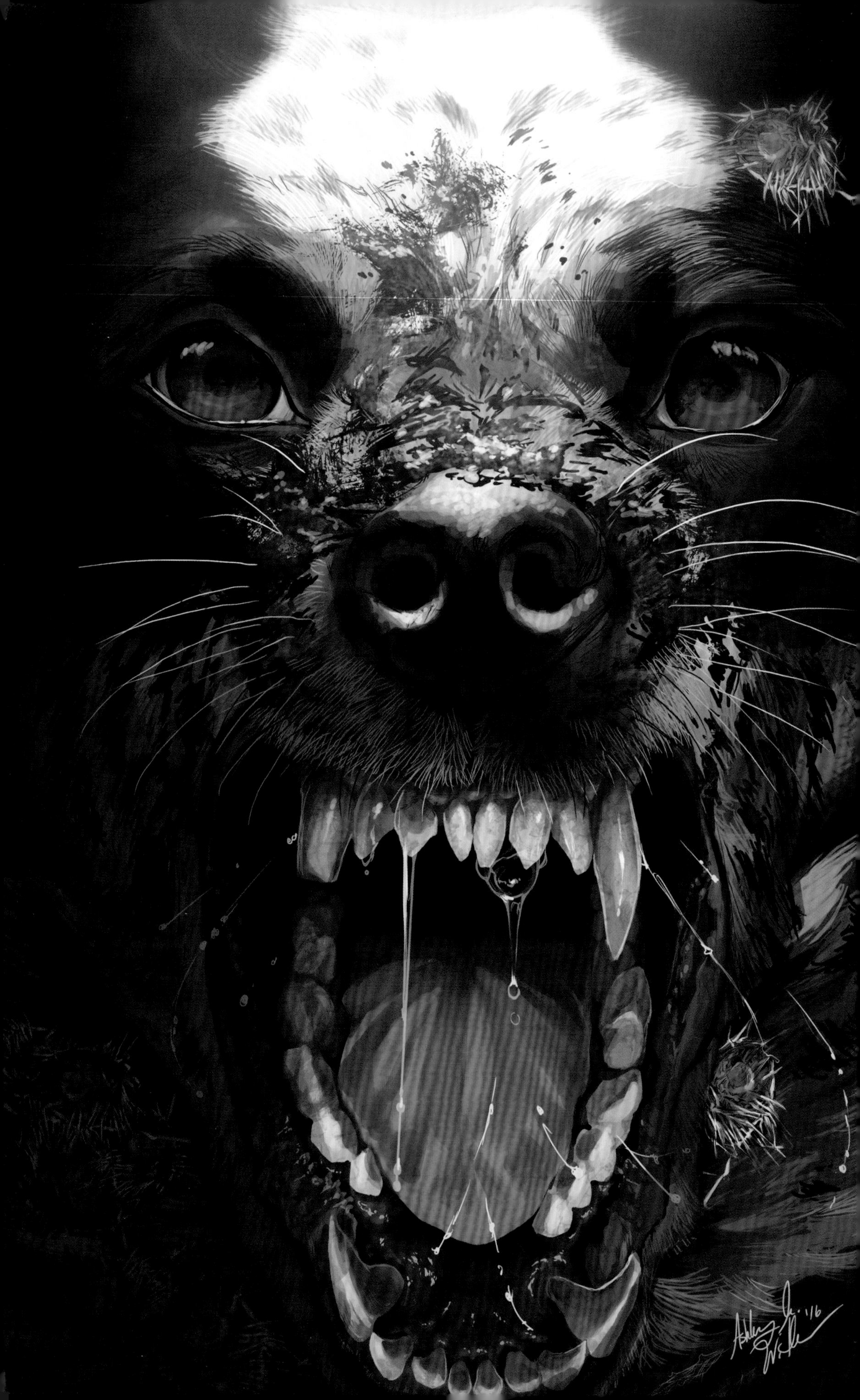

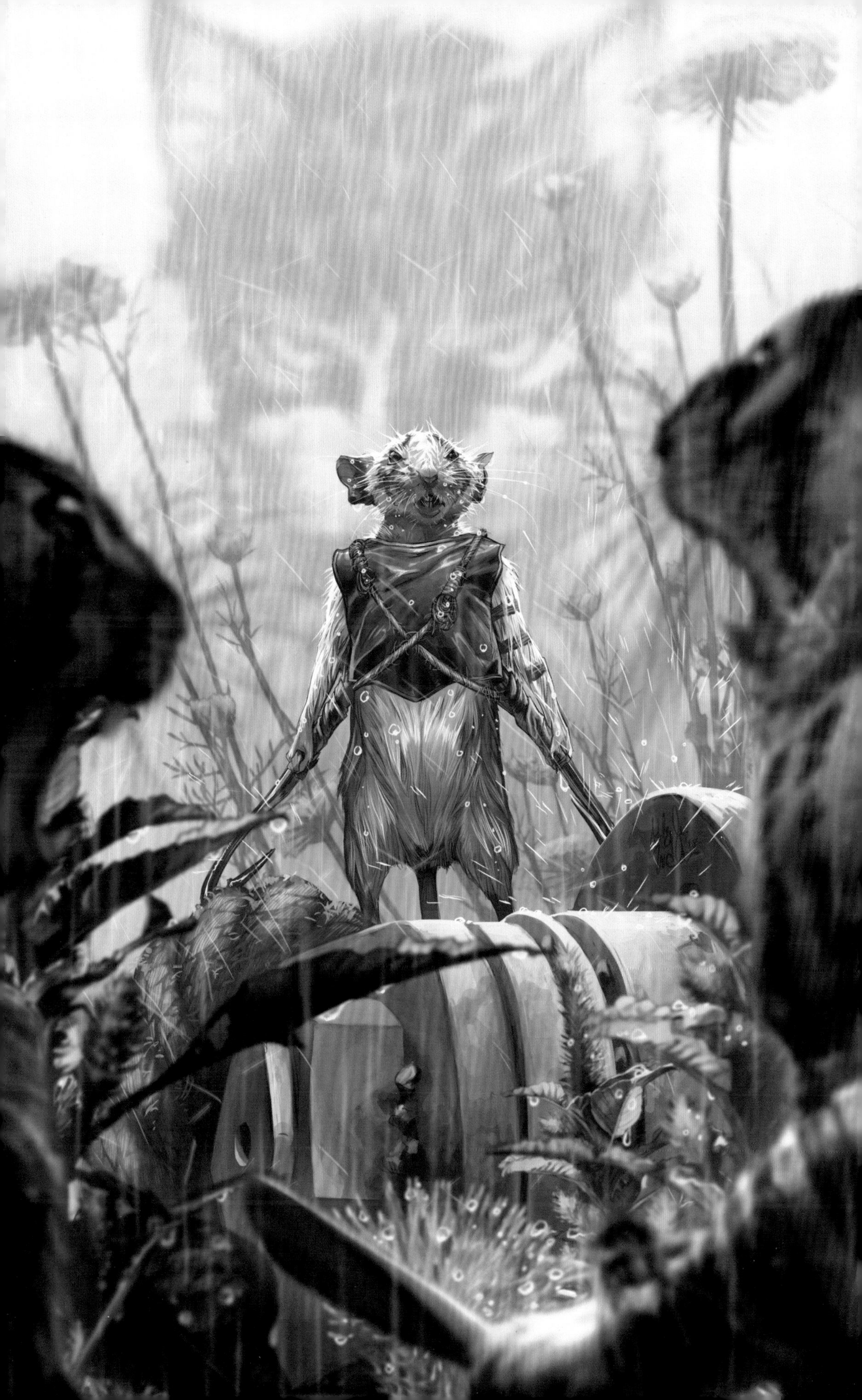

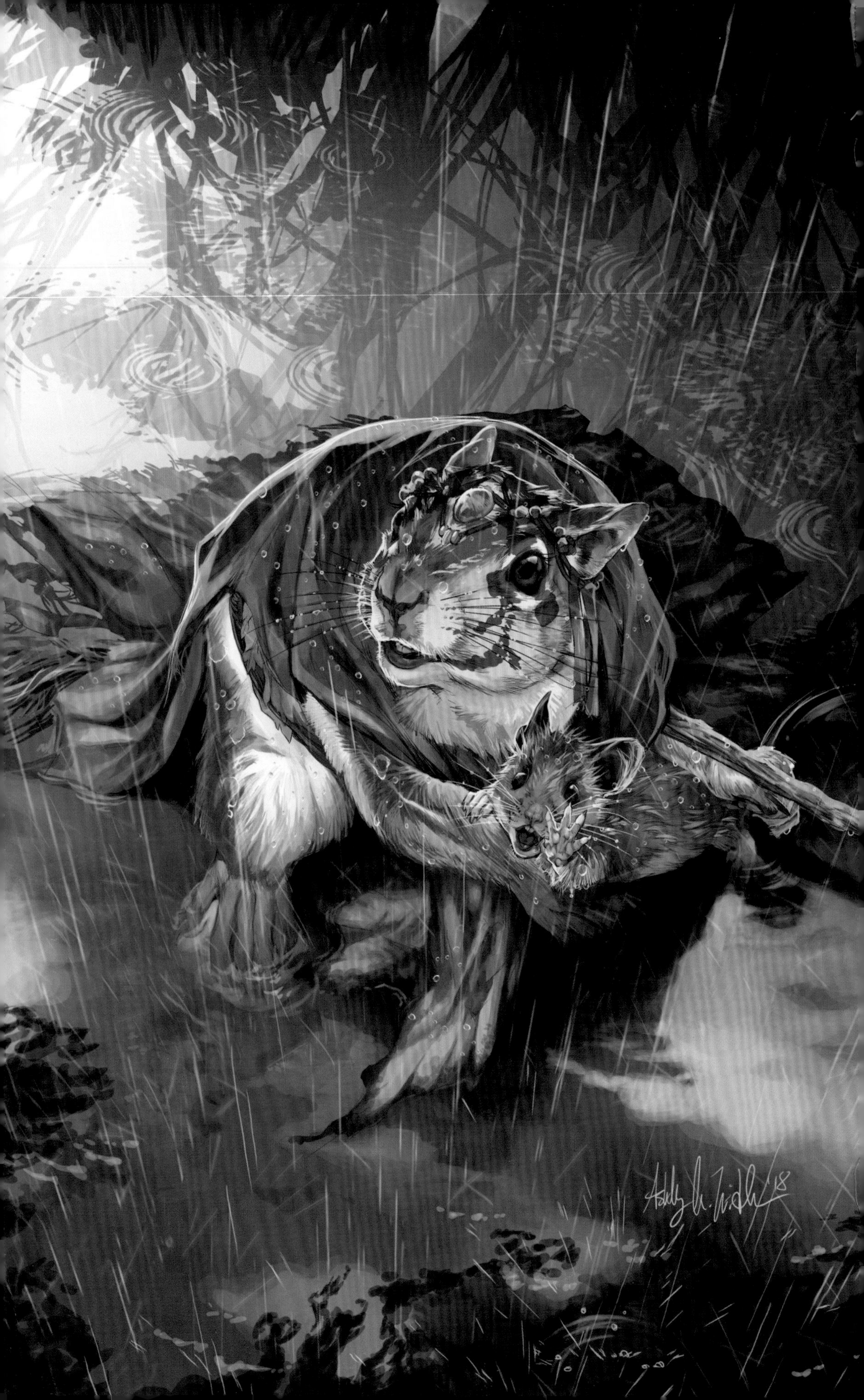